D0891536

Abandoned by Lincoln

ABANDONED BY LINCOLN

A Military Biography of
General John Pope

Wallace J. Schutz
and
Walter N. Trenerry

University of Illinois Press
Urbana and Chicago

© 1990 by the Board of Trustees of the University of Illinois
Manufactured in the United States of America
C 5 4 3 2 1

This book is printed on acid-free paper.

Library of Congress Cataloging-in-Publication Data

Schutz, Wallace J.
   Abandoned by Lincoln: a military biography of General John Pope / Wallace J.
Schutz, Walter N. Trenerry.
      p. cm.
   Includes bibliographical references.
   ISBN 0-252-01675-0 (alk. paper)
      1. Pope, John, 1822–1892.   2. Generals—United States—Biography.
3. United States. Army—Biography.   4. United States—History—
Civil War, 1861–1865—Campaigns.   I. Trenerry, Walter N., 1917–
   II. Title.
E467.1P76S37   1990
973.7′092—dc20
   [B]   89-36543
                                                                  CIP

TO

Jean

AND

Mary Jane

Justice, slow sometimes, comes to us all at last, and the present case, be assured, will be no exception. Time makes all things even, and will make up the record in due season.

JOHN POPE to Mrs. Philip Kearny
October 30, 1862

Contents

MAPS

Preface

This is the first formal biography of General John Pope, who is the only commanding general of a major Union army in the Civil War not to have had one. Because there is not much material about the personal John Pope, earlier writers may have given up. Pope wrote his only reminiscences in an article about the Second Battle of Bull Run, written when he was sixty-four. He did not keep a diary. His family and friends did not keep many of his letters. Few outsiders wrote about him.

In history books Pope strides abruptly into the center of things in 1862, captures Island No. 10, loses the Second Battle of Bull Run, and strides off into obscurity. Yet Pope spent forty-eight years in the regular army, including four years at West Point, and took part in most of the great dramas of his day.

The authors hope to put the man in his proper setting and to clear up some misunderstandings about what he set out to do, as opposed to what people seem to think he set out to do, in his Virginia campaign. How and why he became Lincoln's abandoned general will become clear in the discussion of the Second Bull Run campaign and the armed politics of 1862.

Acknowledgments

Thanks for invaluable help are due to Kenneth T. Morse, Reference Librarian and Bibliographer, University of Rhode Island Library, whose professional knowledge and personal interest called the writers' attention to sources not previously used. Dr. Richard N. Ellis, Head of the Department of Southwest Studies, Fort Lewis College, Durango, Colorado, made helpful suggestions and kindly allowed us to quote from his excellent book, *General Pope and U.S. Indian Policy*. Dr. Rodney C. Loehr, Professor Emeritus of History at the University of Minnesota and a Civil War Round Table member, urged us to undertake this biography and at all times continued to support our efforts.

Continuous encouragement also came from the late Professor E. B. Long of the University of Wyoming, Laramie. Lois Stanley of St. Louis went beyond the call of duty in her research of Pope's Missouri assignments. Douglass R. Cadwallader of Minneapolis, a great-grandson of William Pope, the general's brother, provided family information, as did Helen Bacon of Washington, D.C. Dorothy Kebker of Genoa, Ohio, did the investigation on the Horton family. Gratitude must also be expressed for valuable aid given by the late Mary A. Pope of Walla Walla, Washington, granddaughter of the Popes, who supplied us with family records.

In the realm of encouragement, our wives, Jean Schutz and Mary Jane Trenerry, were ever ready to listen to our plans and problems, and exhibited a patience that matched their encouragement. In addition, credit must be paid Jean Schutz and Amy Schutz for their work in drawing the original maps. Acknowledgment should also be made to the University of Minnesota Geography Department's cartography lab for producing the final versions.

Thanks are also given to the staffs of numerous libraries and institutions. Without the help of these devoted people and the great libraries and institutions that were consulted, this biography could not have been undertaken. The blemishes are our own.

PART 1

UPHILL

Chapter One

YOUTH

JOHN POPE, WHO STANDS characterized forever in American history books as the Union general who lost the Second Battle of Bull Run, served forty-eight years in the United States Army. His career opened with promise, ripened, and dwindled into frustration and disappointment. He seems to have had every good quality, including an unfounded trust in subordinates and an unrewarded faith in the democratic government that handled him roughly. In the end he lacked the deviousness that went with success.

Pope was born in Louisville, Kentucky, on March 16, 1822, but grew up in the village of Kaskaskia, Illinois, on the Mississippi River. His heritage blended the best of North and South. On his father's side he could claim to come from a First Family of Virginia; on his mother's, from Pilgrims.

The general-to-be began his life not only well born but well connected. When he was born his father, Judge Nathaniel Pope, was the only United States district judge in Illinois. John's maternal grandfather, Elijah Backus, headed the Illinois Land Office in 1807. Both men held top-rank presidential appointments, showing that they had been important to administrations handing out patronage.

The Pope family was founded in 1635 by Nathaniel Pope, who left England to become a Virginia planter. He came into the mainstream of American folklore when his daughter Ann married George Washington's great-grandfather.[1] A century later one of his descendants, William Pope, John Pope's grandfather, served in Washington's army and after the war married a Virginian, Penelope Edwards. Penelope's nephew, Ninian Edwards, became the first governor of Illinois Territory and his son, also named Ninian, married a sister of Mary Todd Lincoln.

On his mother's side, John Pope's ancestors included Reverend William Hyde, who in 1636 joined the Reverend Thomas Hooker in founding Hartford, Connecticut, and its democratic form of government; John Haynes, governor of Massachusetts Bay in 1635 and convert to Hartford democracy in 1639; and Matthew Griswold, deputy governor of Connecticut during the American Revolution.[2]

John Pope's father, Nathaniel Pope, grew up in Lexington, Kentucky, where the Pope family was well known. He was personally acquainted with Henry Clay, the up-and-coming leader of the Kentucky bar. After studying for a time at the new Transylvania University, Nathaniel Pope returned to reading law, possibly in Henry Clay's law office, and was admitted to the Kentucky bar in 1804 at the age of twenty. In that year Nathaniel moved to Ste. Genevieve, Missouri, and set up his law practice across the Mississippi from Kaskaskia. Here his future wife, Lucretia Backus, was keeping house for her father, Elijah. The young couple met, fell in love, and were married in 1808. They lived in Ste. Genevieve about one year and then moved to Kaskaskia, their permanent home.

Kaskaskia was not a haphazard choice. In 1809 Congress set up the territory of Illinois and fixed Kaskaskia as its capital.[3] In that year Nathaniel Pope's older brother, John, happened to be serving as senator from Kentucky with Henry Clay. In an understandable sequence the president appointed Ninian Edwards governor of the new territory and Nathaniel Pope the territorial secretary.[4]

After editing the first compendium of Illinois laws in 1815[5] Nathaniel Pope was elected territorial delegate in 1816 and was Illinois's first member of Congress until 1819. As territorial delegate Nathaniel helped add two amendments to the act enabling Illinois to become a state, earning the double titles the Man Who Made Chicago and the Father of the Illinois School System.

Pope's first amendment secured the Chicago area for Illinois by setting the line of 42°40' north latitude as the state's northern boundary, in place of the proposed south shore of Lake Michigan. His second amendment set aside 3 percent of the proceeds of state land sales as a school fund and 2 percent for roads[6] in place of the 5 percent for roads assigned in other states growing out of the Northwest Territory.

In spite of his good work for Illinois, Nathaniel Pope lost the race for Congress in 1818 and in 1819 found himself out of a political job for the first time since 1809. But a defeated politician with connections rarely suffers, and when a timely act of Congress created a new judicial district of Illinois entitled to a United States district judge,[7] the appointment went to Nathaniel Pope.

In 1819 Nathaniel saw this only as a stepping stone to higher office, a base from which to climb and to which he could return if he happened to fall. He ran for the United States Senate in 1824 and lost. In 1826 a vacancy opened in the Supreme Court of the United States. Nathaniel spent several weeks in the capital knocking on doors and pleading with friends but the appointment went to another. In 1828 he ran again for the United States Senate and lost. Perhaps feeling that it was not to be, he entered no further political races and remained a district judge until his death in 1850.

Until 1820 Judge Pope belonged to Jefferson's Democratic Republican party, but in 1820 the Missouri Compromise forced people to look into their consciences and take sides on slavery. Judge Pope joined the antislavery wing of his party without hesitation. In 1834, the same year that Lincoln entered his first political race as a Whig, Judge Pope joined Henry Clay's new Whig party.

In his day Nathaniel Pope was a well-known Illinois character. Of middle height, stocky, with an oversized head, he cultivated a rough manner, postured, and roared. People either praised him for his oddities or detested him as a crude frontier blowhard. A lawyer from Rockford, Illinois, remembered, "He had a head like a half-bushel, with brains enough for six men. He was learned, but rough and gruff. He had a wonderful knowledge of human nature and was utterly without fear. General Pope has many of his father's qualities."[8]

After he became a member of the Illinois bar in 1836, Abraham Lincoln practiced in Judge Pope's court, and the same Rockford lawyer recalled how the crusty judge softened his manner when Lincoln had a case:

> The Judge was rough toward everyone, but his roughness toward Lincoln had a touch of tenderness in it. He would sometimes rebuke him, but in a sort of fatherly way. . . . Many people wondered at the favor shown to John Pope by Mr. Lincoln during the war. . . . Lincoln understood the sort of roar in John

Pope's proclamations which many people thought gasconnade.
That roar he got from his gruff old father; it was the roar of the
lion and Lincoln had heard it a thousand times.[9]

The future general grew up in Kaskaskia under this booming
guidance with the advantage of having met most of the leading
Illinois lawyers who would have national power when Lincoln
became president.

The Popes seem to have had a close family life in the amiable
setting of Kaskaskia, where many people still spoke French on the
streets and where the larger homes with private libraries, owned by
men and women of taste, gave the village the name of Little Paris.[10]
John Pope had an older brother, William (born 1816), sisters
Penelope (born 1818) and Elizabeth (born 1820), and twin sisters,
Cynthia and Lucretia (born 1824).

When he had time, Judge Pope worked at being pedagogue as
well as father, trying to guide his children's literary tastes toward
the English, Greek, and Latin classics, teaching them what French
he knew, encouraging them to use his library freely, and taking
them to his court to watch trials and to meet the men in frock coats
and stovepipe hats who gathered there. He could do little more. If
John Pope was a fair sample, however, Judge Pope was a tremendous influence on his children, leaving them, in John's case, with
the lion's roar but also leaving them with a lifelong respect for
learning, scientific curiosity, and the United States Constitution
and system of government, as well as a lifelong hatred of slavery.

John Pope absorbed his father's bookishness. His brother and
sisters called him the "family student" because he always seemed to
be reading something about science or history. Although nothing
is known about it, he probably had an early interest in warriors and
battles.

In 1838 John Pope was sixteen years old, a stocky, barrel-chested
young man of medium height, given to roaring, posturing, and
swaggering, and educated as far as his father and Kaskaskia could
educate him. John presumably got his formal education in elemen-
tary and secondary schools in Kaskaskia, but there is no record of
his education or of the schools themselves. His parents had wanted
him to enter college but the judge knew that his judicial salary of
$1,000 a year[11] would not stretch far enough to pay tuition at a

leading private college, and since 1836 he had been working to get John appointed a West Point cadet.

This would not necessarily mean an army career. In 1838 the United States Military Academy was the foremost American technical school and its graduates the leading American engineers in private life as well as in the army. The tiny United States Army of 1838 could not take all the academy's graduates and many of them left for civilian life. In 1861, for instance, West Point graduates in civilian life included Ulysses S. Grant, merchant; William Sherman, street railway executive; George McClellan, railroad president; and Stonewall Jackson, mathematics teacher.

Academy appointments went by congressional districts. Each member of Congress had one appointment about every four years. Since these appointments were scarce and members of Congress were politicians, appointments usually went to pay off political debts or to create political debts payable in the future. What Judge Nathaniel Pope had to trade for an appointment never surfaced, but thanks to William R. May of the Third Congressional District of Illinois, the secretary of war was pleased to appoint John Pope a cadet, to graduate, if all went well, with the class of 1842. His letter of acceptance, dated March 20, 1838, bearing his father's endorsement and consent, is still in his personal file.[12]

John Pope could now see how he liked army life. He would serve under President Martin van Buren, Secretary of War Joel R. Poinsett, and General of the Army Winfield Scott. He would be much closer to Major Richard Delafield, Superintendent of the Academy, and Captain Charles F. Smith, Commandant of Cadets. 1838 was not a bad year to enter the army. The United States had had much turmoil that might lead to military action and speedy promotion: the Texas War of Independence in 1836; the murder of the abolitionist Elijah P. Lovejoy in Alton, Illinois, in 1837; and the British seizure of the American ship *Caroline* on Lake Erie, also in 1837.

NOTES

1. Rev. G. W. Beale, "Col. Nathaniel Pope and His Descendants," *William & Mary Quarterly* 12:192 (July 1903). All material on John Pope's ancestors, except his father, comes from this article.

2. Reuben H. Walworth, *The Hyde Genealogy,* 2 vols. (Albany, N.Y., 1864), 2:920.
3. Act of Feb. 3, 1809, 2 Stat. 514.
4. Paul M. Angle, "Nathaniel Pope, 1784–1850, a Memoir" (Illinois State Historical Society Pub. no. 43, Springfield, 1936), 121–22. Unless otherwise noted, all material on Nathaniel Pope comes from this publication.
5. Nathaniel Pope, ed., *The Laws of Illinois Territory,* 2 vols. (Kaskaskia, 1815).
6. Act of Apr. 18, 1818, 3 Stat. 428, secs. 2, 6.
7. Act of Mar. 3, 1819, 3 Stat. 502.
8. Angle, 177.
9. Ibid., 178.
10. Merlin G. Cox, "John Pope, Fighting General from Illinois" (Ph.D. diss., University of Florida, 1956), 12–13.
11. Act of Sept. 23, 1789, 1 Stat. 72.
12. John Pope to Joel R. Poinsett, Mar. 20, 1838, RG 94 NA, John Pope.

Chapter Two

THE ARMY

AFTER TRAVELING MORE THAN 1,000 miles, John Pope reached West Point in June 1838 to enter a form of society new to him. Without exposure to military life, he found everything strange, from the gray stone buildings to the bugle calls and drum beats, from the rows of cadets marching, eyes front, in their 1814-style uniforms, to the stiff formalities of salutes and formations.[1] Even the Hudson River countryside was strange. It was settled, dotted with well-kept country homes still owned by the descendants of patroons, nothing like frontier settlements along the Mississippi that Pope knew.

Pope had little time to take this in consciously because he first had to pass the entrance exam. In the act that set up the military academy, Congress specified it should be made up of "cadets well-versed in reading and writing and arithmetic."[2] Superintendent Sylvanus Thayer, who headed the academy from 1817 to 1832, interpreted this to mean that each appointee had to pass a written examination before he could be enrolled.[3] On a June day in 1838, John Pope and ninety-eight other nervous, sweating boys wrote an examination in reading, writing, spelling, and arithmetic through decimal functions, scratching some of their answers in chalk on blackboards in the presence of the thirteen uniformed officers of the examining panel.[4] Pope survived.

The survivors then listened to an officer read the Articles of War, swore to serve the United States well and faithfully as a soldier, and were issued gray cadet's uniforms. Pope was now a cadet in the army and under military discipline. His officers would call him Mr. Pope. The West Point upperclassmen would call him by the far less dignified title of "animal" living in "Beast Barracks."[5] Not much more than twenty years later John Pope and some of the other animals would be generals on fields of battle: N. J. T. Dana, Abner Doubleday, and William S. Rosecrans fighting for the Union; D. H. Hill, Mansfield Lovell, Lafayette McLaws, Earl Van Dorn, and Pope's nemesis of August 1862, James Longstreet, fighting for the Confederacy.

These cadets of June 1838, however, were looking no further ahead than the next step in their military education, basic training. On July 1 Pope and the class of 1842 went into summer camp for the ninety days' field training required each year by law.[6] Pope and his classmates would not leave West Point again until their sixty-day midway furloughs on July 1, 1840, and after that, not until graduation on July 1, 1842.[7]

Summer camp ended in the latter part of August, and on the first of September Pope began his West Point training. His day began at 0500 and ended with roll call at 2100. In his sixteen-hour day he spent four hours in drill, eight hours in class and military exercises, at least two hours in study, and his remaining two hours in eating three meals in the mess hall, reading mail, writing letters, and, if not too tired, in some kind of amusement. It was spartan and relentless. Until 1837 cadets had to sleep on the floor; Pope and his classmates had the new luxury of iron cots.[8]

In 1838 Superintendent Richard Delafield continued Sylvanus Thayer's guidelines for running the academy. Thayer had spent two years studying in France under a former aide to Napoleon[9] and had made the academy an offshoot of the French École Polytechnique, so much so, in fact, that cadets learned French and used French textbooks.[10] Napoleon was the model for training soldiers as well as using them. His ideal corps was comprised of more or less interchangeable officers who had undergone a standard course of training and would give and receive orders in a standard way. Training should stress performance as much as formal learning.

At West Point this meant that each cadet had a class standing made up of an average of academic grades and military performance. The top students in a class then had the first choice in picking their branches of service.[11] Each cadet started each academic year with an allowance of 200 demerits ("skins" or "gigs"). If a cadet overran his allowance in any year, he was expelled.[12] Trifling offenses like being late to formations brought a trifling number of demerits, but more serious offenses like sleeping on post or failing to salute officers brought many more. The only cadet to spend four years at the academy without earning a single demerit was Robert E. Lee, second in the class of 1829.[13]

The law fixed the number of cadets at 250.[14] At the opening of the academic year the faculty divided each class into sections of fifteen; those keener in academic subjects entered accelerated sections. Each cadet recited once each day in each subject. Instructors enforced military discipline in classrooms and civilian instructors held assimilated military rank. For outstanding academic work the faculty awarded an Order of Merit. For outstanding military performance, a cadet could earn military promotion; he might become a corporal in his second year, and in his third, a sergeant. As in the École Polytechnique, the West Point faculty also served as an academic board to keep subject matter and teaching methods up to date, and a board of eighteen to twenty-five visitors appointed by the secretary of war served as general overseers, coming to the academy at least once each year to monitor examinations.[15]

Academy records do not show section assignments for the class of 1842 but do set out the curriculum: chemistry, drawing, engineering (civil, military, and practical), ethics, French, geography, geology, history, mathematics, mineralogy, and natural and experimental philosophy (physics). Although not required, the West Point faculty gave a class in English.[16] Some military subjects were classroom subjects, like the art of war, artillery, and the tactics of infantry, cavalry, and artillery. Others were obviously not for the classroom, such as swordsmanship and, after 1840, horsemanship, taught by a riding master.[17] When a cadet finished the curriculum successfully, West Point awarded him a B.S. degree as well as his commission as an officer.

While nothing in West Point records shows anything about Pope's personal life, his academic record shows that he absorbed his studies better than most of his classmates. At the end of his first year he was fourteenth in artillery tactics and ethics; fifteenth in chemistry, engineering (civil and military), geology, and mineralogy; and twenty-second in infantry tactics.[18] At the end of his second year, Pope stood about the same: fourteenth in geology and mineralogy, seventeenth in natural and experimental philosophy, and a low forty-nine out of fifty-six in drawing. Seth Eastman, the painter of Plains Indians, was assistant instructor in drawing at this time and may have given Pope this sour grade.[19]

Of course life at West Point was not all recitation, parades, and polish. The academy held 250 lively young men, most of them away from home for the first time. Pope very likely joined the rest in reaching for the forbidden fruits of extra snacks, whiskey, cigars, and prostitutes, and probably risked the penalty of seven days' confinement to quarters by visiting Benny Havens's famous tavern, known to be a favorite hangout of William Sherman of the class of 1840.[20]

Pope did get into some kind of scrape, as a letter from his father to his mother disclosed: "enough had transpired to awaken the keenest anxiety, but as you are unwilling to believe I kept them to myself. He is at the most dangerous age and it is to be hoped that his time will be so fully employed that there will be no danger of a relapse."[21]

On June 30, 1840, Pope finished his second year at West Point and used his sixty-day furlough to go home. A cadet of the class of 1843 noted Pope's return to the academy in the fall:

> John Pope, better known as Gen. Pope, when on furlough returned to West Point with nice linen pants, with straps at the bottom and open down the front, which was found very convenient for a soldier who had to wear a waist belt; and although it shocked the sense of propriety of some maidenly ladies, it caught the eye of Major Richard Delafield, Superintendent of the Academy. His hobbies were economy and practical utility. He saw the advantage of Pope's breeches over the broad flap buttoned at the side, and notwithstanding the protest of Mrs. Delafield—who was reported to have said "the cadets thus dressed should not come in person to the house with their account books for orders"—and some other ladies, that stern old soldier gave the tailor permission to make the cadet pants open in front, and that consigned to oblivion the broad flap pants.[22]

Pope's fly pants never got the renown they deserved but probably gave more comfort to more generations of soldiers than McClellan's famous saddle ever did.

In September Pope took up the academic routine again but with no better results. At the end of his third year he stood fourteenth in

French, sixteenth in mathematics, nineteenth in English, and twenty-third in drawing.[23] In 1840 the academy added horsemanship to the curriculum and in this Pope excelled. Nearly fifty years later, Pope's classmate Longstreet remembered: "I was graduated with Pope at West Point. He was a handsome, dashing fellow and a splendid cavalryman, sitting his horse beautifully. I think he stood at the head for riding. He did not apply himself to his books very closely. He studied about as much as I did, but knew his lessons better."[24]

In his fourth year Pope studied the art of war and learned the doctrine that would control, to a disheartening extent, the moves of Civil War commanders in 1861 and later. Pope's teacher was Dennis Hart Mahan, number one in the class of 1824, father of the naval strategist Alfred Thayer Mahan, and teacher of almost every high-ranking Union and Confederate commander in the Civil War.

Mahan had studied in France and was the first American to write seriously on the theory of war.[25] Sylvanus Thayer chose him for his West Point assignment. Mahan saw the art of war as Napoleon's art of war as interpreted by Baron Antoine Henri Jomini, who served on the general staff of Marshal Ney, on the general staff of Napoleon, and became an aide to Czar Alexander I of Russia. Jomini wrote several books on Napoleon's campaigns and deduced from those campaigns lasting principles of warfare.[26]

As interpreted by Mahan, Jomini favored the attack but only from positions of strength. In a campaign the commander should seize and hold strategic territory, strike from interior lines without risking cut communications, and reduce or nullify all fortified places ahead before moving beyond them. A formal pitched battle usually decided a campaign. George McClellan's peninsular campaign of 1862 with its formal siege of Yorktown pointed out how well McClellan, second in the class of 1846, learned his lessons from Mahan and how closely he applied them.

While Pope might not have agreed with what Mahan taught, and Pope's later words and acts show that he did not, he could hardly escape Mahan's influence when he sat in Mahan's classroom after hearing his superior officers speak of Mahan as an authority. Pope was under that influence as late as 1862 when he served in General Henry Wager Halleck's command. Halleck graduated first in his class in 1839, and from 1839 to 1840 taught at West Point as

Mahan's assistant,[27] presumably chosen as the best man to teach Mahan's doctrine. In later years Halleck proved himself as rapt a follower of Jomini as Mahan, beating Mahan into print in 1846 with a book echoing some of Mahan's teachings based on Jomini[28] and in 1864 bringing out a translation of Jomini's *Life of Napoleon.*[29]

Pope had already studied tactics, which at West Point meant the tactics laid out in General Winfield Scott's manual.[30] After Scott became General of the Army in 1841 his rules naturally became doctrine for the whole army, including West Point teachers and cadets. Scott entered the army in 1808 and his Manual of Tactics looked back to the pre-Napoleonic warfare of eighteenth-century Europe in which professional armies did the fighting, relied more on maneuver than attack, avoided battle if possible, and waged limited wars to seize strategic territory.

The theories of Jomini, as taught by Mahan, and of Scott both focused on seizing territory as the true end of war, and in the spirit of the Age of Reason, were supposed to furnish final, closed systems resting on unchanging principles. As Civil War commanders found in the field, Jomini and Scott failed to take into account, among other things, the enlarged striking power of huge conscript armies, the risk in leaving any enemies under arms, the "fortunes of war," and, above all, the political background giving rise to war and furnishing the milieu in which wars take place.

Jomini did not need to weigh the effects of politics. His model, Napoleon, was a dictator-commander who served himself. In Napoleon's realm as much as Louis XIV's, the sovereign, council, and field marshal were one. The United States Army, however, served a democratic government in which every citizen turned critic and complained about anything and everything. With votes in hand, American citizens controlled the Washington bigwigs who controlled generals, and wise tactics for American general officers included keeping one eye on the White House and one eye on Congress while trying to focus both eyes on the enemy.

Mahan and any other West Point teacher would have been unwise to commit this truth to print, but John Pope and his classmates would have profited from hearing it said informally while they were cadets. They would get a jolt the first time they found out how much trouble and risk they faced in serving the actual government set up under such idealistic documents of freedom as the Declaration of Independence and the Constitution. If Pope could have read German he would have known that an antidote to Jomini was already in print.[31] Carl von Clausewitz fought against Napoleon, admired Napoleon's military genius, and wrote a penetrating study of war after musing on Napoleon's battles. Clausewitz saw that war and politics went hand in hand and that a commander must never forget that acts on the battlefield were political acts.

War, said Clausewitz, was no more than carrying out political aims by other means. Commanders try to impose their will on the enemy to achieve political ends. They would do it best and most speedily by destroying the armed forces of the enemy, but could also do it by destroying the enemy's resources or undermining the enemy's will to resist. In years to come Pope reached the same conclusions on his own and tried to carry them out in his race to defeat Jackson in 1862; Sherman likewise reached the same conclusions and applied them with success in making Georgia howl in 1864. In 1841 and 1842 these theories suited general staff officers far more than cadets likely to face Indian warriors of forest and prairie. Standing at the bottom of the ladder and far from strategic or even tactical responsibilities, Pope and the class of 1842 probably put this esoteric theorizing in the back of their minds to think about later when they had more power.

Having tasted such learning at least, John Pope finished his four years on June 30, 1842, standing number seventeen in a class of fifty-six. Nathaniel and Lucretia Pope came from Kaskaskia to see their son graduate, the judge grumbling that John should have finished higher than he did.

Pope chose the Topographical Engineers as his branch of service. In 1842 cadets who stood one through eight could choose the Engineers; nine through twenty-six any branch but the Engineers; those below twenty-six had only a choice between the Infantry and the Dragoons.[32] The Topographical Engineers had existed only since 1838 and had a full strength of thirty-six officers including the commanding colonel.[33] When Pope graduated, the corps was full, but the law allowed a graduating cadet to serve in brevet grade as supernumerary in any branch that was full. When a vacancy opened, the supernumerary would fill it and drop the brevet.[34]

Pope never said why he chose the Topographical Engineers. This was not a fighter's corps, but then neither was the Corps of Engineers, kept open year after year only to the academy's top graduates. Pope had already quietly made the most important choice of his life: he would be a soldier. He left West Point on July 1, 1842, to spend his ninety-day leave showing off his new uniform in Kaskaskia, after which he would await his first assignment.

NOTES

1. Thomas Fleming, *West Point: The Men and Times of the United States Military Academy* (New York, 1969), 22. The uniforms were those of General Winfield Scott's men at the Battle of Chippewa in 1814.
2. Act of Apr. 29, 1812, 2 Stat. 359.
3. Fleming, 38.
4. Lloyd Lewis, *Captain Sam Grant* (New York, 1950), 68.
5. Ibid.
6. Act of Apr. 29, 1812, 2 Stat. 359; Fleming, 38.
7. Ibid.
8. Fleming, 96–97.
9. Ibid., 25.
10. Ibid., 26.
11. See entries for the class of 1842 in G. W. Cullum, *Biographical Register of the Officers and Graduates of the United States Military Academy,* 2 vols. (Washington, 1891).
12. Fleming, 95.
13. Lewis, 81.
14. Act of Apr. 29, 1812, 2 Stat. 59.
15. Fleming, 31, 37.
16. Lewis, 82.
17. "Cadets Arranged in Order of Merit in Their Respective Classes, as Determined at the General Examination in June 1840" (West Point, 1840).
18. Ibid., 1839.
19. Ibid., 1840.
20. Fleming, 93; Lewis, 69, 73.
21. Paul M. Angle, "Nathaniel Pope, 1784–1850, A Memoir" (Illinois State Historical Society Pub. no. 43, Springfield, 1936), 165.
22. Samuel G. French, *Two Wars: An Autobiography* (Nashville, 1901), 11.
23. "Cadets Arranged," 1841.
24. Clarence C. Buel and Robert U. Johnson, eds., *Battles and Leaders of the Civil War,* 4 vols. (New York, 1887), 2:524.
25. Russell L. Weigley, *The American Way of War: A History of United States Military Strategy and Policy* (New York, 1973), 82, 87.
26. Baron Antoine Henry de Jomini, *Precis de l'Art de la Guerre* (Brussels, 1836).

27. "Cadets Arranged," 1839, 1840.
28. Henry W. Halleck, *Elements of Military Art and Science* (Boston, 1846).
29. Baron Antoine Henri de Jomini, *Vie Politique et Militaire de Napoleon,* Henry W. Halleck, trans. (New York, 1864).
30. Winfield Scott, *Infantry Tactics* (Washington, 1834).
31. Carl von Clausewitz, *Vom Kriege,* 3 vols. (Berlin, 1832); *On War,* Col. J. J. Graham, trans. (London, 1873).
32. *Biographical Register.*
33. Act of July 5, 1838, 5 Stat. 256.
34. Act of Apr. 29, 1812, 2 Stat. 359.

Chapter Three

ACTIVE DUTY

BREVET SECOND LIEUTENANT JOHN POPE'S ninety-day graduation leave came to an end on October 5, 1842, when he opened a letter from Colonel J. J. Abert, Chief of the Corps of Topographical Engineers, assigning him to active duty at Palatka, Florida, under the command of Captain Joseph E. Johnston.[1] Johnston had spent the years of 1838 through 1842 in Florida as a topographical engineer during the First Seminole War. When the war ended in 1842 he had the further assignment of helping the battered settlers resume their lives. Under the Armed Occupation Act of 1842[2] Congress awarded 160 acres of Florida land to any person who would settle on it and agree to bear arms. This way Florida residents could handle their everyday defense against marauders and leave the army free for other assignments. This meant surveying the public lands and laying out roads and canals to give access to them.

Pope reported to Johnston and spent the rest of 1842 trudging through the north Florida pineries with his compass, telescope, rods, chains, and field notebooks in the company of mosquitoes and rattlesnakes. By 1843 he left and somehow struck out on his own to Washington to arrange a better assignment. He fell into company with Lieutenant George H. Thomas of the class of 1840 and the two of them experienced the primitive pleasures of railroad travel in that day: "On the way to Norfolk the rails were covered with frost and the driving wheels slipped so that we all had to get out of the cars and help push the train over a slight ascent to a bridge."[3]

Pope reached Washington and managed to get a change of station to Savannah, Georgia, but after a year, Savannah, too, lost its charm and Pope started to pull strings outside military channels. He made no secret of wanting to join the command of Lieutenant Colonel Stephen H. Long at Louisville. At that time Long was famous as the explorer of Minnesota, Wisconsin, and part of the Rocky Mountains, and Pope very likely wanted to share in the glory of laying out new trails in far-away places. Sometime in 1844 Pope bypassed everyone in the army and wrote directly to Senator James Semple of Illinois asking help in getting assigned to Long's command. Knowingly or unknowingly, the senator let the procedure slip when he wrote directly to Colonel Abert, Chief of Topographical Engineers, asking Abert to give Pope the assignment.[4]

In the army writing to a politician over the heads of commanding officers is unpardonable, and Abert exploded. He wrote Pope's commanding officer on February 4, 1844:

> I have just received a note from Mr. Semple of the Senate in which he says that he has been requested by Lieut. Pope to make known his wish to be transferred to some station on duty in the West. Mr. Semple has been informed that Lieut. Pope's request could not be complied with without severe prejudice to the public service.
>
> The irregularity of Lieut. Pope's course deserves some rebuke and is the more surprising as it was presumed that his education would have imbued his mind with more correct notions of military propriety. If the positions and duties of officers could be influenced by applications of this kind, the command of the Corps should cease to be in its Chief but would be actually in any public man to whom an officer might apply.
>
> Lieut. Pope has in his application not only violated sound military principles, but also the regulations which define the course which officers should pursue on any matter connected with their public relations.[5]

After playing this poor opening gambit, Pope compounded it when on September 14, 1844, he bypassed the whole Corps of Topographical Engineers to write directly to the Adjutant General, asking for three weeks' leave because "Business of a private and personal nature requires my presence in the west & it is absolutely necessary for me to be there."[6]

This letter, too, came back to Colonel Abert's office but Abert was away and his deputy approved the request.[7] When Abert returned he saw Pope listed as absent on three weeks' leave, now extended to sixty-seven days by Abert's deputy.[8] The colonel also read a letter from Major James D. Graham asking for a topographical engineer to serve on the American-Canadian Boundary Survey under the 1842 Webster-Ashburton Treaty.[9] Abert had just the man in mind. If Pope disliked Florida and Georgia, he could see how well he liked one of the real military outposts. On October 23, 1844, Abert ordered Pope to report to Major Graham at Houlton, Maine.[10] Pope must have been dismayed. His "business of a private and personal nature" keeping him on leave was a medical problem that he had not disclosed to his chief and one that left him unfit for active duty. He had no choice but to tell.

He wrote Abert enclosing a certificate from his friend and physician Dr. Alex Hope of Alton, Illinois:

> I have carefully examined this officer and find that he is suffering under the effects of secondary syphilis and that he has been afflicted with the disease for five weeks & that as a consequence thereof he is in my opinion unfit for active duty. I further declare my belief that he will not be able to resume his duties in a less period than three weeks as exercise of any description will greatly retard his recovery.[11]

Pope accompanied the certificate with a request for further leave. Abert replied that he had forwarded Pope's request to the Adjutant General.[12] Pope came back with an astonishing plea for additional leave and for assignment to Stephen H. Long's command.[13] The exasperated Colonel exploded again, writing:

> In reference to your leave of absence, allow me to say that the issue of these indulgences in your case already exceeds that of any officer in the Corps who has been as short a time in commission as yourself and I doubt if there be many cases of similar extent of indulgence in the whole Army.
>
> Upon your application to be placed on duty with Col. Long, I have to say that the reasons assigned by you are altogether insufficient being entirely matters of personal convenience. Moreover it is not allowable that the younger officers of the Corps should select their duties. I must presume that when you chose this branch of the service, it was with the desire and the ambition of becoming useful in it, of acquiring a knowledge of its duties, a knowledge of the use of instruments, and of the

various methods of collecting facts of a survey, reducing them to form, and of exhibiting them in properly made drawings. The Chief of the Corps is the best judge of what posting will the sooner enable a young officer to acquire that knowledge, and therefore takes it upon himself to assign the officer.[14]

As late as December 28, 1844, Pope still hung back in Kaskaskia, but after getting a no-nonsense prod from Colonel Abert, left reluctantly for his Maine assignment.[15] He would serve among the "one or more officers of the corps of topographical engineers . . . to aid and assist" in the Canadian-American boundary survey.[16] Major Graham had charge of the first leg. Graham went with Long on Long's first expedition west, and since 1837 had headed an American survey of the Maine–New Brunswick boundary.[17] He was as crusty as Abert, but like Abert was a capable officer who would also find Pope difficult.

The survey crew had to run a 600-mile line from Eastport, Maine, the mouth of the St. Croix River, to Rouse's Point, New York, headwaters of the St. Lawrence. This line ran through forest and field, mountain and valley, and over land and water. Pope reached his station in the coldest part of winter and one of Major Graham's reports shows the boreal conditions facing these surveyors: "On the morning of the 12th of December at 7^{h}30^m A.M. the thermometer outside of my tent stood at 34° below zero of Fahrenheit scale. The proportion of stormy and cloudy weather is so great in this Latitude after October that we . . . were compelled to prosecute our observations whenever the weather was clear, without regard to temperature."[18]

For a year and a half, including the winters of both 1845 and 1846, Pope tramped the hills of Maine "without regard for temperature" as he helped to mark the international boundary line. When in his report for 1845 Major Graham praised his Topographical Engineers as soldiers "who uniformly acquitted themselves in a manner highly useful to the country"[19] without mentioning Pope by name, Pope sat down in his tent and wrote a "memoir" of his own describing his work on the survey and certainly not underplaying his role. He sent his memoir directly to Colonel Abert, over Major Graham's head, and Abert, spluttering about "proper channels" and "irregularity" sent it to Major Graham.[20] The memoir has now disappeared but lasted long enough to surface later in Pope's career and provoke more hot-headed correspondence. For the time being, Pope's work in the far North was over. On June 2, 1846, he left Maine to join General Zachary Taylor's forces on the Rio Grande, leaving to others the boring business of reworking field notes and drawing maps. Pope marched off to test his good opinion of himself in war.

He was twenty-four years old. During his life the United States left the Era of Good Feelings to enter an Era of Tension,[21] although in the course of his exhausting routine at West Point and his military assignments that sent him to remote frontiers, Pope may have felt he spent these years in a vacuum. President followed president: Adams, Jackson, Van Buren, Harrison, Tyler, Polk. The last great men of the Revolution, Adams and Jefferson, died on July 4, 1826. Secretaries of War John C. Calhoun and Lewis Cass improved the army. A Seven Years' War with the Seminoles upset Florida from 1835 to 1842 and destroyed the reputation of more than one military commander. While making a Canadian boundary treaty with Great Britain, Americans still talked of annexing Canada, tried to seize Cuba, and protested an 1837 British seizure on Lake Erie of an American supply ship to Canadian rebels. Westward, Americans shouted "Fifty-Four Forty or Fight!" in another boundary quarrel over Oregon.

Slavery, brought into public discussion by the Missouri Compromise in 1820 and the Nullification Crisis in 1832, began to split the Union and take precedence over any other issue. In the Senate, Daniel Webster of Massachusetts debated Robert Hayne of South Carolina over who ruled under the Constitution, the Union government or the states. In the House, former president John Quincy Adams went straight to the moral issue by denouncing slavery as evil. For the time being a national itch for expansion in the name of Manifest Destiny held North and South together in a crusade that proslavery and antislavery forces tried to bend to their own purposes. Texas furnished the excuse for a slavery battle.

In 1836 Texans won their war of independence from Mexico and set up the slaveholding Republic of Texas. Nine years later on the petition of Texas, the United States annexed the former republic in spite of Mexican warnings that annexation meant war, and in so doing started a boundary dispute between Texas and Mexico.

President James K. Polk welcomed the boundary dispute as an excuse for meddling even though he had made it a Democratic party measure to buy from Mexico the lands making up Arizona, California, Colorado, Idaho, Nevada, New Mexico, and Utah. He felt sure that Mexico would sell but still wanted extra reassurance.

In secret negotiations with Polk, recently ousted Mexican president Antonio Lopez y Santa Ana promised to sell the lands if Polk would help him get back to Mexico from his exile in Cuba. Santa Ana told Polk that any sale would have to appear as though it were made under duress and suggested where the American army could take a threatening stand. Polk accordingly sent General Zachary Taylor to Fort Jesup, Louisiana, with a corps of observation that became an army of observation when it moved to Corpus Christi, Texas, and in the end became the army of occupation when Taylor led it across the Rio Grande heading for Monterrey.[22]

Meanwhile, Santa Ana, fifty-two and one-legged, sailed through the American blockade of Mexico's east coast with his fifteen-year-old bride, "The Flower of Mexico," beat his opponent, raised an army of liberation, and swore to drive the last foreigner from the soil of Mexico. Polk began to wonder about his agreement, as did all the politicians who thought they had an agreement Santa Ana would honor.

Unsure of what the Mexicans claimed as their northern boundary, Polk ordered Taylor to cross the Nueces River, which Taylor did without incident. But when Taylor followed Polk's further orders and crossed the Rio Grande, the Mexicans made it clear they would stand and fight. Armed hostilities opened with American victories at Palo Alto on May 8, 1846, and at Resaca de la Palma on May 9;[23] Congress formally declared war on May 13.[24] Taylor's strategy, dictated by Polk, would be to invade northern Mexico and hold it as security for the sale promised by Santa Ana.

Polk's strategy was fueled by politics. President Polk was a Democrat who staked the future of his party and his own political future on getting the Mexican lands that he wanted. Both of the seasoned generals available were Whigs. Polk chose Zachary Taylor to carry the Democratic party program into effect; Taylor was not only a Whig, but a Whig with plans for the White House. Polk found himself in a spot like that of Lincoln in 1861 or that of Franklin Delano Roosevelt in 1942. Without a real choice of generals, whatever he did would begin a political rivalry. While the Democrats would claim any Taylor victories for the administration, the Whigs would call them the triumphs of their next presidential candidate. If Polk tried to run a low-key military campaign, Whigs would scream "politics!" and Taylor might plunge ahead anyway. If Polk ordered vigorous moves, Taylor would come out the hero of the hour if he succeeded or Taylor might find it more advantageous politically to drag his feet until American voters started to complain about the cost of a long, drawn-out war. Taylor could use the excuse that the administration failed to support him properly; the Whigs would argue the need for a change.

When John Pope reached camp in June 1846, he found himself assigned to General Taylor's staff and in a good place to watch how a veteran of war and politics conducted himself in the field with his eye on the voting public. Pope probably knew little about the Machiavellian background of this campaign, though. He spent his time, like the other topographical engineers, designing and helping to lay out roads and bridges and making reconnaissances to map the enemy's position, the advantages and disadvantages of ground held by the enemy, and the best routes for attack.[25] He served under the immediate command of Captain Thomas B. Linnard along with Lieutenant William B. Franklin, who would let him down in a crisis in 1862, and with Lieutenant George G. Meade who would turn the Confederates back at Gettysburg in 1863.

Major Joseph Mansfield, with Captain Robert E. Lee on his staff, commanded all the engineers. In Taylor's army Pope would run across most of the men who would be top officers in the Civil War: Jefferson Davis, rifle regiment commander; Ulysses S. Grant, infantry officer; Joseph E. Johnston, his former commanding officer in Florida; and Braxton Bragg, artillery battery commander. While nearly all the future Union generals were serving in the army in Mexico, their future commander-in-chief, Abraham Lincoln, was sitting in the House of Representatives in his one and only term in Congress, denouncing the Mexican War as unjust and fought only to extend slavery.

During the hot months of June, July, and August, 1846, Pope and the other young officers spent most of their time learning their duties and working on campaign plans as volunteers came into camp to take basic training and get their assignments. The young men spent the rest of their time analyzing the senoritas, noting that "their bosoms were not compressed in stays, or mantled in cashmeres, but heaved freely under the healthful influence of the genial sun and balmy air."[26]

When training ended in August 1846, Taylor thought he might be able to rely on his unruly volunteers for some kind of duty, so the army began to march in columns westward along the Rio Grande. At times the temperature reached 110°.[27] On September 13, all columns met at Cerralvo[28] in the desert south of the Rio Grande. On the march Pope rode with the scouts and engineers ahead of the main body, mapping the country, outlining march and supply routes, and marking good points for supply depots.

Taylor was on the way to Monterrey and expected the Mexicans to surrender the city without a fight, knowing Polk's secret agreement with Santa Ana. Santa Ana ordered the city abandoned, but Generals Pedro de Ampudia, Mariano Arista, and Francisco Mejia commanding the Mexican troops in Monterrey refused to obey an order they thought shameful and prepared to stand and defend. Taylor knew he had to take the city, defended or undefended. In May Thurlow Weed, a Whig Party boss later to become a Republican, had whispered in Taylor's ear that the Whigs had their eyes on him as their candidate for president in the coming election of 1848.[29] To take Monterrey, Taylor thought, could clinch his nomination.

On September 19, the American soldiers could see the city of Monterrey looming above them to the south. A giant unfinished cathedral now used by the Mexicans as an artillery post commanded the approach. Taylor saw that he must seize or outflank this "Black Fort" to take the city.[30] Under Major Mansfield's direction Pope and the other topographical engineers made reconnaissances, picked a campsite for the troops in El Bosque de San Domingo, and went on to survey passages around the city the army could use in cutting the road to San Luis Potosi and Mexican communications with the South.[31] It was Pope's first experience in sighting and sketching in the open while armed enemy soldiers watched him through telescopes.

Using information gathered in these reconnaissances, Taylor planned his main attack on the city from the south accompanied by two diversionary attacks from the north, violating the military maxim against splitting forces in the face of the enemy. He had about 3,000 regulars and 3,500 volunteers. General Ampudia, commanding the Monterrey defenses, had 7,000 regulars, 3,000 conscripts, and a growing body of American deserters, largely Irish immigrants, known as the Legion de Estrangeros, but better known as the San Patricio Battalion.[32]

Although they outnumbered the Americans, the Mexicans did not attack but stood still to await the American attack. On September 20, the American Second Division followed one of the routes laid out by Pope and the other topographical engineers, outflanked the Mexican defenders under heavy fire, and seized the San Luis Potosi road. On the next morning the Second Division stood ready to launch the main attack from the south.[33] While the Second Division got ready to open the main attack, Taylor ordered Major Mansfield to lead elements of the First Division in a reconnaissance from the north, which would be the first of the two planned diversionary attacks to test the enemy's strength.[34] As a member of Major Mansfield's command, Lieutenant John Pope took part and finished his military training by going into combat.

Mansfield's reconnaissance found the enemy very strong. The Americans had rough going as they fought their way through narrow streets under fire from rooftops. After forcing their way past two redoubts they found themselves facing the Mexican bridge-head of La Purisima, next to General Mejia's headquarters, where Mexican artillery not more than one hundred yards away could use them as massed targets. Stalled and in danger of being cut off, the commander recalled his detachment.[35] During the fight Mexican infantry bounced two bullets off the scabbard of Pope's saber and struck down a topographical engineer, Captain Williams. While still under fire, Pope got off his horse, picked up Williams, and carried him into a house.[36] Mexican rifles also hit Major Mansfield, who crawled into the same house where Lieutenant Ulysses S. Grant remembered seeing all three.[37]

Although nothing has survived that Pope said or wrote about his feelings when under fire for the first time, his superiors saw that he acted cool, self-possessed, and energetic, as if battle gave him new life. Major Mansfield wrote that "Lieut. Pope executed his duties with great coolness & self-possession & deserves my highest praise."[38] Colonel Garland reported that Pope "deported himself as a gallant soldier under the heaviest fire of the enemy."[39] If he had fears, he overcame them. In 1862 a by no means uncritical reporter would call Pope cool and brave during the final debacle at Second Bull Run. He sat calmly on his horse watching the battle while bullets hummed past him and shells burst above him while he exposed himself to the same risks that his troops faced.

The battle for Monterrey lasted another two days until September 23 when the tired Americans knew that their ammunition was running low and began to feel that they would never take the city. Suddenly, the Mexican General Ampudia asked for an armistice; Taylor promptly granted one for eight weeks. Ampudia and his army marched out of Monterrey to head for San Luis Potosi, 300 miles to the south.[10]

In his official report of the battle for Monterrey, General Taylor praised his topographical engineers for their "valuable and efficient assistance" and wrote specifically that "Lieutenant Pope ... was active and zealous throughout the operations."[41] This mention would go into Pope's service record and Taylor's report would reach the secretary of war, the president, and Congress. In addition to being mentioned in three official reports, Pope earned a welcome promotion, becoming brevet first lieutenant as of September 23.[42]

Illinois politicians were keeping their eyes on Illinois citizens in the armed forces. On December 14, Lieutenant John Pope was one of two honored in a resolution of the General Assembly that stated his "brave and noble conduct" would "give us fully the power to assure our fellow-citizens of Illinois, that her sons who left their homes to fight the battles of their country, will well sustain the character of their native and adopted State."[43] The General Assembly followed this on January 20, 1847, by awarding Pope a sword for his courage in "carrying off the field, while exposed to the most imminent danger, amidst showers of balls, covering him with dust, a wounded fellow-officer."[44]

For the time being Pope could do no more than read the resolutions in copies sent by mail. He would sit with the army of occupation for the next five months while the army occupied Northern Mexico in hopes of forcing Santa Ana to hurry his promised sale of about half his country.

Serving on Taylor's staff gave Pope a chance to watch at close range the maneuvers of a soldier-politician on the upswing. On December 10, 1846, while still commanding an army in the field,

Taylor formally offered himself to the Whigs as their candidate for president in 1848.[45] Polk had expected this and made a counter-move to subdue Taylor and force Santa Ana to act. Polk gave command of a separate army to the other Whig general, Winfield Scott, with orders to land at Vera Cruz, march inland, and take Mexico City; he then ordered Taylor to stay in Monterrey but to ship most of his regular army troops to Scott. Taylor could see that President Polk meant the two rival Whigs to kill each other off politically or at least split the party into two factions. Taylor did not mind. He had his Monterrey victory safely in his pocket and had no interest in further battles that he might lose. Scott still had to win his victory and he could slip anywhere in his literally uphill fight from the beach of Vera Cruz up the mountains to the Halls of Montezuma.

Pope undoubtedly watched Taylor and may even have heard him discuss his plans. At headquarters nothing stayed hidden and Taylor himself, rough, genial, and talkative, made no secret of his ambition. In spite of an insider's view, Pope, however, seems to have stuck to his father's lifelong belief in democracy instead of becoming cynical about it. Even in 1876 Pope was writing in all seriousness to President-elect Hayes urging him in the name of morality to rise above party and give his all for civil service reform.

Early in 1847 the army of occupation's five months' lull nearly came to a disastrous end. Santa Ana decided that he would rather be a patriotic Mexican than a land broker for Americans. Seeing Scott's army move toward Vera Cruz, he reasoned that Taylor's unsupported army left in Monterrey might be an easy prize. He reasoned further that Taylor would not look for an attack from the south when 300 miles of desert stood between his army and the nearest sizeable Mexican settlement. To carry out his surprise plan he garnered 20,000 soldiers to serve with him, and on January 27 began a forced march north from San Luis Potosi.[46] His troops came in sight of the Americans on February 20.

At that time Taylor and his army of 5,000, nearly all volunteers, sat in camp on a high plateau near a farm called La Hacienda de San Juan de la Buena Vista, ten miles south of their Saltillo base and thirty miles north of the village of La Encarnacion. Suddenly patrols reported the arrival at La Encarnacion of 20,000 Mexican troops led by Santa Ana. Taylor had time to do no more than call in his outposts and wait for the attack that came on February 23. Santa Ana planned skillfully to envelop the American army from west and north, but he had failed to give his tired troops enough time to rest from their long desert march, and had failed to give enough credit to American artillery.

The Battle of Buena Vista lasted until the afternoon of February 24. Taylor's volunteers fought astonishingly well, and after Captain Braxton Bragg carried out Taylor's order, " 'Double-shot your guns and give 'em hell, Bragg,' " the Mexican line broke and the army fell back. The Americans had won a tremendous victory under the poor odds of one to four. Taylor could count on being the next president.[47] Santa Ana withdrew his troops in good order, and after his council advised against another attack he marched the army south. The still-outnumbered Americans had no thoughts of pursuit.

During the battle Pope rode into the thick of things along with General Taylor as one of Taylor's staff. He later drew the battlefield map for Taylor's official report, which read in part: "Lts. Pope and Franklin, Top. Engrs., were employed before and during the engagement in making reconnaissances and in the field were very active in bringing information and in conveying my orders to distant points."[48] This added another official mention to Pope's service record and again, as at Monterrey, brought Pope another promotion. As of February 23 he was Brevet Captain Pope.[49]

The rest of Pope's Mexican service was anticlimactic as the war came to its end. Taylor left the army for active politics on November 26, but Pope was still on duty in Mexico as late as April 1, 1848.[50] Santa Ana left the turmoil of Mexico for the quiet of Jamaica on May 5, 1848.[51] American and Mexican commissioners traded ratifications of the Treaty of Guadelupe Hidalgo on May 30, 1848, and Polk got his lands.[52]

Pope had reached the first peak in his life but would have to go back to the valleys for the next thirteen years. At twenty-six he was a seasoned combat officer, valued by his superiors, and egotistical, though with good reason. Away from the backbiting and paperwork of peacetime, he had found himself in the life of action. On October 27, 1849, Brevet Captain John Pope appeared in the Illinois House of Representatives at Springfield to receive from the hand of Governor French the sword voted by the Illinois legislature in 1847. Pope made a short acceptance speech with faint overtones of the coming conflict even then seen as irrepressible, saying in part, "I am neither virtuous nor stoical enough to say to you that this sword shall never be drawn but in a just cause, but I here devote both it and myself to the service of this my native state, whether right or wrong."[53] Memories of action, however, were fading away. Pope already knew that his next assignment would take him to the Minnesota frontier.[54] He did not know that he would stay on frontiers, far away from the mainstream, for the next ten years.

NOTES

1. Abert to Pope, Oct. 5, 1842, RG 77 NA.
2. Act of Aug. 4, 1842, 5 Stat. 502.
3. Samuel G. French, *Two Wars: An Autobiography* (Nashville, 1901), 24.
4. Abert to J. MacKay, Feb. 6, 1844, RG 77 NA.
5. Ibid.
6. Pope to R. Jones, Sept. 14, 1844, RG 94 NA.
7. Ibid.
8. Pope to Abert, Sept. 10, 1844, RG 94 NA.
9. Abert to J. D. Graham, Oct. 22, 1844, RG 77 NA; Abert to Graham, Dec. 2, 1844, RG 77 NA.
10. Abert to Pope, Oct. 23, 1844, RG 77 NA.
11. Certificate, Alex W. Hope, Oct. 25, 1844, RG 94 NA.
12. Pope to Abert, Oct. 25, 1844, RG 94, NA; Abert to Pope, Nov. 4, 1844, RG 77 NA.
13. Abert to Pope, Dec. 2, 1844, RG 77 NA.
14. Ibid.
15. Abert to Pope, Dec. 28, 1844, RG 94 NA.
16. Act of Mar. 3, 1843, 5 Stat. 623.
17. Act of Mar. 3, 1837, 5 Stat. 163.
18. Report, J. D. Graham to J. J. Abert, Nov. 5, 1846, RG 77 NA.
19. Ibid., Oct. 4, 1845, RG 77 NA.
20. Abert to Graham, May 29, 1846, RG 77 NA.
21. For a good general treatment of American history including this era, see Allan Nevins and Henry Steele Commager, *A Pocket History of the United States,* 7th ed. (New York, 1981).
22. K. Jackson Bauer, *The Mexican War 1846–48* (New York, 1974), 225–26.
23. Ibid., 52–57, 59–63.
24. Ibid.
25. Report, J. D. Graham to J. J. Abert, Oct. 4, 1845, RG 77 NA.
26. B. F. Scribner, *Campaign in Mexico* (Philadelphia, 1850), 19.
27. Bauer, 88.
28. Ibid., 90.

29. Ibid., 360.
30. Ibid., 90.
31. Ibid., 92.
32. Ibid., 89.
33. Report, Maj. J. F. K. Mansfield to Gen. Zachary Taylor, Oct. 9, 1846, RG 94 NA; J. Frost, *The Mexican War and Its Warriors* (New Haven, 1849), 75.
34. Ibid.
35. Ibid.; Bauer, 94.
36. *Illinois State Journal* (Springfield: Oct. 30, 1849).
37. E. B. Long, ed., *Personal Memoirs of U. S. Grant* (Cleveland, 1952), 55.
38. See note 33.
39. Report, Col. John Garland to Brig. Gen. David E. Twiggs, Sept. 24, 1846, RG 94 NA.
40. Bauer, 99–101.
41. *General Taylor and His Staff* (Philadelphia, 1848), 47–48.
42. Service Record, John Pope, RG 94 NA.
43. Joint Resolution 6, Laws of Illinois, 15th Gen. Assem., 1846–47, 179.
44. Joint Resolution 16, Laws of Illinois, 15th Gen. Assem., 1846–47.
45. David Lavender, *Climax at Buena Vista,* (Philadelphia, 1966), 88–89.
46. Bauer, 206.
47. Ibid., 216–17.
48. Report, Gen. Zachary Taylor to Adj. Gen., Mar., 6, 1847, RG 94 NA.
49. Service Record, John Pope, RG 94 NA.
50. Bauer, 224; Pope to Linnard, Apr. 1, 1848, RG 77 NA.
51. Bauer, 385.
52. Ibid., 387.
53. *Illinois State Journal* (Springfield: Oct. 30, 1849).
54. Abert to Pope, Apr. 20, 1849, RG 77 NA.

Chapter Four

FRONTIERS

POPE'S FIRST POSTWAR ASSIGNMENT took him to Fort Snelling, Minnesota, to join a survey party under Major Samuel Woods, who had orders to follow the Red River of the north to Pembina on the border between Minnesota and Prince Rupert's Land in search of sites for army posts.[1] In 1849 the federal administration wanted an American military presence on and near the Canadian border to keep the British and Minnesota's quarrelsome Indians in check.

Although resolving the Oregon border in 1846 settled some disputes, British-American relations remained tense. At the Minnesota border the British gave sanctuary to Indians running from angry Minnesotans, barred Minnesota fur traders from crossing the boundary to hunt, and quietly let Hudson's Bay Company fur traders slip south into Minnesota.

Minnesota Indians caused endless uproar because the Chippewas had an ancient dispute with the Sioux, who had an ancient dispute with the Winnebagoes. Feuding tribes fought each other whenever and wherever they met, in woods, in fields, or on village streets. To add to the turmoil, mixed-bloods at Pembina complained the United States government abandoned them. Since they were considered neither white nor Indian they did not receive protection from either.

Brevet Captain Pope boarded a riverboat at St. Louis on May 16, 1849, and reported at Fort Snelling six days later.[2] He found that he had to mark time until his party took off, and spent his first two weeks in Minnesota riding around St. Paul and St. Anthony, shaking hands with territorial officers and other Minnesota settlers whom he would meet again in 1862 on his second assignment to Minnesota.

On June 6 Major Woods and his party marched on a fifty-six-day hike to Pembina after covering 497 miles, as measured by Pope, traveling about nine miles a day.[3] Although Pope said his trip was without adventure, the party had one memorable night when lightning struck a tent and knocked a lieutenant unconscious. Pope and the other soldiers then christened the two nearby lakes the "Lightning Lakes."[4]

Throughout his trip north and his return to Fort Snelling, Pope seems to have ruffled his superior deliberately, almost looking for trouble and daring anyone to punish him when he found it. Like other veterans, he was not finding it easy to readjust to the peace-time army. As the party's one topographical engineer, Pope acted as though his orders issued in Washington and signed by a corps chief put him in a class apart from the detachment. Although Pope carried out his duties—measuring distances on his wagon-wheel odometer, taking azimuths, calculating mean time, latitude, longitude, and magnetic deviations from true north, sounding the Red River—he worked alone, commanding in his mind an expedition of one.[5] Furthermore, he disobeyed and meddled.

At Pembina Major Woods visited the forty-ninth-parallel monument set up by Major Stephen H. Long in 1823 to mark the British-American boundary. Pope wanted to resurvey the line and, if Long had made a mistake, to relocate it. Woods told Pope to leave it alone. That was not the tone to take with Brevet Captain Pope, who crossed the border at once and began to question British soldiers and Canadians, including the Hudson's Bay Company's chief factor, about what they remembered of the 1823 survey. When Woods heard about Pope's inquiries, he gave Pope a peremptory order to forget about Long's monument and to stay on the Minnesota side of the border; Pope obeyed.[6] If Long erred in 1823, Pope's discovery of the error in 1849 would at best make Pope look good, but at worst could lead to an international incident.

Barred from Prince Rupert's Land, Pope wandered around the Pembina settlement talking to the dissatisfied mixed-bloods (kin of the mixed-bloods who in 1870 and 1885 would rise with Louis Riel). These fur traders poured out their complaints about the British, the Hudson's Bay Company that owned Prince Rupert's Land, and the United States government that left them without protection from either the British or the company. They asked Pope to help them put their case before the government. Pope was cautious enough not to mention these talks to Major Woods, but the case for the mixed-bloods appeared at length in the report that Pope wrote later.[7]

Without much to do at the border and kept from following his own inclinations by Major Woods, Pope asked Woods if he could return to Fort Snelling alone. The Major agreed with enthusiasm, adding that Pope could have the company of another officer. "I did not think their presence with the command would be of any service to it," Woods wrote later in his official report.[8] Pope's return was more the ceremonial voyage of a territorial magnate than the everyday backtracking of a lieutenant. Stretching orders allowing him to hire four men for "special duties," he bought a thirty-three-foot canoe, loaded it with pemmican and buffalo meat, and hired eleven mixed-blood paddlers. Pope and his companions shoved off at Pembina on August 26, paddled up the Red and down the Crow Wing and Mississippi rivers, and reached Fort Snelling on September 27 to find that Woods and the main party had beaten them by twelve days in an overland march.[9] Pope left Fort Snelling quickly on a riverboat for St. Louis, where his orders allowed him to write his report.

On this assignment, as on every peacetime assignment up to this point, Pope did little but build up his name as a self-centered braggart, all too free in criticizing his superiors. In his official report of the Pembina expedition published by Congress, Major Woods wrote of his detached topographical engineer: "Brvt. Capt. Pope joined the expedition, continued with it, and left it, with the most ridiculous assumption of position, which he endeavored to maintain by misrepresentation and a wasteful extravagance of public monies placed at his disposal. His duties were neglected and he left his post (Fort Snelling) without authority in my absence."[10]

Pope, however, could handle a quill as deftly as Major Woods, and on February 5, 1850, finished a separate thirty-eight-page report for the Corps of Topographical Engineers. Congress ordered it published and Pope's report became a classic description of early Minnesota as seen in the light of Manifest Destiny.[11] To Pope the place had a limitless future. At the outset Pope wrote that he meant his report to be "entirely practical in its nature," unlike the "spritely narrative or the recital of wild adventure" that his forerunners and superior officers J. J. Abert, Emory, Fremont, and Long had written about their expeditions that had "furnished materials for personal adventure and historical incident."[12]

Leading off with some lyrical prose about Minnesota as a garden spot destined for immense commercial growth, Pope came to his practical recommendations. Indians, Pope said, were nuisances in the way of white settlement; they must go as quickly as possible. The United States should extinguish their remaining land titles and move the Minnesota tribes to places north and west.[13] While they remained, army detachments at posts scattered throughout the Indian country could send out daily patrols to enforce peace.[14] This was the first appearance in print of Pope's lifelong argument that Indian control rested on making them conscious that soldiers were watching them twenty-four hours a day.

Taking up the mixed-bloods' cause, Pope recommended a strong fort at Pembina backed by a smaller fort at the meeting of the Red River of the north and the Sioux Wood River. The Pembina fort would protect the mixed-bloods from the British and the Hudson's Bay Company, while furnishing a governmental center that these settlers wanted. Enlisted mixed-bloods could garrison the fort. A fort at Pembina was never constructed, but in 1858 Fort Abercrombie was built on the west side of the Red River sixteen miles north of its junction with the Sioux Wood River.[15]

Pope took care of Major Woods by recommending the sale of Fort Snelling, which Major Woods commanded. This fort between the growing villages of St. Paul and St. Anthony, Pope maintained, was already far from Indian country and was needless.[16] In a few years the United States did sell the fort, only to buy it back for use as an outpost and training center in the Civil War.

To develop Minnesota resources fully, Pope said, the territory needed money to build military roads, make streams navigable, and make land grants for railroads. If Congress took care of these, Pope foresaw a huge Minnesota transportation network for gathering Red River Valley wheat into the coming world depots and world ports of Duluth and St. Paul, and from there shipping it over Lake Superior and down the Mississippi River and all over the world.[17]

He must have had faith in his own rhetoric. At the end of his report he pleaded with someone in authority: "I have become so much interested in the country, and so fully convinced of the rapid progress it will make in wealth and population, that it would not only be a high honor but a deep gratification to me should I be so fortunate as to be selected for the purpose of continuing the explorations yet to be made within its borders."[18] As yet, however, those in authority did not feel like entrusting this to a twenty-seven-year-old lieutenant.

Along with Pope's report went a map labeled "by Capt[n] John Pope, Corps Top Eng[rs]."[19] Dotted lines showed the march to Pembina and Pope's cruise back to Fort Snelling. Nothing on the map showed that Pope was using a base map drawn by Joseph R. Nicollet in 1843, although the report did credit Nicollet with marking certain points of latitude and longitude in Minnesota.[20] Failing to give credit for the base map was an error that would cause Pope more trouble later when he made the same mistake again.

Major Woods had already seen Pope's map. In his official report Woods commented, "The sketch left me by Captain Pope, of the route traveled over, is marked with some accuracy, but I would infinitely have preferred a map of Mr. Nicollet's which I would have corrected myself and sent with this report as a reference."[21] By the time Major Woods's report and his own report appeared, Brevet Captain Pope was in St. Louis after the death of his father in January, at whose funeral Abraham Lincoln delivered the eulogy.

Pope spent most of 1850 and some months of 1851 in St. Louis on extended leave supposedly "attending affairs of great personal consequence."[22] One of these affairs repeated his earlier indiscretion of trying to go around channels to get a new assignment, this time apparently the command of a projected arsenal. As usual, Colonel Abert found out about it, and as usual, had something sharp to say:

> The Bureau has no knowledge of these efforts to which you refer, to have you placed in direction of the works at Chicago, or in the direction of the contemplated works in Minnesota. . . . To yield to them would be to yield the command of the Corps to extraneous influence. . . .
>
> The younger officers of the Corps . . . cannot and should not expect such commands. They should first learn its other duties,

and go through a course of experience in relation to them as others have done.[23]

A brief tour of duty with his old commander, Joseph E. Johnston, now a colonel in San Antonio, came to nothing in the late fall of 1850 and Pope came back to St. Louis to enjoy further leave until April 8, 1851. On that day Colonel Abert appointed him chief topographical engineer of the Ninth Military District and ordered him to report to Brevet Colonel Edwin V. Sumner, district commander, at Fort Union in the New Mexico territory bought from Mexico at the end of the last war.[24] Pope began his trip to Fort Union three weeks later, starting at Fort Leavenworth, Kansas, and following the old Santa Fe Trail. Although the Trail was well marked on the ground, Colonel Abert asked Pope to furnish him with an accurate map of it.[25]

Crossing the Trail usually meant forty to sixty days of hard going. Beginning at Westport, Missouri, it ran to Council Grove, Kansas, and on to Fort Dodge, Kansas, where it branched. The north branch followed the Arkansas River to the Big Timbers and then turned south to cross the 7,800-feet high Raton Pass. The south branch crossed a sixty-mile waterless stretch called the Cimarron Desert to go along the Cimarron River all the way into the pueblo of Santa Fe.

Pope made his first crossing without trouble, reaching Fort Union well ahead of his commander, who took nearly two months marching troops from Fort Leavenworth. When the tired Colonel Sumner met Pope, he ordered Pope back over the Trail almost at once to see if he could find some easier way to cover the distance. Pope started back on August 8[26] with Edward M. Kern, a civilian topographer. Kern had had experience riding with Fremont in the 1840s and on this trip kept a field book in which he noted courses and distances, sketched landmarks, and recorded some of their adventures.[27] Although no map of the Pope-Kern trip has survived, Kern's field book did.

Kern's notes show that after starting at Wagon Mound, New Mexico, the two men went north to the Big Timbers, and northeast to the Smoky Hill Fork of the Kansas River, which more or less paralleled the main Santa Fe Trail along the Arkansas River to the south. Following the Smoky Hill Fork to a point north of Great

Bend, Kansas, they turned back south to rejoin the main Trail along the Arkansas River. They reported finding plenty of grass, wood, and water all the way.[28] Along the Trail they ran into excitement without real peril. Once a group of Apaches strolled into their camp to do nothing more threatening than offer courtesies. "One old fellow wanted to get a Muchacha for me," Kern recorded.[29] At night a band of Arapahoes stampeded the pack and draft animals, leaving Pope and Kern with a total of eleven horses and mules.[30]

When the two men reached Missouri they pushed on to St. Louis where they jointly drew a map based on Kern's field notes and where Pope sat down to write another of his separate reports in the form of a long letter to Colonel Abert. Kern left St. Louis to go to Philadelphia, taking Pope's report and delivering it to Colonel Abert by hand. The report would bring to life and set in movement echoes and resentments stretching all the way back to 1845. Pope's report of September 18 covered not only the Santa Fe Trail, which Abert had asked him to write about, but tried to cut down to size another group of superior officers, and wound up by offering advice on Indian policy and the deployment of military units to carry that policy into effect.[31] Pope, as usual, held a magnifying glass to his own achievements and a minifying glass to those of others.

His route was new and it made the Santa Fe Trail easier by avoiding mountains and deserts and shortening the overall distance. Pope wrote Abert, "I have been successful beyond my most sanguine expectations."[32] His job would have been easier, he said, if he had not had to use the "entirely inaccurate and useless maps made by Capt. Fremont" that erred by miles in locating Bent's Fort and the Big Bend of the Smoky Hill Fork.[33] These statements would rapidly get him into trouble. The novelty of his shortcut was questionable and Fremont's maps were quite accurate.

Leaving his role as explorer for the role of strategist and Indian policymaker, Pope reported that army posts in New Mexico were exactly as they were in 1846. "It is difficult to understand the motive which influenced commanding officers to retain the same posts," he admonished.[34] Colonel Sumner agreed with Pope's recommendations to break up the few large garrisons and disperse the soldiers in numerous small posts located throughout the Indian country: "It is intended to force the Indians who may be disposed to commit depredations upon the Inhabitants, to pass a military post both in going and returning [,] a thing which it is well known they are very loath to do. The presence of troops in their country and in their immediate vicinity will exercise a very great influence in preventing hostilities."[35] Pope ended his report by giving specific recommendations for troop assignments.

Colonel Abert in Washington had Pope's map in hand as well as Pope's report when he responded to Pope's suggestions on October 2. The colonel wrote coldly:

> The route which you described has been previously indicated in print. It is presumed that all of your sketch or map except the traces of your route, is compiled from some authority. The fact of its being compiled, or the authority in such cases, should always be stated, that the officer making the compilation need not be accused of taking to himself a credit which does not belong to him or of being uninformed in such matters.
>
> This remark refers with some force to your map, sent in, of the expedition to the Red River of the North, of which all, but the route traveled by you, is evidently taken from Nicollet's map of that region, but credit for that is not given on your map.
>
> Particular care should be observed by you in these matters, as Col. Graham, under whom you served some time, does not compliment your accuracy of observation and reported to me that nearly all your work on the N.E. boundary line was rejected by him & had to be done over.[36]

As the colonel knew, his touchy subordinate had a habit of setting pen to paper when his feelings reached the boiling point, and whether or not he deliberately goaded Pope, the colonel could not have been surprised to get Pope's furious answer of October 11.

> If the routes from the "Big Timbers" of the Arkansas to the Cimarron have ever been explored it will be news to the people of New Mexico and I am very certain that no officer at present with the H^d Quarters is at all aware of the fact. . . . I should be glad to know the name of the person who has examined this route before as I have been in complete ignorance of the fact that such an examination had been made.

As for the maps of his new trail and of Minnesota in 1849:

The title of the sketch I forwarded to the Bureau expressed in my opinion precisely what it was: A Sketch of the new route pursued by me, & not a map of the Cimarron or Bent's Fort route—So far as my experience goes, it has always been the custom to copy a skeleton map & fill up any portion with the work of the exploring officer. Such was the case while in Mexico & it was never considered necessary to give all the authorities since the title explained precisely what portion of the sketch was made by the officer who forwarded it—As to the map of Minnesota referred to I have never dreamed that anyone supposed I had made any thing except the survey of the route pursued in going to and returning from the Red River of the North—It was very distinctly stated what portion of the work was mine & it never occurred to me that any person on earth could have supposed I claimed any thing else.

As to the sharp criticism of his work in Maine and the statements that he was incompetent:

As to any remarks or statements made by Maj Graham and of which the Bureau has thought proper to inform me for the first time after a lapse of six years, I have only to say, that as I have always endeavored to do my duty without fear & without favor the compliments or censures of any officer of the Corps are alike indifferent to me—

In the matter referred to on the N.E. Boundary my only duty as an assistant to Lieut. Warner was to accompany the men who were chaining, place the mile posts & monuments & note the crossing of roads, streams and ridges. It appears to me that no great error was allowed to occur in such duty & notwithstanding Maj Graham's remarks I must be permitted to doubt as to the *errors* I committed. . . .

After my arrival in Washington from the north east boundary I wrote a sort of military memoir with a sketch which was accepted by you & afterward fell into the hands of [the] Commanding General. Maj. Graham upon ascertaining that I had presumed to interfere with his prerogative demanded this paper from me. I informed him that it was in your possession & that if I had infringed any of his rights that you as Colonel of the Corps were responsible for it, as I had given you the memoir I had written. Maj Graham as I afterwards learned got possession of the paper with some difficulty—and it is this presumption on my part that I am indebted for Maj. Graham's conduct to me. I was young & inexperienced at the time & as you yourself had sanctioned the writing of the memoir & had afterward received it from my hands I could not suppose I was so far lost to propriety as I have understood Maj Graham said at the time—At all events Major Graham has never exhibited any friendly feeling toward me since & I can well understand now that the "memoir" was the greatest error I was guilty of in the North Eastern boundary.[37]

Pope was lucky he was not court-martialed for passing blame on his corps chief. At the same time he was trying to defend himself against charges of impropriety, the hotheaded lieutenant again bypassed all command channels to write directly to the adjutant general in hopes of getting leave to stay in St. Louis.[38] Army records do not show any answer or show that Pope's letter got back to Colonel Abert. Even without this further insulting letter, Colonel Abert had still plenty to say when he wrote again on October 27:

The "inexperience" to which you appeal would call for a more subdued tone of remark, and for efforts of careful and exact observation. Lieut Col Graham reported your loose and errone-ous operations at the time, and it is only within a few days that I have been informed, that nearly all your operations, while of that command, were done over again during the last summer.

In your report you indulge in much freedom of remark upon the operations of your predecessor in the same field, Captain Fremont. You speak of his "entirely inaccurate and useless map" of that part, etc. In such cases the inaccuracy should be pointed out and be clearly proven, or it would be better not to condemn so positively.[39]

Although he found Pope's sneer at Graham "unbecoming," Colonel Abert was willing to consider it "more thoughtless than deliberate"[40] and closed this interchange with forgiveness. Pope's squabble with his corps chief had been at the least "unbecoming" in a second lieutenant, but it was not unique in the paper battles in the army of that day. At twenty-nine Pope was admittedly unconventional, but in 1851, even high ranking army officers had very little to do and used up time by writing long letters.

After Abert rejected Pope's claim of opening a new trail, Pope settled down to the topography of his present time and place. He was as self-assured as ever, and claimed, "With competent assistance I hope to be able within two years to make a complete exploration of this territory."[41] In June, July, and August of 1852 he was riding with Colonel Sumner on a great sweep of New Mexico. At the Acoma Pueblo on July 1, Sumner signed a treaty with the Mimbreño Apaches, and Pope's signature appears as witness to the X of Chief Mangas Coloradas whose son-in-law, Cochise, later became chief of the Chiricahuas.[42]

Later in that year Sumner let Pope answer an inquiry from member of Congress J. S. Phelps of Missouri about the feasibility of running part of a proposed transcontinental railroad line across New Mexico. As soon as the Mexicans transferred their lands to the United States in 1848, transcontinental railroad fever broke out. By 1852 it had developed two strains, northern route and southern route, after the failed Wilmot Proviso of 1846 and the enacted Compromise of 1850 reheated the slavery issue. Although Pope opposed slavery, he was working in the southern route territory, which could be a territory of opportunity for him.

On October 26 he finished a closely spaced eleven-page letter to Phelps in which, after paying respect to Manifest Destiny and homage to a "plan so gigantic and fraught with results of such incalculable importance to the commercial world," Pope recommended a central New Mexico route from Santa Fe to Albuquerque to San Diego, California. Since he was writing to a member of Congress from Missouri who had business leaders as constituents, Pope also recommended Independence, Missouri, as the line's eastern terminus.[43] "Carson, Leroux, and Hatcher, celebrated among the guides and mountain men of this country," approved his choice of route, Pope wrote Phelps, and if asked would accompany any expedition to survey it. Colonel Sumner approved the report, endorsed it, and asked Abert to assign Pope to the survey.[44]

By this time Pope's luck was beginning to turn. On March 3, 1853, he got his first permanent promotion and became First Lieutenant.[45] On April 27, the new secretary of war, Jefferson Davis, ordered Pope relieved from duty in the Ninth Military District and assigned him to the Pacific Railroad Survey.[46] Pope was beginning to climb upward. He could never bear to leave an assignment, however, without writing a report to remind everyone how well he had performed his duties, so before quitting Fort

Union he gave Colonel Abert a long account of New Mexican affairs in 1853.[47] Again entering into the role of strategist and military philosopher, Topographical Engineer Lieutenant Pope outlined what he saw as the problem of New Mexico and gave his recommendations for solving it.

Mainly, the conquered New Mexicans had to adopt the ways of their American conquerors, including American self-government. At present this was impossible because marauding Apaches kept New Mexicans in a state of terror. Only the army could handle the Apaches, who complicated the problem because they struck by night and hid by day and would not stand and fight. In the end soldiers could only keep the peace by setting up forts in the Apache country linked to each other by military roads and by sending out dragoon patrols from the forts to march through or past every Apache pueblo every day. Pope appended to his report a map showing existing forts and recommended sites and routes for new forts, patrol paths, and military roads.[48]

The file wrapper shows that Pope's report reached Colonel Abert's desk on November 11, 1853.[49] Nothing shows that he read it or that anyone else ever read it, and New Mexican historians have made little use of this sharp-eyed observer's overview of their state shortly after New Mexico parted from old Mexico. It was probably unimportant to Pope. He looked forward, not back, and was already thinking about the problems of a railroad survey.

NOTES

1. Abert to Pope, Apr. 20, 1849, RG 77 NA.
2. Brvt. Capt. John Pope, "The Report of an Exploration of the Territory of Minnesota," S. Ex. Doc. 42, 31st Cong., 1st Sess., 1850, 13.
3. Ibid., 25.
4. Ibid., 18; Warren Upham, *Minnesota Geographical Names*, Minnesota Historical Society Collections, St. Paul, 1920, 17: 434.
5. Pope, 42.
6. Brvt. Maj. Samuel Woods, "Report of Brevet Major Samuel Woods in Relation to His Expedition to the Pembina Settlement," H. Ex. Doc. 51, 31st Cong., 1st Sess., 1850, 19.
7. Pope, 31, 32, 10.
8. Woods, 19.
9. Pope, 34, 40.

10. Woods, 19.
11. Pope, 13.
12. Ibid., 2.
13. Ibid., 9, 15.
14. Ibid., 10.
15. Ibid.
16. Ibid., 12.
17. Ibid., 41.
18. Ibid.
19. Ibid., Map Supp.
20. Ibid., 43.
21. Woods, 19.
22. Pope to Abert, Nov. 11, 1850, RG 94 NA.
23. Abert to Pope, Aug. 27, 1850, RG 77 NA.
24. Abert to Pope, Apr. 8, 1851, RG 77 NA.
25. Ibid.
26. Edward M. Kern, Manuscript Field Book, Henry E. Huntington Library and Art Gallery, San Marino, Calif.
27. Ibid.
28. Ibid.
29. Ibid.
30. Ibid.
31. Pope to Abert, Sept. 18, 1851, RG 77 NA.
32. Ibid.
33. Ibid.
34. Ibid.
35. Ibid.
36. Abert to Pope, Oct. 2, 1851, RG 77 NA.
37. Pope to Abert, Oct. 11, 1851, RG 77 NA.
38. Pope to Gen. R. Jones, Oct. 20, 1851, RG 77 NA.
39. Abert to Pope, Oct. 27, 1851, RG 77 NA.
40. Ibid.
41. See note 31.
42. Treaty with the Apaches, July 1, 1852, 10 Stat. 979.
43. Pope to Hon. J. S. Phelps, Oct. 26, 1852, RG 77 NA.
44. Sumner to Abert, Oct. 27, 1852, RG 77 NA.
45. Service Record, John Pope, RG 94 NA.
46. Pope to Abert, n.d., 1853, RG 77 NA. File wrapper shows receipt on Nov. 11, 1853.
47. Ibid.
48. Ibid.
49. Ibid.

Chapter Five

RAILROADING

ON ITS FINAL WORKDAY OF ITS legal existence, March 3, 1853, the outgoing Congress of the outgoing Fillmore administration tacked a clause onto the Government Appropriation Act of 1853, which it then passed. The clause authorized the secretary of war to make "such explorations as he may deem advisable, to ascertain the most practicable and economic route for a railroad from the Mississippi River to the Pacific Ocean."[1] The clause also authorized the secretary to use officers of the Corps of Topographical Engineers in making surveys, and required all survey parties to wind up their work and report their findings and recommendations by the end of 1854.

Since the act did not specify any routes, the secretary of war could use his discretion in instructing survey parties, but Jefferson Davis, the new secretary of war, knew well that the Pacific Railroad route was a hot political question and that for the sake of peace in Congress on this issue at least, he had better exercise his discretion. The Southerners who dominated Congress demanded a southern route, which Davis favored since he was from Mississippi, as did Virginians in the army such as Colonel Joseph E. Johnston, Pope's commanding officer, and Colonel J. J. Abert, chief of Pope's corps. Northerners insisted on a hearing for a northern route.

Davis handled the two-sided pressures ably by stretching his appropriation to cover surveys along four parallels of latitude, the thirty-second, the thirty-fifth, the thirty-eighth, and the forty-seventh, practically blanketing all the passable trans-Mississippi routes between Mexico and Canada. In October 1853, Lieutenant John Pope assumed command of the party surveying the eastern half of the thirty-second parallel route. Lieutenant John G. Parke commanded the party surveying the western half.

The central point of this route was Dona Ana, New Mexico, near Las Cruces. Pope's eastern half ran from Dona Ana northeast across the treeless desert of west Texas's Llano Estacado to the hamlet of Preston, Texas, on the Red River of the south near Denison. Parke's western half ran from Dona Ana to the Gila and Mojave rivers. If built along this thirty-second parallel route, the transcontinental railroad would end at San Diego, California. Pope and his party marched away from Dona Ana on February 12, 1854, and reached Preston on May 15.[2] Their dusty trip carried them past the natural limestone reservoirs called the Hueco Tanks near El Paso, across the Guadelupe Mountains near Salt Pass, on to the falls of the Pecos River, then across the Llano Estacado to Sulfur Springs on the Colorado River, and from there to the Clear Fork of the Brazos River and on into Preston. They were tired but no one suffered illness and the party had no troubles.

It was Pope's first independent command, which seems to have supplied the final element he needed in maturing and accepting his life in the army. He had wanted responsibility. Now he had it and handled it well. While he would never shed his bellow and brag or his tendency to belittle his superiors, his service record would show no more reprimands for sloppy work or deliberate insubordination.

Pope headed a sizeable command including a detachment of twenty-five from the First Dragoons under Lieutenant Louis H. Marshall, who remained Pope's friend and a member of Pope's military family for years. Marshall was a Southerner and a nephew of Robert E. Lee, who in the war years did not scold his nephew for staying loyal to the Union, but could not understand why Marshall stayed loyal to Pope and served on Pope's staff. Marshall was one of the few to see that under Pope's public facade, which looked coldly egocentric, was a private Pope who could be warm, relaxed, and a friend worth cultivating.

Outside the Dragoon escort, a group of fifty civilian teamsters handled Pope's transport and supply. In addition, all the survey parties carried scientific teams with them to study the animals, vegetables, and minerals in these still unexplored sections of the country; with Pope were Captain J. F. Taplin, mineralogist; Dr. William L. Diffenderfer, surgeon and botanist; and John H. Byrne, mathematician and diarist. The party had no geologist, and as a result all members had to gather geological specimens as well. Lieutenant Marshall was assigned to collect fish, land reptiles, and insects while commanding the military escort. While the scientists worked their areas Pope and his crew laid out their proposed railroad line, fixing latitude and longitude, shooting azimuths, sighting topography and grades, noting the location of wood and water, and in the end mapping the whole route. So far as existing records show, scientists and surveyors worked amiably together without the quarrels or jostling for attention characteristic of specialists working alongside other specialists.

At the end of the trip reports and specimens traveled several ways. Dr. Diffenderfer shipped his collection of birds, animals, and grasses to Professor John Torrey of Princeton, known in 1854 as the foremost American botanist. Lieutenant Marshall sent his finds off to Professor Spencer F. Baird of the new Smithsonian Institution, who later became known as the Father of the Smithsonian and succeeded to Torrey's title as first of American botanists. Pope's team had its modest part in feeding these reputations.

On October 17 Pope finished his official survey report and sent it to Secretary of War Davis.[3] In time it appeared as part of an eleven-volume series printed by order of Congress and now one of the great classics of Western exploring. Pope quite naturally recommended his thirty-second parallel route, emphasizing that this route had gentle grades for more than half the way between Preston and Dona Ana, and that it ran through forests that could supply wood for fuel and building timber. Water, unluckily, was quite another thing. For the 125 miles that the route took across the Llano Estacado, the surface was absolutely dry.

Lack of water was an admitted hindrance, but not a hindrance without remedy. Pope had been reading recent scientific literature and wrote in his report that he believed that water lay under the Llano Estacado and would come to the surface in artesian wells. Four wells, each about 600 feet deep, spaced at 25-mile intervals between the falls of the Pecos River and Big Spring on the Colorado River, should furnish enough water in the 125-mile desert stretch. Although in 1855 he could only find rudimentary geological studies of this area, Pope felt confident that beneath the dry plain he would find rocks in the classic formation for artesian wells: porous water-bearing layers trapped between solid layers, tilted downward, fed by rainfall at remote outcrops, and under enough pressure to force water to or near the surface after a drill pierced overlying solid layers. Pope wrote further that in this area wells would surely draw settlers and that the War Department should consider placing a fort at each well site. Garrisons of these forts could control the Indians and guard settlers from Indian and desperado attacks.

Secretary of War Davis combined Pope's report with the reports of the other survey teams and forwarded everything to Congress, which tabled the whole Pacific Railroad project until 1862. If that were not enough to stop the project, in 1854 Senator Stephen A. Douglas succeeded in getting his Kansas-Nebraska Bill enacted into law. This act specifically repealed the Missouri Compromise of 1820, opened to slavery all United States territories whatever, north or south of the 36°30' line, sent tempers flaring, and made the coming conflict irrepressible. Agreement on a Pacific Railroad route was impossible. As the year ended, it looked as if Lieutenant John Pope would have to wait for another assignment and could only hope that it would be another independent command.

As matters turned out, it was. Jefferson Davis was a West Pointer who had served on the frontier and with distinction in the Mexican War. Now, as secretary of war, he was one of few who thought seriously about military strategy. Pope's report had overtones of the railroad as a new element in warfare, and even without railroads, a commander in the southwest with access to local water supplies would have an edge over one who had to transport water from a far-off source. Davis thought it worthwhile to test Pope's recommendations for the Llano Estacado.

On January 5, 1855, Secretary Davis appointed Pope chief of a party to try "the experiment of testing the practicability of procuring water by artesian wells on the arid plains."[4] Pope again commanded a mixed detachment of soldiers, scientists, and roustabouts, and marched off to the camp at the falls of the Pecos River that he had used in his survey. He made this his base camp and built stone and adobe buildings as well as supply sheds and shops. The site was known locally as "Pope's Well" until it vanished under the waters of the Red Bluff reservoir, and was for a time a regular stop on a cattle trail.

Pope spotted his first drillsite some fourteen miles east of his camp and began drilling on June 1. The tubing broke twice and he had to abandon the effort, but he had reached water at a depth of 641 feet and the water rose 390 feet in the hole. Looking on the bright side, Pope wrote Davis, "The success of the experiment was fully established. . . . The existence of these streams of water . . . sufficiently established the object of the experiment, and I therefore closed the work. . . . The present operation was a mere experiment."[5]

Marching his party into New Mexico to his old base camp at Dona Ana, Pope began another well at the second drill site on November 1. The tubing collapsed on February 10 when the well reached 293 feet without reaching water. Pope had other problems as well. His workers had been living on salt provisions and began to come down with scurvy; his mules gobbled their forage ahead of schedule and had to eat less nutritious desert grass; his two geologists began to argue with him, telling him as well as Secretary of War Davis that the second drill site was a mistake.[6]

Dr. Thomas Antisell, one of Pope's geologists who would make a name for himself in medicine after the Civil War, argued that Pope's whole experiment in the Llano Estacado was doomed because the region could not produce true artesian wells. These, Antisell said, brought water to the surface without pumps and needed heavy rainfall on the outcrops to furnish the needed pressure. Since the water-bearing rocks under the Llano Estacado surfaced in New Mexico, an area that received little rain, they could never meet the requirements.[7] Pope thought this nonsense. The English used pumps to bring water to the surface from artesian wells, he reminded Antisell. He reminded him further that he was drilling under orders for "testing the practicability of procuring water by artesian wells," whatever his civilian geologists might think about his location for the second or any other drill site.[8]

Pope's second geologist, G. G. Shumard, who would also make his name in medicine after the Civil War, had other objections. Shumard claimed the Llano Estacado had the wrong regional dip for artesian wells, and igneous dikes (lava plugs from ancient volcanoes) dotted the Llano Estacado and would act as dams to stop water flowing through porous rocks.[9] To Pope this was more nonsense. Pope had spent the four years between 1851 and 1855 mapping New Mexico and recording regional dip and strike. To his own knowledge, he said, regional dip on the Llano Estacado was right for artesian wells. Pope had run across igneous dikes and was as well qualified to judge their effect as Shumard. Pope claimed that when water in the rock met an igneous dike, the water would simply flow around the dike.[10]

Having become his own scientific adviser, Pope marched his crew back to his base at the falls of the Pecos, located his third drill site some five miles from the first, and began drilling again on April 1. This well got to 861 feet when the equipment failed yet again. Here he had found water at 676 feet, and the water had risen to within 110 feet of the surface. Pope wanted to drill farther but discovered that he had spent his appropriation.[11]

At this point Pope could call his artesian well experiment neither a success nor a failure. In any case it seems to have led to another satisfying permanent promotion. On July 1, at the age of thirty-four, First Lieutenant John Pope became Captain John Pope.[12] He knew that in the little army of 16,000, it would be a long time before he became a major. He also knew that it would do him no harm to take assignments that brought him under the eyes of top ranking superiors. In that line of duty he was already doing well; he had as one of his correspondents the secretary of war himself.

While his team drilled wells Pope had had time to satisfy his natural curiosity by making extracurricular scientific studies. He mapped his drill site areas, which was routine, but he also surveyed and marked the southeast corner of New Mexico. He set up astronomical stations to find latitude and longitude but he also used them to collect information about phenomena such as meteor showers. He recorded magnetic compass deviations from true north but also measured the magnetic intensity and magnetic dip of rocks.[13] Pope also dabbled in electrical studies by measuring electricity in the air. He speculated about the effects of ozone, which was formed when a powerful electric charge, usually lightning, passed through air and changed the molecular structure of oxygen. From what he saw, bolstered by what he read in scientific papers of the day, Pope decided that ozone gave cool, dry climates their relative freedom from epidemics and could carry away the "noxious and injurious vapors" of hot, humid ones.[14] He was not far wrong, because scientists in the twentieth century would use ozone to purify air and water.

Although Pope was no Francis Bacon, he had the scientific interests of a learned amateur, and he had Bacon's faith in his own line of experiments. On November 22 he was in Washington finishing his report to Jefferson Davis. The artesian well experiment should go on, Pope wrote, and he "would cheerfully devote four years of my life on the plains in the conduct of such a work."[15] To Pope, the government had a duty to open the Southwest to settlement by making water available, which in turn would make railroads possible and tie the new settlements to older areas of the country. In speaking of his drilling, Pope had to admit that "expenditures of the expedition have greatly overrun the original estimates,"[16] but said that now he and his workers were experts who could cut time and costs. A modest appropriation would support the work for two more years.

Although no one recorded what happened between November 1856 and March 1857, it is probably fair to assume that Pope and Davis met in person and that each tried to influence people in the capital. On the last business day of the outgoing Pierce administration, the lame-duck Congress enacted the Army Appropriation Act for 1857–58, which included an appropriation for "continuing the experiment of sinking artesian wells upon the public lands."[17]

The new secretary of war, John B. Floyd, kept Pope in command and sent him back to the falls of the Pecos to reopen, deepen, and complete the third well abandoned in 1856. This time Pope wanted no mistakes. He hired the superintendent, crew, and steam drilling rig of the company that dug the most recent artesian well in St. Louis, and set off for his old location with a military escort of one hundred at Fort Sam Houston in San Antonio.[18] After cleaning out the old hole, the team began drilling late in September, and drilling went on through foul weather, another outbreak of scurvy, and exasperating mechanical breakdowns, until midway in 1858 the hole reached 1,049 feet without finding water. Pope called off further digging; Secretary Floyd agreed.[19]

Pope and Secretary Floyd still believed in the experiment in spite of technical failures, and Floyd now sent Pope into camp at Anton Chico, New Mexico, at the headwaters of the Pecos. Pope made a new location, putting his fourth drill site at Galisteo, New Mexico, fifty miles west of his camp. Drilling began on December 1. More than six months later the drillers cut into a water-bearing formation at 1,301 feet, and natural pressure sent the water to within twenty feet of the surface. Pope had his technical success, but his technical success used up the appropriation; Pope capped the well on July 1, marched his crew across the Santa Fe Trail to Fort Leavenworth, and paid off the last worker in St. Louis on August 15.[20] So ended the War Department's experiment in finding artesian wells on the Llano Estacado. In the frenzy of 1859 following John Brown's attack on Harper's Ferry and his capture, trial, and hanging, Congress would hardly listen to a request for further appropriations. But Pope and his team did contribute to later success. In the 1890s and early 1900s drillers with geological information and machinery unknown in Pope's day dug artesian wells at Artesia and Roswell, New Mexico. Because of this, part of the desert came under cultivation.

When he said goodbye to his drilling crew in St. Louis, John Pope finished his apprenticeship. He was thirty-seven years old, a West Point graduate, a bachelor, and a regular army captain with seventeen years of active service in peace and war. He had been changing little by little from a hotheaded youngster bent on using influential connections to get his own way into a quieter man nearing middle age who accepted his place as a subordinate in a larger system. Time had not changed his personality, though it may have mellowed him. He was still the large-headed, barrel-chested son of Judge Nathaniel Pope of Kaskaskia, a reader, a thinker, a man of boundless self-confidence who had no time for fools and who publicly roared, postured, and spoke his piece no matter who heard him. Few knew that he had a quieter private personality.

Until 1859 Pope spent all his life on frontiers except for leaves spent in St. Louis and occasional temporary duty in Washington. His military experience was about the same as that of his contemporaries who also served in an army regularly used by the government in carrying out civil projects like surveying and mapping, road and bridge building, and railroad planning. Now and then a frontier unit guarded remote hamlets from Indian attack. Apart from the Mexican War, hardly any army officer commanded or even saw a unit larger than a battalion. Pope's commands, although of mixed soldiers and civilians, were larger than he would have had in the infantry, in which one hundred normally made up a company. Moreover, his commands gave him in miniature the problems and experience that he would need when maneuvering larger units: food, forage, clothing, equipment, arms, ammunition, transport, camp layout, health and sanitation, defense against attack, and carrying out his mission despite obstacles, especially hostile Indians.

Pope's life was about to change abruptly. After leaving the frontier he would find himself assigned to Cincinnati, close to the center of public affairs, close to those with political power. He would shoot upward in the army. Within three years his life would reach its climax and enter its bitter anticlimax of thirty years. If Pope had stayed on frontier duty he would probably have become a paternal figure in Western folklore as friend of both the Indians and the immigrants, but that was not his fortune. Like others before him he could not resist a tempting offer that might let him dominate the American scene.

NOTES

1. Act of Mar. 3, 1853, 10 Stat. 189.
2. Bvt. Capt. John Pope, "Report of the Exploration of a Land Route from the Red River to the Rio Grande," *Pacific Railroad Surveys*, 12 vols., H. Ex. Doc. 129, 2:1ff.
3. Ibid.
4. Lee Myers, "Pope's Wells," *New Mexico Historical Review* 37, no. 4 (October 1963): 282.
5. Pope to Jefferson Davis, Nov. 16, 1855, RG 48 NA.
6. Ibid.
7. Ibid.
8. Myers, 282.
9. See note 5.
10. Ibid.
11. Pope to Davis, Nov. 22, 1856, RG 48 NA.
12. Service Record, John Pope, RG 94 NA.
13. Pope to Davis, Feb. 10, 1856, RG 48 NA.
14. Ibid.
15. See note 11.
16. Ibid.
17. Act of Mar. 3, 1857, 11 Stat. 200.
18. William Wallace McCullough, Jr., *Dr. William Dennis Kelley, 1825–1888, Texas Physician and Surgeon* (Galveston, 1961), chap. 7: 6.
19. Myers, 295.
20. Ibid.; McCullough, chap. 7: 8.

PART 2

AT THE TOP

Chapter Six

COMMAND

EARLY IN THE FALL OF 1859 Captain John Pope received orders assigning him to Cincinnati to plan and design Great Lakes light-houses under the hybrid Light House Board, a branch of the treasury empowered to use army, navy, and civilian engineers.[1] A little earlier he had accepted another assignment, becoming a husband.

Pope closed his well-drilling experiment by paying off his crew in St. Louis on August 15. One month later, to the day, he married Clara Horton, eldest daughter of Valentine B. Horton of Pomeroy, Ohio, owner of mines and a fleet of tugboats and a member of Congress.[2] Horton was as well connected in Ohio as Pope was in Illinois, a personal friend of Ohio's Governor Salmon P. Chase, who saw himself as head of the Republican party.

No Horton or Pope letters survive to show how, where, or when the young couple met, but they may have become acquainted in Washington in 1857 or 1858 when Pope had temporary duty at the War Department. It is also reasonable to think that Representative Horton had something to do with Pope's assignment to a station so near his new wife's family home. Pope's orders were dated October 3, nineteen days after his wedding, and the circumstances suggest that his orders to Cincinnati rounded out a planned sequence.

Before 1859 Pope served away from political centers and on the far edge of politics; in Cincinnati Republican politics surrounded him. Republican politics meant antislavery politics under the leadership of Governor Chase and his Ohio lieutenants, including Pope's new father-in-law. The issue was kept literally in view. Covington, Kentucky, was just across the Ohio River and Cincinnati residents could peer across to see slaves at work.

Pope designed lighthouses by day; he could hardly escape politics by night. On May 16, 1860, the Republican National Convention in Chicago made Abraham Lincoln the candidate for president. This upset Chase, who felt entitled to the nomination, and Chase's followers, but could hardly upset Pope; Lincoln was a family friend and shirttail relative. To the Illinois army captain seeing his country split and on the way to war, Lincoln as president could be a friend where one counted. Pope's father-in-law could get Chase's ear but Pope came to Ohio only in 1859, long after Chase had accrued priority political debts to native Ohioans.

Republicans of Horton's district renominated him for Congress. Chase cultivated his own Republican followers to help him return to the Senate, which he had left in 1855. On election day American voters elected Abraham Lincoln their president, the first Republican to hold the office, and Ohio voters reelected Horton. In a short time the Ohio legislature sent Chase back to the Senate.

The "Great Secession Winter of 1860–61"[3] followed. States of the lower South seceded from the Union, one after another, formed the Confederate States of America, and elected Jefferson Davis as their president, with whom Pope had been on good terms from 1853 to 1857. Beginning in December 1861, Southern politicians and militia commanders marched into arsenals, mints, customhouses, treasury offices, post offices, and forts of the United States, coolly taking these properties as their fair share. James Buchanan, the repudiated outgoing Democratic president, wrung his hands and did nothing.

When on January 9, 1861, Confederate soldiers in a Charleston fort seized and fired United States ammunition to turn back an unarmed merchant ship[4] sent to supply the last Charleston fort still held by the United States, President Buchanan did not act. Pope decided it was time to move. War was coming, and to an army officer war meant promotion. Since opportunities for promotion were limited, officers without field service, or without at least commissions in the fighting arms of infantry, artillery, or cavalry, had to hurry to call attention to qualifications that entitled them nevertheless to commands.

Pope wrote a letter to his old friend President-elect Lincoln on January 21, 1861, to advise a civilian about the army. Pope warned that army officers in key posts might be disloyal and advised

Lincoln that he should require every officer to sign a statement promising to take any assignment and obey any order whatever. If anyone hedged or refused, the president should transfer that officer far away from the action, such as Puget Sound.

Pope also advised Lincoln on politics, something army protocol advised officers to avoid: "There should be no effort to conciliate until rebellion is at an end and secession as a right explicitly abandoned. . . . The fact whether we have a government, and whether it has the right to enforce its laws and protect its officers, must be brought to speedy issue."[5] Nothing shows that Lincoln answered Pope's letter, but he kept it, and must have read it.

A little less than three weeks later, Captain Pope spoke to the Literary Society of Cincinnati, probably at the invitation of his father-in-law. Pope spoke on "Our National Fortifications and Defenses," and could assume that his largely Republican audience felt as strongly as he did about President Buchanan's shilly-shallying while Southern mobs overran and seized fourteen United States forts. Secession meant nothing more than inexcusable unconstitutional rebellion, Pope began. The federal government must enforce its laws, put down the rebellion, recover property stolen from the United States, and dispose of disloyal army officers. By 1861 the art of fortification had almost reached "perfection," Pope said, and to let traitors take fourteen forts, almost impossible to retake, was stupid, suicidal, and treasonable. If John B. Floyd, secretary of war and Democrat, had kept the garrisons in all forts up to authorized strength, the United States could have nipped this piracy at the outset.

The North could take up arms, Pope said, or the South could backtrack. The latter was impossible. "I firmly believe," he said, "that war is inevitable, whether we resist or yield to secession." President Buchanan had proved himself worthless. Pope lashed the tumbledown administration: "It is impossible to control the astonishment and indignation which every American must feel when he considers in what a position a few months of the administration of a bad or weak man have placed this great and prosperous country. If we overcome this damage, it will at least serve as a warning, and a most impressive one, to the American people, to be careful for the future in the selection of a chief magistrate." He concluded with offhand remarks about the "treasonable conspiracies" of Buchanan's advisers and Buchanan's "corrupt and infamous cabinet,"[6] and sat down "enthusiastically applauded" for his "patriotic sentiments."[7]

Two days later Pope was in Springfield, Illinois, taking his place as one of four officers detailed as military escorts on the train carrying President-elect Lincoln and his family to Washington. The little train of one locomotive, one tender, one passenger car, and one baggage car steamed out of the Springfield station after Lincoln's moving farewell to his neighbors, and after zigzagging through the North came to its Washington roundhouse on February 24.[8] Pope is credited with suggesting that Lincoln and his family stay at Willard's Hotel until outgoing president Buchanan and his niece and housekeeper, Harriet Lane, left the White House on March 4.[9]

Being on the list of passengers on the Lincoln train of 1861 had a political value equal to the social value of having an ancestor on the roster of the *Mayflower*. To have ridden with Lincoln meant holding a key that opened nearly every political door. Almost every prominent person in the Republican party boarded it for a short ride. Pope found himself in the company of names that made headlines for forty years: Lincoln and his family, Davis, Yates, Lamon, Browning, Hay, Nicolay, Ellsworth.[10] Pope's old commander, Colonel Edwin V. Sumner, headed the escort, and after Lincoln tired himself in making speeches and shaking hands by day, Sumner and Pope helped him relax by telling him funny stories. The realities of ambition being what they are, Sumner, Pope, and any other rider must have gotten in a few words about the political impasse of 1861 and what Lincoln should do about it.

Over Colonel Sumner's strong protest, Lincoln made his famous secret exit from the train at Harrisburg and arrived in Washington alone. Pope and the escort stayed on the train to the end, and when no longer needed, made their separate ways back to their posts. Pope must have arrived in Cincinnati on February 25 or 26. His father-in-law and Chase were still in Washington as members of the Ohio delegation to the peace conference called by the Virginia legislature on February 4. By the time that Pope reached home it was clear that the conference would accomplish nothing beyond restating what the North and South would fight about.

Pope was in for his own fight when he received a War Department special order setting March 4 as the date for a general court-martial at Newport Barracks, Kentucky, "for the trial of Captain

John Pope, corps of Topographical Engineers, and such other prisoners as may be brought before it."[11] The charge: violating the Fifth Article of War;[12] the specification: making remarks derogatory to the president of the United States in a speech to the Literary Society of Cincinnati on February 9, 1861.

Buchanan was still president. Pope had made remarks calling him a bumbler if not a criminal. For not the first time in his life, Captain John Pope found that words have their consequences and that his words might end his army career just when he was becoming more prominent. Since his speech appeared in full in several newspapers and Pope had not asked for corrections or deletions, he could not deny the specification. War was coming and Pope could see himself confined to some disciplinary barracks for the duration. Almost like a *deus ex machina* in some Euripidean tragedy coming from the sky to resolve the moral dilemma, another War Department special order dated March 2 quashed the court-martial because of "the President having expressed to this Department his conviction that the language of the said Captain Pope . . . would not in any manner affect him injuriously."[13] Either Buchanan wanted to leave office in an atmosphere of benevolence or Pope had friends who rallied swiftly and drove bargains.

Saved at the edge of disaster, Pope now spent most of his time angling for the highest command he could get; most of the other officers were doing the same thing. The army of 1861 was miniscule and resigning Southern officers shrank it more. While Pope and other captains might look presumptuous as they pulled wires to become major generals overnight, the fact was that when Lincoln took office the United States Army had exactly 794 officers.[14] With so few officers and such a need for a large army, any officer had the chance for promotion.

As an Illinoisan Pope did not like Lincoln's appointment of Simon Cameron as secretary of war. Cameron was a Pennsylvania political boss sure to save the icing on any cake for Pennsylvanians if he could. Pope thought that he could circumvent Cameron's effectiveness by writing Cameron's chief. On April 11 Pope went around military channels as usual and wrote directly to Ward Hill Lamon asking appointment as Lincoln's aide and military secretary, rank unspecified.[15] Pope reasoned accurately that Lincoln knew little about the army and could use day-by-day advice. At that time

Lamon, who was one of Lincoln's close friends, was acting unofficially as Lincoln's appointment and patronage secretary. Lamon endorsed Pope's letter, but instead of handing it to Lincoln, turned it over to Cameron as a War Department matter. Cameron left the letter unanswered, but as things turned out this was immaterial.

On April 12, and before Pope's letter could have reached Lamon, the South Carolinians opened Civil War hostilities by starting their bombardment of Fort Sumter. War had come and Pope resolved more firmly not to fall behind in the race for military position. By sundown he had gone outside military channels again to offer his services to Richard Yates, Governor of Illinois. "I prefer to do my devoir under the banner of my own State," Pope wrote.[16] Yates wired him to come at once. On April 15 Major Robert Anderson surrendered Fort Sumter, Lincoln called for 75,000 volunteers to help suppress powerful "combinations" in the South, and a War Department special order detailed Captain John Pope to Chicago as mustering officer of Illinois volunteers.[17]

Pope took his Illinois assignment gladly, but with no intention of staying a captain. On April 16 he wrote to Judge David Davis, Lincoln's 1860 campaign manager, asking Davis to remind Governor Yates to use care in choosing officers for Illinois troops.[18] On April 20 Pope wrote Lincoln that he was going to Springfield to start troop training.[19] On May 15, he wrote to Lincoln again, this time asking flatly for a commission as brigadier general in the volunteers serving with the Illinois troops.[20] While his request awaited action, Pope ran into an old acquaintance from West Point and Mexico, Ulysses S. Grant, who was working in the Springfield mustering office as a civilian. Grant later replaced Pope as mustering officer and still later served with Pope in Mississippi in 1862. He had a chilly recollection of Pope in 1861: "He was a native of Illinois and well acquainted with most of the prominent men in that State. I was a carpetbagger and knew but few of them. . . . On one occasion he said to me that I ought to go into the United States service. I told him I intended to do so if there was a war. He spoke of his acquaintance with public men of the State, and said he would do all he could for me. I declined to receive endorsement for permission to fight for my country."[21]

After waiting a month for an answer to his request to Lincoln, Pope received a temporary commission on June 15, naming him brigadier general of volunteers, to rank as such from May 17.[22] Major David M. Hunter, another member of Lincoln's military escort in February, received the same volunteer rank at the same time. What Pope would have grabbed a month earlier, however, he saw now as a stingy gift. Even though he had not asked for it, Pope felt Lincoln should have given him a permanent commission as brigadier general in the regular army.

When Fort Sumter surrendered, Congress was not in session. In all the excitement of the time Lincoln issued a proclamation on May 3 enlarging the regular army.[23] It was an unconstitutional act[24] that Congress had to cure in July,[25] but Lincoln had gone ahead to appoint officers in his enlarged regular army: George B. McClellan as major general, plus one brigadier general, one colonel, and three lieutenant colonels. All the new regular commissions went to Pennsylvanians. Pope blamed Cameron, but Lincoln must have taken personal interest in McClellan's appointment since they knew each other. McClellan finished second at West Point, served with distinction in the Mexican War, went to the Crimea as military observer in 1854, and from 1857 to 1860 was civilian chief engineer and vice president of the Illinois Central Railroad at the same time that Lincoln was general counsel. In 1858 he took the trouble to attend the Lincoln-Douglas debates. Until 1862 Pope and McClellan had hardly met, but McClellan's appointment as major general over Pope's head in 1861 seems to have been the first irritation in the coming struggle between these two that would lead to disaster for both of them.

After one day's fuming, Pope wrote the president directly as one Illinoisan to another:

> I think it not unreasonable under the circumstances that Illinois should have one of the Brigadier Generals in the new regular forces and as the sentiment of that State has been unanimously and earnestly expressed for me I hope I shall not be asking too much in applying for the appointment. . . .
>
> I could not with honor hold my commission after being thus oversloughed by my juniors and by civilians for what seems to me no better reason than that they are personal or political friends of the Secretary of the War. . . .
>
> I trust you will give this matter some inquiry & that consideration to which it is entitled.[26]

On the same day Pope also wrote directly to Senator Lyman Trumbull of Illinois, also a friend, asking Trumbull to protest to Lincoln about McClellan's appointment.[27] Getting no immediate reply from either Lincoln or Trumbull, Pope began to worry about losing even his volunteer commission, and on June 23 wrote Trumbull that he would accept the volunteer commission and take command of the Illinois troops stationed at Alton. He knew, Pope wrote, that Trumbull and the Illinois congressional delegation would not let him suffer by his decision.[28]

Even after taking the field Pope had no intention of letting a powerful senator forget him. On July 3 he wrote again to warn Trumbull that the War Department might waste Illinois troops by sending them out piecemeal instead of under command of an Illinois major general. Senator Trumbull must know a man of military experience who was qualified for this assignment, Pope wrote, and should address himself to this issue.[29] This letter, to which no answer survives, appears to have ended Pope's personal letter-writing campaign.

At thirty-nine, Brigadier General John Pope had not commanded so much as a platoon, but in that respect his experience was the same as many who later became high-ranking officers. He had the greater drawback of being a topographical engineer whose weapons were transit and drawing board, and whose wartime service was on a general staff. What he knew about tactics and strategy came from his West Point textbooks, hazy memories of 1846–47, and his reading.

On July 3 the War Department created a Department of the West that included Illinois and set it under the command of John Charles Fremont, a major general commissioned directly from civilian life as a political gesture. Fremont was an explorer with Kit Carson, a prominent anti-slavery Republican who ran for president in 1856, and the mapmaker whose talents Pope called into question in 1851.[30] Fremont had once been a first lieutenant in the army but resigned in 1847 under a cloud. He probably did not hear Pope's criticisms in 1851.

On July 18 Fremont ordered Pope to cross the Mississippi at Alton, march to St. Charles, Missouri, and begin quashing riots in North Missouri.[31] In July 1861, Missouri was one of four border slave states flirting with secession[32] that Lincoln felt justified in using force to keep from seceding. When Pope and his troops marched into St. Charles they found themselves in a state with two separate governments, each of which had some claim to be the lawful one, and one of which supported the Confederacy.

Late in 1860 the Missourians had elected members to a convention to discuss secession. The convention met, voted not to secede, and adjourned; it was not dissolved. In November 1860, Missouri held its regular general elections. The voters elected a Democratic governor and a majority of Democratic senators and representatives in the legislature. The new governor and legislators favored secession. Under American constitutional dogma, all law comes from the people and the people may override constitutions and laws by expressing their will. Missouri Republicans now argued that the 1860 convention, elected by popular vote, embodied the supreme will of the people and could exercise that supreme will until the convention was dissolved. Republican leaders accordingly had officers of the 1860 convention recall it to order for further business. The convention met again, came to order, continued its adjourned session, deposed all the Democratic state officers and legislators, and substituted a Republican slate.

Hamilton R. Gamble became the Republican, or convention, governor. Claiborne Jackson, theoretically deposed, remained the Democratic, or constitutional, governor. Inasmuch as Jackson and his Democratic associates in office and in control of the Missouri militia refused to obey their ouster, Gamble had nothing to govern until he could put his administration into office by force. Gamble was a brother-in-law of Edward Bates, Lincoln's rival in the Republican National Convention of 1860 and attorney general of the United States. Gamble knew the powerful Blair family in Missouri, including Postmaster General Montgomery Blair, that chose to support the Union in 1861. Doubtless advised by Bates and the Blairs, President Lincoln welcomed the Republican administration of Gamble as the agent for holding Missouri in the Union.

Union forces in Missouri had to make the Gamble administration effective and uphold it. Lincoln knew that an administration called into being by the convention had the same questionable authority as the various Ordinances of Secession but Lincoln was not a man to worry overmuch about legality in accomplishing his wartime ends. In effect, Gamble headed a military government of Missouri.[33] Lincoln and his military advisers saw rightly that Union strategy called for holding Missouri to use as a base for future operations down the Mississippi River. The northernmost slave state could be used by Confederates to take control of Iowa, Illinois, Kansas, and Nebraska.

When Pope arrived he found northern Missouri seething. While the Union held St. Louis and key central points, Confederate sympathizers roamed openly in the areas between St. Louis and the Iowa border. In a pattern familiar from bushwacking days in Kansas in the 1850s, gangs of wreckers roamed by night to smash communication lines and hinder the coming of Union troops. Pope's Illinois troops straddled the North Missouri Railroad, running north and south, and the Hannibal and St. Joseph Railroad, running east and west. Pope knew that he had to keep the railroads running to move and supply the army in spite of guerrilla attacks. As yet, however, he had no orders and no commander; Fremont was still in New York.

Relying on his experience in the military government of northern Mexico in 1847–48, Pope went ahead on his own. On July 21 he announced his general policy: people living along the railroad had the duty to guard it from harm. Superintendents named by Pope would administer a series of ten-mile sections of track. If any part of a line suffered damage, the army would repair it, but would assess the cost and collect payment from the superintendency in which the damage took place.[34] Pope was taking his chances. His order rested on no authority from a superior and acted upon civilians in a Union state. Under the circumstances, he could well face civil suit and criminal prosecution in the courts of Missouri, since American law made soldiers answer to civil courts in peace and war alike and there were few precedents for when civil authority must bow to the military.

On the day after Pope announced his policy, Union and Confederate troops met at Bull Run in the first major battle of the Civil War. When the Confederates held their ground Confederate sympathizers interpreted this as a victory; the effect in Missouri was to make guerrillas bolder and more active. General Fremont did not reach St. Louis until a week later. On July 29 Fremont appointed

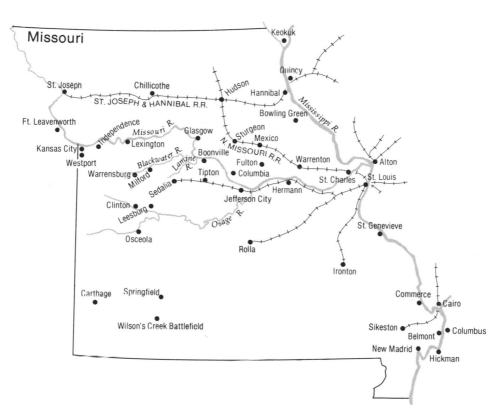

Missouri

Keokuk

Quincy

St. Joseph   Chillicothe   Hudson   Hannibal

ST. JOSEPH & HANNIBAL R.R.   Bowling Green

Ft. Leavenworth   Independence   *Missouri R.*   Glasgow   Sturgeon

Kansas City   Lexington   *Missouri R.*   Mexico

Westport   *Blackwater R.*   Boonville   N. MISSOURI R.R.   Warrenton   Alton

Warrensburg   Milford   *Lamine R.*   Fulton   St. Charles   St. Louis

Sedalia   Tipton   Columbia   Hermann

Clinton   Jefferson City

Leesburg   *Osage R.*   St. Genevieve

Osceola

Rolla

Ironton

Carthage   Springfield   Commerce   Cairo

Wilson's Creek Battlefield   Sikeston   Columbus

Belmont

New Madrid   Hickman

Mississippi R.

General Pope's Military Operations, 1861–62

Brigadier General John Pope the commander of the District of North Missouri, which meant all of Missouri north of St. Louis.[35] Pope moved his headquarters to Mexico, Missouri, and divided his large district into subdistricts.[36] One subdistrict fell to a subordinate and long-time acquaintance, Colonel Ulysses S. Grant.

For the time being the army's business remained the same: holding Missouri and keeping it quiet by putting down opposition, rounding up dangerous agitators, and smashing guerrilla bands or driving them out of the state. Now backed by Fremont's formal order, Pope created a network of local informers and issued an order subjecting to arrest all persons bearing arms against the United States and all persons taking part in unlawful assemblies, with the proviso that no one should suffer for merely speaking an opinion without trying to incite listeners to act.[37] He shortly made a slight revision in his system of guarding the railroads. Now each county would have a five-member Committee of Public Safety empowered to draft local residents for guard or patrol duty. If any part of a railroad line suffered damage, the army would repair it but levy on private property within the county to collect the cost.[38] Three men favoring the Union and two men favoring secession, picked by local army commanders, made up each committee. Pope felt that having Southern sympathizers on these committees formed the key to his plan, writing somewhat later: "When once the secessionists are made to understand that upon peace in their midst depends the safety of their families and property, we shall soon have quiet again in North Missouri."[39]

Complaints poured in to Pope, to newspapers, to General Fremont over Pope's head,[40] but Pope stood fast and enforced his orders to the letter. When freebooters in Marion County fired on trains, Pope acted like his commander-in-chief, Lincoln, in ignoring the Constitution. In the face of the Third Amendment[41] Pope quartered troops on the residents and kept them quartered until a Marion County delegation called to apologize and to promise to keep strict order in the future.[42] On August 25 Pope and Fremont met in St. Louis to go over Pope's orders and the civilian complaints against him piling up at headquarters. Fremont approved everything that Pope had done.[43]

To this point Pope's campaigning in Missouri was only administrative service, but combat was coming. Open warfare broke out in

southern Missouri near the Arkansas border. Former Governor
Sterling Price with his secessionist Missouri militia joined Confederate General Ben McCulloch in northern Arkansas. A small Union
force moving south to attack them was defeated at Wilson's Creek,
Missouri, on August 10. What was left of the Union forces retreated
northeast and left southern Missouri open to Confederate invasion.
Fremont should have acted at once to concentrate his troops and
march them all southwest to meet and defeat the Confederates, but
he was no man of action. He contented himself with a proclamation setting all Missouri under martial law and freeing the slaves of
all Missourians who took up arms against the United States.[44]
Almost as soon as Fremont issued it, Lincoln revoked the proclamation so far as it dealt with slavery. He could not risk antagonizing
the loyal slave states. By a coincidence of history in 1865 it fell to
Pope to revoke the rest of the proclamation dealing with martial law.

Meanwhile, as Fremont knew, Price and 10,000 Confederate
troops were marching north along the western border of Missouri
ready to strike at a still uncertain target. Fremont could nevertheless see nothing but guerrillas and sent Pope out on a guerrilla
chase that opened his Missouri field service. Pope was to march
west to meet General Samuel D. Sturgis marching east. Their forces
should encircle and trap 1,500 wreckers and looters under their
irregular leader Martin Green, a onetime militia colonel.[45] Pope
took the field, marched, and met Sturgis; the trap caught nothing.
On September 12 Pope wired Fremont that Green crossed the
Missouri River at Glasgow, heading west, and had probably left
north Missouri for good.[46]

On the same day Fremont began to get intelligence that Price's
troops looked as if they meant to attack Lexington, Missouri, then
garrisoned with only 2,500 troops. This would cut the communications between St. Louis and Kansas City. Finally prodded into
acting, the department commander began to send frantic telegrams
to commanders of his widely scattered detachments ordering them
to round up their troops and hurry off to Lexington. Pope heard
about the danger to Lexington while he was on the way to Keokuk,
Iowa, to take charge of incoming recruits. He wired that he was
sending 4,000 soldiers and four artillery pieces and hoped that they
could reach Lexington within two days.[47] But Pope's troops ran
into such hot enemy fire that a necessary river crossing became an

unacceptable risk. Reinforcements sent by others also failed to reach the city. Fremont seemed never to have imagined an enemy attack in his department and had not set up a supply system, collected transport, or arranged for draft animals.

Under the circumstances Lexington's commander, Colonel James A. Mulligan, surrendered the city and his army of 2,600 on September 20. His surrender was the second Union disaster in Missouri and underlined Fremont's first-class incompetence. Pope had been charged with trying to undercut Fremont by deliberately holding his troops back so that they could not reach Lexington in time,[48] but as far as surviving records show, Pope heard about Lexington from Sturgis on September 15, had no word from Fremont, and went ahead promptly on his own.[49]

After the fall of Lexington Fremont reorganized his troops into an Army of the West with five divisions and planned a great sweep south and west to drive Price and McCulloch from Missouri.[50] Pope commanded the second division and was ordered to concentrate at Boonville, march to Leesburg, and stop at Leesburg before taking position as the army's right wing in a march south along Missouri's western border.[51] By the time Pope reached Leesburg he knew that the Confederates had marched back to their southern Missouri refuge after failing to get recruits in central Missouri. Fremont's planned campaign was already useless. Pope also knew that Fremont was in hot water in Washington. Officers had seen Secretary of War Cameron and Adjutant General Alonzo Thomas in St. Louis and knew this visit meant no good for their commanding general.

Lincoln actually relieved Fremont from command in an order dated October 24, 1861,[52] but Fremont was in the field and did not get it until later. He was busy planning to catch Price and McCulloch and on November 1 Fremont gave Pope orders to move out at once and go to Springfield, Missouri, by forced marches.[53] Although he knew it was useless, Pope sent one regiment off to Springfield. The troops scurried away, marched to the city, and found it free of Confederate soldiers. By that time Fremont no longer commanded the Department of the West.[54] Pope had nothing to do but await orders from a new, yet unnamed commander, and to speculate about a shakeup in top army command.

Lincoln took a political gamble in removing Fremont. Although incompetent in the field, Fremont became the idol of the growing radical wing in the Republican party when he delighted the abolitionists by trying to abolish slavery in Missouri on his own. After listening to complaints about Fremont's removal, Lincoln decided that it would be politically expedient to give the man another command, which he did, not foreseeing that Fremont's ineptness would put the capital at risk and add to Pope's headaches.

Lincoln took, or was maneuvered into, another political gamble when on November 1 he prodded General Winfield Scott into retirement and appointed George B. McClellan as general-in-chief of the Army. Scott was a long-standing Whig, Lincoln's original party, who stood as a symbol of American continuity, a military Uncle Sam, because of his continuous army commands since 1812. He was also a Virginian who set an example of loyalty to the Union. McClellan was a known Democrat with political ambitions, already ticketed by Tammany leaders as a coming candidate, indifferent toward slavery, and determined to carry on a chivalrous war, which to Republicans meant being soft toward the enemy. Moreover, Lincoln was delivering into McClellan's hands an army that could become a powerful Democratic political bloc if McClellan led it to success. The Congress quickly set up a Joint Committee on Conduct of the War to keep an eye on such possibilities and any moves in support of them.

To Pope, McClellan's appointment had to be another slight given by Lincoln. Pope had once protested to Lincoln against this Pennsylvanian's promotion over the head of his seniors. Now he found McClellan his top commanding officer. Pope was a Republican, firmly against slavery, a longtime friend of the Lincolns, connected through his own family and his wife's family with Republicans in leading offices, and until May of 1861 McClellan's senior on the regular army rank list. The fortunes of war, however, were favoring McClellan, but the mutual distaste between Pope and McClellan was growing.

McClellan turned out to be an excellent organizer and an inspiring commander. He also brought order to Union strategy by making an overall plan that would supersede the existing haphazard system of many separate commands with objectives more or less at the whim of commanders. Under McClellan's strategy, McClellan himself would lead the Army of the Potomac to victory and end the rebellion by taking Richmond. One supporting western army would campaign down the Mississippi to keep the Confederates of the trans-Mississippi busy and split the Confederacy in two. Another supporting western army would keep the Confederates between the Appalachians and the Mississippi so occupied that they could not send reinforcements or supplies to the defenders of Richmond. It was simple, which was a military virtue, and it was convincing, if McClellan assumed correctly that taking Richmond would end the war. McClellan and most of the other commanders North and South saw no reason to question the assumption. They had all learned it at West Point.

On November 9 McClellan appointed Henry Wager Halleck the new commander of the Department of the West, which covered Illinois, Iowa, Minnesota, Missouri, Wisconsin, Arkansas (a Confederate state), and Kentucky west of the Cumberland River. Halleck reached St. Louis and assumed command on November 19.[55] Pope must have known his new commanding officer at West Point. Halleck was in the class of 1839, and in 1839–40 taught the art of war under Mahan while Pope was there.

Pope's first experience of the new chain of command came when a 6′4″ redhead appeared at Pope's headquarters in Sedalia, Missouri, and started to give direct orders to the Second Division to call in its scattered detachments and concentrate. The redhead was General William T. Sherman, fresh from Kentucky and serving as inspector at Halleck's headquarters. At that time Pope's military intelligence reported no organized Confederate forces in the area and Pope had spread his troops out in detachments. Pope complained about this interference to Halleck, who promptly recalled Sherman.[56] At this time Sherman was the victim of newspaper harrassment in articles calling him "crazy" and the endless pressure could have driven him into such overstepping.[57]

The fact that no Confederate troops were in Pope's area in November did not mean that they could not come in December, and in December Pope learned that Price was again heading north. Pope, commanding the area between the Osage River on the south and the Missouri River on the north, concentrated his Second Division after all and moved west on December 15 to get between Price's troops and any supplies and recruits coming to them from north Missouri. After sealing off a north-south passage at Warrensburg he sent out forces under Colonel Jefferson C. Davis, later a general, to meet and destroy the main body. On December 18 Davis found the Confederate force encamped near the Blackwater River. He cut off all retreat routes and forced a surrender. For once the Union Army in Missouri gathered the real fruits of a victory: 1,300 prisoners, 500 draft animals, 73 wagons, 1,000 stands of arms, and a store of military supplies.[58] This was the Battle of the Blackwater River that brought credit to Davis, Pope, and Halleck, and valuable journalistic coverage overplaying the victory, as usual, in hopes of driving from memory the earlier Missouri disasters at Wilson's Creek and Lexington.[59] The little battle had the practical effect of breaking up the Confederate forces and making them withdraw to Missouri's southern border.

Halleck had a victory celebration in St. Louis, sent Pope his personal congratulations, and later appointed Pope to command of the District of Central Missouri, adding, "you will certainly have a suitable command if I can give it to you."[60] The army moved into winter quarters and Pope had time to reflect on the extraordinary year which had passed. He should have been satisfied with his record in the field. It was as outstanding as anyone else's, certainly on a par with that of Sherman and Grant. If Halleck's words about a "suitable command" meant anything, Pope could reasonably look ahead to larger assignments that might lift him from divisional command to army command.

NOTES

1. Special Order (hereafter SO) 215, Adjutant General's Office (hereafter AGO), Oct. 3, 1860, RG 94 NA; Service Record, John Pope, RG 94 NA; Act of Mar. 3, 1851, 9 Stat. 627; Act of Aug. 31, 1852, 10 Stat. 112; Act of Aug. 9, 1854, 10 Stat. 335.
2. *Meigs County Telegraph*, Sept. 20, 1859.
3. The phrase is that of Henry Adams.
4. *The Star of the West.*
5. Pope to Lincoln, Jan. 21, 1861, Robert T. Lincoln Papers, Library of Congress, Washington.
6. Cincinnati *Daily Gazette*, Feb. 13, 1861, Public Library of Cincinnati and Hamilton County.
7. Minutes, Literary Society of Cincinnati, Public Library of Cincinnati and Hamilton County.

8. See Ward H. Lamon, *The Life of Abraham Lincoln, From His Birth to His Inauguration as President* (Boston, 1872), 519 ff.; Henry Villard, *Memoirs of Henry Villard,* 2 vols. (Boston, 1904), 1:151 ff.; Victor Searcher, *Lincoln's Journey to Greatness* (New York, 1960).

9. Ward H. Lamon, *Recollections of Abraham Lincoln* (Chicago, 1893), 34.

10. Villard, 1:150.

11. SO 60, AGO, Feb. 27, 1861, RG 94 NA.

12. Act of Apr. 10, 1806, 2 Stat. 59, c.5: "Any officer or soldier who shall use contemptuous or disrespectful words against the President of the United States, against the Vice-President thereof, against the Congress of the United States, or against the chief magistrate or legislature of any of the United States, in which he may be quartered, if a commissioned officer, shall be cashiered, or otherwise punished as a court-martial shall direct; if a non-commissioned officer or soldier, he shall suffer such punishment as shall be inflicted upon him by sentence of a court martial."

13. SO 66, AGO, Mar. 2, 1861, RG 94 NA.

14. Maurice Matloff, ed., *American Military History,* reprinted and partially revised (Washington, 1973), 188.

15. Pope to Lamon, Apr. 11, 1861, Robert T. Lincoln Papers.

16. Pope to Yates, Apr. 12, 1861, John Pope Papers, Illinois State Historical Library, Springfield.

17. SO 106, AGO, Apr. 15, 1861, RG 94 NA.

18. Pope to Davis, Apr. 16, 1861, Illinois State Historical Library.

19. Pope to Lincoln, Apr. 20, 1861, Robert T. Lincoln Papers.

20. Pope to Lincoln, May 15, 1861, Robert T. Lincoln Papers.

21. Ulysses S. Grant, *Personal Memoirs of U.S. Grant,* E. B. Long, ed. (Cleveland, 1952), 121.

22. See Pope to Lincoln, June 16, 1861, Illinois State Historical Library.

23. Proclamation of May 3, 1861, 12 Stat. 1260.

24. Article I, sect. 8, cl. 3 of the United States Constitution reads: "The Congress shall have Power . . . To raise and support Armies."

25. Act of July 29, 1861, 12 Stat. 279.

26. See note 22.

27. Pope to Trumbull, June 16, 1861, Illinois State Historical Library.

28. Pope to Trumbull, June 23, 1861, Illinois State Historical Library.

29. Pope to Trumbull, July 3, 1861, Illinois State Historical Library.

30. General Order (hereafter GO) 40, AGO, July 3, 1861, RG 94 NA.

31. Fremont to Col. E. D. Townsend, Assistant Adjutant General (hereafter AAG), July 18, 1861, Official Records (*The War of the Rebellion,* hereafter OR) II: 404.

32. The others were Delaware, Kentucky, and Maryland.

33. For a summary of the Missouri tangle, see John Fiske, *The Mississippi Valley in the Civil War* (Boston, 1900). For a detailed study of the whole Civil War, see J. G. Randall and David Donald, *The Civil War and Reconstruction,* 2d ed. (Lexington, Mass. 1969).

34. Notice, John Pope, Commanding North Missouri, July 21, 1861, OR III:403–4.
35. SO 10, Dept. of West, July 29, 1861, OR III:415.
36. GO 1, Dist. of N. Missouri, July 29, 1861, OR III:415.
37. Ibid.
38. GO 3, Dist. of N. Missouri, July 31, 1861, OR III:417.
39. Pope to Col. William F. Worthington, Aug. 2, 1861, OR III:422.
40. See, for example, St. Louis *Weekly Missouri Democrat,* Aug. 6, 1861; J. T. K. Hayward to Fremont, Aug. 10, 1861, OR III:433–35.
41. "No Soldier shall, in time of peace, be quartered in any house, without the consent of the Owner, nor in time of war, but in a manner to be prescribed by law." (Congress had not acted in 1861.)
42. See Pope to Gen. J. C. Kelton, Aug. 17, 1861, OR III:447.
43. See Pope to Fremont, Aug. 25, 1861, OR III:456–57.
44. Proclamation, Aug. 30, 1861, OR III:466.
45. Fremont to Pope, Aug. 6, 1861, OR III:473.
46. Pope to Fremont, Sept. 12, 1861, OR III:487.
47. Pope to Fremont, Sept. 16, 1861, OR III:176, 497 (Three messages).
48. Allan Nevins, *Fremont, The West's Greatest Adventurer,* 2 vols. (New York, 1928), 1:596, 1:607–10, 1:643.
49. Official records contain no communications whatever from Fremont to Pope on this subject and Nevins's statement that Fremont ordered Pope to send help on both Sept. 13 and 14 cites no authority.
50. GO 1, Army of the West, Sept. 21, 1861, OR III:502.
51. GO 16, Army of the West, Sept. 28, 1861, OR III:508.
52. GO 18, AGO, Oct. 24, 1861, OR III:553.
53. J. H. Eaton, AAG, Army of the West, to Pope, Nov. 1, 1861, OR III:559.
54. See GO 28, Army of the West, Nov. 2, 1861, OR III:558 (Issued by Fremont who had not yet received Lincoln's order).
55. GO 97, AGO, Nov. 9, 1861, OR III:567.
56. Gen. Schuyler Hamilton to Fremont, Nov. 28, 1861, OR VIII:391. Sherman later wrote in his defense, "I advised General Halleck . . . to put them into brigades and divisions so as to be ready to be handled, and I gave some preliminary orders looking to that end. But the newspapers kept harping on my insanity and paralyzed my efforts." William T. Sherman, *Memoirs of William T. Sherman* (1875; reprint, Bloomington, Ind., 1957), 215.
57. See J. G. Randall and David Donald, *The Civil War and Reconstruction,* 2d ed. (Boston, 1966), 202; James M. McPherson, *Battle Cry of Freedom: The Civil War Era* (New York, 1988), 305; and Benjamin J. Lossing, *The Pictorial Field Book of the Civil War,* 3 vols. (Hartford, Conn., 1874), 2:78.
58. Report, Pope to Halleck, Dec. 23, 1861, OR VIII:38.
59. See *Harper's Weekly,* 6 (January 1862): 3 and 6 (January 1862): 19.
60. Halleck to Pope, Dec. 20, 1861, OR VIII:452; Halleck to Pope, Jan. 27, 1862, OR VIII:528.

Chapter Seven

GLORY

AT THE BEGINNING OF 1862 General Pope was killing time at his headquarters at LaMine, Missouri, in the general languor that settled on all commands at the end of 1861. General Halleck did not order Pope to pursue and smash the Confederate forces turned back at the Blackwater River and was as content as his predecessor Fremont to see the enemy go into Arkansas to regroup at leisure. Pope could only sit in his Department of Central Missouri waiting for subversives and guerrillas to show their heads or, if he was lucky, for the unlikely reappearance of a Confederate army.

In the East General-in-Chief McClellan trained his huge army and kept putting Lincoln off about setting a definite date for beginning the peninsular attack on Richmond. In General Don Carlos Buell's Department of the Ohio all was quiet until General George H. Thomas gave the Union its first victory of the year at Mill Springs, Kentucky, on January 19.

Any push for attack in Halleck's Department of the West had to come from a subordinate or a superior. Halleck was no fighter and had no more talent for command than Fremont, although that fact did not come out until later. Halleck's questionable nickname, "Old Brains," came from his having taught at West Point, his reading in the theory of war, his little treatise on fortifications, his translations of French military works, and his treatises on international law and California mining law.

As matters turned out a push for attack did come from a subordinate who was a fighter. General Ulysses S. Grant asked and got Halleck's permission to join Commodore Andrew H. Foote at Cairo, Illinois, in a army-navy expedition up the Cumberland and

Tennessee rivers. In their quick, decisive campaign Grant and Foote recaptured both Fort Henry and Fort Donelson, which commanded the strong points of Columbus, Kentucky, and Nashville, Tennessee. Since these two places were now outflanked, the Confederate commander in the West, Albert Sidney Johnston, ordered them abandoned at once. Halleck congratulated Grant and Foote, took unto himself the credit for their victories, and treated the campaign as closed. He ordered no pursuit and no further advance into enemy territory. After the fall of Fort Donelson on February 16, Grant sat with his army of 42,000 while to the East Buell sat with his 50,000. Foote steamed his little gunboat fleet back to anchor at Cairo.[1]

The Confederates moved. Under the overseeing of General Pierre G. T. Beauregard they transferred ordinance and troops to Island No. 10 in the Mississippi, enlarged their existing garrison at New Madrid, Missouri, to support the island, and strengthened Fort Pillow guarding the approach to Memphis on the Mississippi. So much enemy activity in and near his own department startled the bookish General Halleck into doing something. On February 17 Halleck ordered troop transports heading up the Cumberland and Tennessee rivers rerouted to a staging area at Commerce, Missouri.[2] On the next day he ordered Pope to see him at St. Louis. When Pope arrived, he found himself appointed the commanding general of the new Army of the Mississippi that he would have to assemble from new recruits, including those rerouted to Commerce. His mission was to take New Madrid and Island No. 10.[3] Pope would have to agree that this was a suitable command that Halleck promised earlier.

Acting with speed, Pope went to Cairo, visited the arsenal, requisitioned siege guns, picked up recruits, and was back in Commerce, Missouri, on February 24 getting his army ready to march. In a season of rain and spring floods, Pope's greenhorns stepped smartly along the slippery, muddy Sikeston causeway and reached New Madrid in a week, standing before the village on March 3. Pope ordered an attack at once. At that time Confederate General McCown had about 3,000 troops in New Madrid with the remainder on Island No. 10 and the adjacent mainland. In the river he had a little supporting fleet of gunboats commanded by Commodore George N. Hollins, one of the few United States Navy officers to desert to the Confederacy.[4] Spring floods brought the Mississippi almost to the top of the levee, so that Hollins's gunboats rode above Pope's soldiers' heads and the gunners could depress their pieces to fire point blank into the attacking army. Pope had to call off his attack at the close of March 4.

He moved rapidly to make downriver reconnaissances and to set up small posts centered on Point Pleasant to command the Mississippi for ten miles south of New Madrid. He requisitioned more siege guns to reopen his attack on New Madrid on March 12. All during the day of March 13 Pope's artillery pounded the village and scored hits on the Confederate gunboats.

Since he had the only Confederate fleet on the Mississippi, Hollins began to worry about its safety under steady bombardment and decided he ought to get his ships out of artillery range and into shelter; General McCown agreed. On that rainy night General McCown abandoned New Madrid and had his troops ferried across the river to Madrid Bend under cover of Hollins's gunboats. The commodore then pulled his fleet to the left bank of the Mississippi.[5] Pope and his army then took over the deserted village the next day. General Schuyler Hamilton, a grandson of Alexander Hamilton and a personal friend of Pope, took command. The enemy abandoned arms, ammunition, and supplies. Bloodless though it might have been, this was victory for the Union, which for most of the past year had had to swallow news of treachery, bungling, stupidity, and defeat. News reporters and magazine writers played up Pope's victory as "brilliant" and "decisive," making the young general front-page news.[6]

Pope earned some of this excess praise. From the date of his appointment as commanding general on February 17 to the date of his entry into New Madrid on March 14 Pope built his army from the ground up, gathered recruits, fitted them out, supplied them, set them marching, and led them into action. His army did not suffer one casualty.

Halleck duly claimed Pope's success at New Madrid, which for once came in a campaign that Halleck originated. Now placing further confidence in this capable-looking department commander, the War Department gave Halleck command of an enlarged Department of the West that took in Buell's Department of the Ohio. This in effect handed the textbook warrior all Union forces west of the

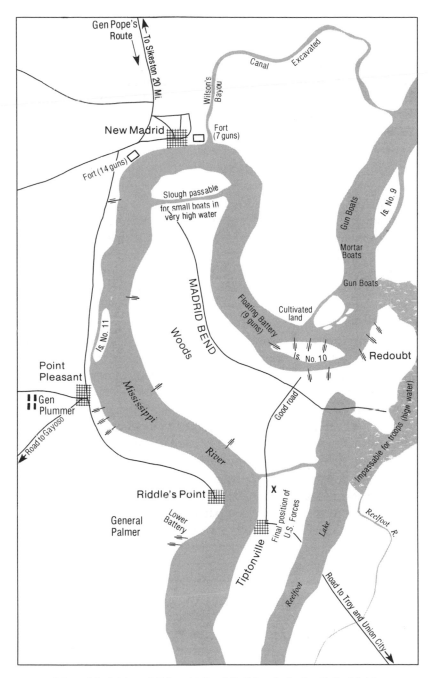

New Madrid and Island No. 10, March 2–April 7, 1862

Alleghenies. Halleck's new command would doubtless mean more action for Pope's Army of the Mississippi. Other contemporary events would affect Pope's future steps. On March 8 Union forces won a victory at Pea Ridge, Arkansas, that ended the Confederate threat to Missouri and to Pope's army at New Madrid. On March 11 Lincoln removed McClellan as general-in-chief of the army when McClellan took the field with his Army of the Potomac. Lincoln and his new secretary of war, Edwin M. Stanton, would try to manage the army themselves. On March 14 General Ambrose E. Burnside set off on an expedition to give the Union Army a coastal base below Richmond.

Pope had little time to muse on high-level changes and far-off campaigns. As a commander he had taken credit himself for Davis's victory at the Blackwater River in 1861 and he could hardly blame Halleck for doing the same thing. It was the army way. More important to Pope at the moment was the fact that Confederates had fortified Island No. 10, blocking passage of the Mississippi. Even before he started his campaign for New Madrid Pope had been thinking about how to take Island No. 10. That he needed naval support was obvious. He asked Halleck for use of the same river fleet that supported Grant in his river campaign; Halleck approved.[7] Commodore Foote still suffered from a leg wound sustained in Grant's campaign but agreed to serve again.[8] On March 14, the day that Pope entered New Madrid, Foote sailed from Cairo in his flagship, the USS *Benton,* with his fleet of nine gunboats, ten mortarboats, and four troop transports. The ships anchored in the Mississippi just North of Island No. 10 on the foggy morning of March 16.[9]

Foote's riverboats were not battlewagons, but really gunboats built at St. Louis in 1861–62, armored only at the bow and sides. They did not have enough power to back against the Mississippi's six-knot current. Since their anchors would not hold against this current they tied up to shore when idle. In spite of their weakness in power and anchor, they had ordnance to reckon with, each gunboat carrying three nine-inch Dahlgren guns, one twelve-pounder, and four forty-two-pounders. Each mortarboat carried one thirteen-inch mortar but mortarboats had no power and had to be towed into position and made fast.[10]

Although he had a second plan in mind, Pope wanted to reduce

Island No. 10 by bombardment if he could. He asked Foote to attack as soon as he arrived. After an all-day pounding on March 17, during which the total ammunition used amounted to more than that used in any other Mississippi River engagement during the Civil War, the Confederates on Island No. 10 were still firing their guns and three of the seven Union gunboats had taken hits. Pope realized that these gunboats simply could not knock out land batteries. He had to use direct assault. That meant getting troops from New Madrid over to the shore opposite Island No. 10 in transports. Foote brought four troopships from Cairo, but the island stood between them and the troops at New Madrid that would embark on them. Pope could get his transports to New Madrid only if gunboats convoyed the troopships and shielded them from the Confederate batteries. Foote refused to allow his gunboats to try this maneuver.[11]

This left Pope the choice of getting his transports to New Madrid by a waterway out of enemy sight and range, which brought his second plan into play. At the campaign's outset, General Hamilton seems to have had the idea of cutting a canal through the land just north of Madrid Bend, the bend in the Mississippi commanded at its south point by Island No. 10. Hamilton recommended this to Pope, who pounced on the scheme, reported it to Halleck, and had engineers working on it within a day after New Madrid fell. The plan called for a canal twelve miles long, fifty feet wide, and four feet deep. Crews would have to cut trees four feet below water level. Using four light draft steamers rigged with underwater saws, working under guard of three gun barges, all sent downriver from Cairo, Pope's engineers finished the work on April 4 after seventeen days of steady plugging.[12] A chain of east-west bayous cut down the distance of actual canal building and speeded the work.

Shallow draft transports could now steam through a canal out of Confederate artillery range, but Foote's gunboats could reach New Madrid only by running past Island No. 10's batteries on the Mississippi. Foote refused to order any of his captains to try this until a personal call from Assistant Secretary of War Scott convinced him to call a council of gunboat commanders to discuss ways and means. The commanders' talks ended in a question: Would anyone volunteer? Captain Henry Walke of the *Carondelet* did. Walke got a volunteer crew and waited for the traditional dark and stormy night, which came on April 4. Walke left his anchorage at 10 P.M. with gun ports closed and lights out. At first the Confederates on watch saw nothing, but when they saw sparks at the top of the ship's stacks, they gave the alarm and Confederate batteries opened fire. Walke luckily ran his gunboat so close to the shore that the fort's artillery could not depress their guns low enough for point-blank fire. All shots went high. The little gunboat chugged on and docked at New Madrid on April 5, at 2 A.M.[13]

This was nearly all that Pope needed. He ordered the transports sent through the new canal and asked Foote to send another gunboat past the island batteries. Foote agreed promptly this time and on the night of April 6, the gunboat *Pittsburg* also reached New Madrid safely.[14] On the next night Pope had the two gunboats silence small Confederate artillery posts across the river, ordered his troops to board the transports, and sent his landing force over the Mississippi to the west side of Madrid Bend. Watching his troops cross from New Madrid was, Pope exclaimed, "the most magnificent spectacle he had ever seen!"[15] The Confederates saw themselves cut off and trapped. Some of the garrison tried to escape through mainland swamps but found the water shoulder high and had to surrender to General E. A. Paine of Pope's army. Those who stayed in the fort surrendered to Commodore Foote. The Confederate gunboat fleet of Commodore Hollins steamed downriver to safety. In this operation Pope captured around 3,800 prisoners, including 276 officers, as well as all the Confederate artillery, arms, and unused ammunition and supplies.[16] Just as at New Madrid, Pope's army sustained no casualties.

Halleck came through with ringing praise: "I congratulate you and your command on your splendid achievement. It exceeds in boldness and brilliancy all the operations of the war. It will be memorable in military history and will be admired by future generations. You deserve well of your country."[17] Assistant Secretary of War Scott, who watched from the sidelines, wired Secretary Stanton, "General Pope's movement has been a glorious success."[18]

Pope let himself do a little soaring on his own in a General Order to his troops: "The conduct of the troops was splendid throughout. To such an Army nothing is impossible, and the general commanding hopes yet to lead them to some field where superiority of numbers and positions will tempt the enemy to give them the opportunity to win the glory they are so capable of achieving."[19]

Newspapers and magazines caught up the victory and praised Pope's speed in handing the Confederates two defeats in the forty-seven days after his appointment to command. Boldface headlines such as "THE VICTORY AT ISLAND NO. 10" led into articles overpraising Pope.[20] His face soon appeared on a patriotic envelope as the newest Union war hero. Calling this capture "one of the most important and brilliant achievements of the war," the editor of *Frank Leslie's Illustrated Magazine* exalted, "where, in the whole history of this country, or of modern warfare, can we point to results so grand achieved without bloodshed? . . . In respect of spoils and trophies of war, this glorious victory yields to the National arms an aggregate exceeding that of Mill Spring, Donelson, and Henry combined. . . . Honor to the patience, the intelligence, and the skill, not less than the bravery and devotion of Com. Foote and Gen. Pope!"[21]

Two weeks later the same editor was still dwelling on Pope's deeds in a feature article about Pope's canal[22] and in a summary of Pope's deeds in and for Missouri: "His brilliant movement in Central Missouri tended as much as anything to restore peace to that State, and his brilliant investment of New Madrid led to the evacuation of that place."[23] On top of this, Pope must have received congratulations from friends, relatives, soldiers, politicians, and from the men and women who read the articles about him. Pope had to feel that at least some of these well-wishers must be right. He could see himself called an outstanding military leader by professionals; he might be willing to hear himself called a military genius.

The springtime surge in Pope's reputation had psychological and political bases beyond the sparse supply of Union heroes in 1862. On the same day that Island No. 10 fell, Generals Grant and Buell barely saved their Union armies in a standoff at Shiloh that cost the Union 13,000 casualties. Pope had yet to lose one soldier. In the East, after countless delays, McClellan and his army were in their twenty-first day of an elephantine march toward Richmond. Pope accomplished all his objectives in forty-seven days. Grant was a political unknown. McClellan was a politically active and ambitious Democrat. Pope was a Republican allied by marriage to a prominent Republican member of Congress and serving a Republican president and Republican-controlled Congress.

As to Pope's real military ability, his victories came in an interregnum in top command. Two civilians, Lincoln and Stanton, were trying to handle military affairs on their own by creating armies, handing out commands, and adopting military strategy. They heard Pope's praises from "Old Brains" Halleck, who still had his unearned reputation as a military mastermind, from an assistant secretary of war actually on the scene, and in articles loaded with the words *splendid, brilliant,* and *decisive.* As yet they had heard nothing contrary to this. Furthermore, Lincoln was all politician. He wanted Republican commanders to deliver Republican victories that he could use for purposes of the Republican party. No one should forget that the Civil War was the only war in American history in which two political parties resorted to arms to maintain their respective party platforms. Republican General Pope had now delivered the Republican party two striking, bloodless victories and looked capable of delivering more. At Shiloh General Grant cost the Confederacy about 10,000 casualties, but cost the Union 13,000. Unexpectedly bloody alongside Pope's comfortable triumphs, Shiloh was not the kind of victory for an administration to use as political capital. Whatever the final assessment, Pope's energetic style of command set in movement forces that would carry him upward. The first payoff came on March 21, 1862, when he became major general of volunteers.[24]

After Pope's victory a brief lull came in the Department of the West. When Halleck duly took congratulations for projects originated and carried out by subordinates, he realized he had to start new campaigns. Pope wanted to take Memphis, Tennessee; Grant wanted to chase the Confederates who, he thought, would regroup and recruit at Corinth, Mississippi. Grant was right; taking cities had no point if armed enemy forces remained intact in the field. Halleck agreed with Grant in principle and, knowing that his chief subordinates had proved themselves in the field and could steer him right, left his comfortable headquarters in the Planter's Hotel in St. Louis to take command in the field. He reached Pittsburg Landing on April 12, assumed command of Grant's and Buell's troops, ordered Grant and Buell to wait for Pope, and ordered Pope to transfer his army from New Madrid to Pittsburg Landing.[25]

Since Fort Pillow still barred the Mississippi at Memphis, Pope had to send his transports north to Cairo and then back south on the Tennessee River. His Army of the Mississippi joined the others on April 22.[26]

Halleck now had about 105,000 soldiers under his command[27] organized in three wings and called in true Napoleonic style the Grand Army of the Tennessee. Pope's Army of the Mississippi was the left wing; the Army of Ohio commanded by Buell was the center; The Army of the Tennessee commanded by George H. Thomas formed the right wing. Thomas took Grant's place because for some as yet unknown reason Halleck removed Grant from an army command and assigned him to the meaningless post of deputy commander of the Grand Army.

On April 30, three weeks after the last armed Confederate hovered near Shiloh and after the Confederates had plenty of time to regroup and plan, Halleck and his huge force stepped out on what would be the Grand Army's Grand March. On May 30 the Grand March ended at Corinth after the marchers covered only twenty miles, strolling at an average pace of 3,432 feet per day. Grant in his duty-free post had time to comment on Halleck's march: "The movement was a siege from the start to the close. The National troops were always behind entrenchments, except of course the small reconnoitering parties sent to the front to clear the way for an advance. Even the commanders of these parties were cautioned 'not to bring on an engagement.' 'It is better to retreat than fight.' "[28]

Pope was about the only commander to come out of the campaign with credit. Grant wrote, "General Halleck kept his headquarters generally, if not all the time, with the right wing. Pope being on the extreme left did not see so much of his chief, and consequently got loose as it were at times."[29] Sherman, who also served in the campaign, agreed that only Pope's wing saw much fighting.[30]

On May 3 and 4 Pope's army advanced to Farmington, only four miles from Corinth, met a sizeable Confederate force, engaged the Confederates, and trounced them. Then, as Grant recalled, "There would have been no difficulty in advancing the center and right so as to form a new line well up to the enemy, but Pope was ordered back to conform with the general line. On the 4th of May he moved again, taking his whole force to Farmington and pushed out two divisions close to the rebel line. Again he was ordered back."[31]

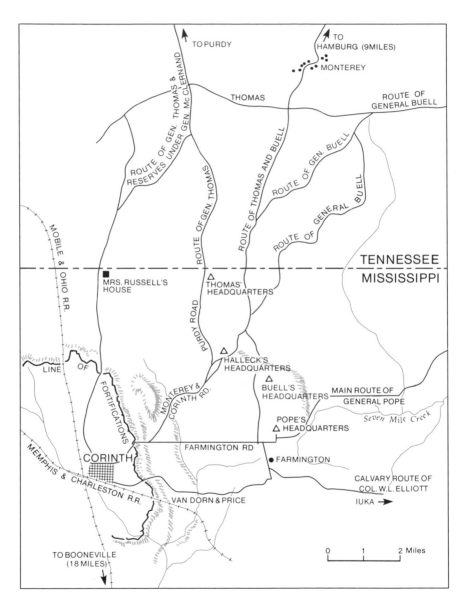

General Halleck's Advance on Corinth

The Grand Army inched along with all wings in line while Halleck sent out reconnaissances in force that seldom saw an enemy. On May 20 the Grand Army reached a point three miles from Corinth, and Pope's soldiers built a ninety-foot tower from which they could see into the town.[32] On May 29 Pope wired Halleck that he could bring on an engagement at any time Halleck gave the order.[33] Since Halleck's textbook apparently did not call for such an order at such a time, he gave none.

By May 29 the Confederates had decided to abandon Corinth. Outnumbered two to one, they could not get reinforcements from the authorities in Richmond who faced McClellan's approach. The troops in Corinth made noise, ran trains in and out of town to give the look of being reinforced, completely deceived their attackers, including Pope, and after sunset rode out of town on the Mobile and Ohio Railroad. At 6:40 A.M. on May 31 soldiers of the 39th Ohio and 42d Illinois, both in Pope's Army of the Mississippi, walked into undefended Corinth and raised the Stars and Stripes on the courthouse.[34] The rest of the Grand Army ambled into town a little later.

During the Corinth campaign Pope had been working on ways to make better use of the cavalry and to strengthen it. Existing army practice kept cavalry units small and in the control of subordinate commanders. Pope saw that fragmenting the cavalry into small detachments violated the sound military principle of keeping forces concentrated and also created time-wasting "friction" when army commanders had to order division commanders to order brigade commanders to order cavalry commanders to send out separate arrays of cavalry, get their separate reports, and combine reports all the way back up the line.

Pope wanted to set up mobile striking forces under control of army commanders, forces strong enough to carry out actions on their own in addition to carrying out the usual cavalry duties of gathering information, screening troop movements, raiding, and harrying a defeated foe. He began to experiment on the way to Corinth, first putting two cavalry regiments together to make a cavalry brigade under a commander who reported directly to Pope. He got better results, he found, and better information than commanders Buell and Thomas did when using cavalry in the traditional way.[35] When he could, Pope meant to carry the experiment a step further. His chance came when Corinth fell. Pope had already combined two cavalry brigades into a cavalry division under Colonel Gordon Granger. Now he sent Granger's division out as a separate striking force to cut off the Confederate retreat by wrecking the Mobile and Ohio Railroad. Riding 180 miles in four days, Granger and his troops accomplished their mission of destroying tracks, bridges, and warehouses, but could not catch the enemy army. They found only hordes of stragglers, and the sick and wounded left behind by the Confederates.

On June 3 Pope wired Halleck: "The roads for miles are full of stragglers from the enemy, who are coming in in squads. Not less than 10,000 men are thus scattered about, who will come in within a day or so."[36] Halleck rephrased this in a wire to Stanton, saying that Pope "already reports 10,000 prisoners and deserters,"[37] which *Harper's Weekly* picked up and spread.[38] Halleck's wishful thinking brought Pope the name of liar when the 10,000 prisoners did not materialize. After the war Pope tried to get Halleck to correct the record but Halleck would not.[39]

On June 9 Halleck ordered Pope to take a "strong defensive position" to the south of Corinth, which left Pope nothing further to do. Once at Corinth, Halleck seemed to think that he had done all a general could. He sat in his conquered village, fortified it like Gibraltar, and ordered no action. His Grand Army shortly dissolved under his feet. Taking Corinth was the pinnacle of his campaign to nowhere, in which he displayed in full his mature skill in directing military pirouettes.

Pope entered the Corinth campaign still hearing praise for his acts in Missouri and ended the campaign with a reputation as a decisive and successful commander. Pope knew as well as Grant that the only way to win a war was by meeting and destroying enemy armies, but he had never been in a position to do it, being generally tied by orders from Fremont or Halleck giving him geographic objectives and never allowing him to bring on an attack or carry on a pursuit. The public, and probably even Lincoln and Stanton, still believed in capturing cities rather than defeating armies. But like other Union commanders, Pope still had to revise his battle strategy. He still believed in Jomini's doctrine of investing and besieging fortified places before moving ahead; his siege gun requisitions showed that. He wanted to seize Memphis rather than chase Confederates to Corinth.

While his acts helped to open the Mississippi, which was sound strategy, a closer analysis of his conquests than reporters usually made would show them spotlessly bloodless but nearly toothless; and his greatest feat, the Island No. 10 canal, sprang from another's mind. In the end what both soldiers and civilians saw in Pope was a man of dash who organized well, moved fast, and carried out what his superiors wanted without wasting time. By June of 1862 Pope had done as well as any other Union general, which was not yet saying much, and he could accept public applause feeling that he had earned it.

NOTES

1. See Ulysses S. Grant, *Personal Memoirs of U. S. Grant,* E. B. Long, ed., 2 vols. (New York, 1885; reprint, Cleveland, 1952), for the campaign of Fort Henry and Fort Donelson. See Manning F. Force, *From Fort Henry to Corinth,* Campaigns of the Civil War Series, (New York, 1882), for the campaigns of New Madrid, Island No. 10, and Corinth. See Benjamin F. Lossing, *The Pictorial Field Book of the Civil War,* 2 vols. (Hartford, 1874), for all of Pope's campaigns. See also chapter 6, note 33.
2. Halleck to Gen. G. W. Cullum, Feb. 17, 1861, OR VIII:559.
3. Lossing, 2:239.
4. Ibid.
5. Ibid., 2:240.
6. See *St. Louis Missouri Republican,* Mar. 15, 16, 18, 19, 1862; "Truly a great victory and entitled Maj. Gen. Pope to great credit for his management of the Union forces," Mar. 19; "Brilliant and decisive," Mar. 20. See also *Harper's Weekly,* 6 (Mar. 29, 1862): 179 and 6 (Apr. 12, 1862): 179. See also *Frank Leslie's Illustrated Magazine,* 13 (Mar. 29, 1862): 310.
7. Halleck to Cullum, Mar. 17, 1862, OR VIII:595.
8. Foote to Montgomery C. Meigs, Mar. 9, 1862, OR VIII:600.
9. Ibid., 2:241.
10. Ibid.
11. Ibid., 2:244.
12. Ibid.
13. Ibid.
14. Ibid., 2:245. See also Foote to Halleck, Apr. 7, 1862, OR VIII:668.
15. Ibid.
16. Lossing, 2:247. See also Halleck to Pope, Apr. 9, 1862, OR VIII:678.
17. Halleck to Pope, Apr. 8, 1862, OR VIII:675.
18. Scott to Stanton, Apr. 8, 1862, OR VIII:676.
19. GO 30, Army of the Mississippi, Apr. 10, 1862, OR VIII:681.

20. See *St. Louis Missouri Republican,* Apr. 9, 1862. See also *Harper's Weekly,* 6 (Mar. 24, 1862): 194; 6 (Apr. 5, 1862): 212; 6 (Apr. 12, 1862): 228; 6 (Apr. 26, 1862): 257; 6 (May 3, 1862): 283; See also *Frank Leslie's Illustrated Magazine,* 13 (Apr. 5, 1862): 321; 13 (Apr. 12, 1862): 366; 13 (Apr. 19, 1862): 377; 13 (Apr. 26, 1862): 385; 14 (May 3, 1862): 8; 14 (May 10, 1862): 41.

21. *Frank Leslie's Illustrated Magazine,* 13 (Apr. 26, 1862): 385, 386.

22. Ibid., 14 (May 10, 1862): 46.

23. Ibid., 41.

24. Service Record, John Pope, RG 94 NA.

25. Lossing, 2:289.

26. Ibid., 2:290.

27. Ibid., 2:291.

28. Grant 1:195–96.

29. Ibid.

30. William T. Sherman, *Memories of General W. T. Sherman,* 2 vols. (New York, 1875), 1:253.

31. Grant, 1:196.

32. Pope to Halleck, May 20, 1862, OR X, part 2:206.

33. Pope to Halleck, May 29, 1862, OR X, part 2:223.

34. See *Harper's Weekly,* 6 (June 14, 1862): 371.

35. Thomas F. Thiele, "The Evolution of Cavalry in the American Civil War 1861–1865" (Ph.D. diss., University of Michigan, 1951), 95. The classic overall study is Stephen Z. Starr, *The Union Cavalry in the Civil War,* 3 vols. (Baton Rouge, 1979–85).

36. Pope to Halleck, June 3, 1862, OR X, part 2: 249.

37. Halleck to Stanton, June 4, 1862, OR X, part 2:249.

38. See *Harper's Weekly,* 6 (June 21, 1862): 387, quoting Halleck's dispatch.

39. Pope to Halleck, July 3, 1865, and Halleck to Pope, July 5, 1865, OR X, part 2:635.

Chapter Eight

HIGH COMMAND

AFTER RELAXING FOR A WEEK in St. Louis with family, including new daughter Clara Horton Pope, and friends, General Pope found his leave cut short by a telegram from Secretary of War Stanton reading, "I would be glad to see you in Washington."[1] Pope started for the capital at once and reported to Stanton at the War Department on June 22, 1862. While the two men sat alone in Stanton's office, Stanton outlined the military picture in the East. In southeastern Virginia McClellan and his Army of the Potomac stood ready to attack Richmond. In western Virginia, General Fremont commanded an army in the Mountain Department and General Banks, another army in the Department of the Shenandoah. Nearer Washington, General McDowell commanded an army in the Department of the Rappahannock.

Fremont and Banks originally had the mission of coordinating their armies' movements with those of McClellan and keeping Confederate forces in the Shenandoah Valley from either reinforcing Richmond or attacking Washington. General McDowell's corps originally formed part of the Army of the Potomac, but Lincoln detached the corps himself and assigned to McDowell the duty of protecting the capital. Unluckily, Confederate General Stonewall Jackson ranged the Shenandoah Valley after March 23 with the counteraim of protecting the Confederate capital by threatening the Union one. Jackson attacked and defeated both Fremont and Banks. With Jackson still moving freely in the Valley and with the whole Army of the Potomac soon to be fully occupied in a battle for Richmond, the president felt uneasy about the safety of Washington.

Secretary Stanton said that he and the president had decided to combine the three separate commands of Fremont, Banks, and McDowell into a new army. This army would capture Jackson if possible, but would at least keep Jackson away from Washington and his forces from returning to Richmond. If Pope wanted command of the new army, he could have it. Lincoln was out of town, Stanton said. Pope could have time to think about the offer until the president returned.[2] Undecided but probably unsurprised, Pope left Stanton's office to think about the assignment. So far as the records show, this was the first time Pope heard about the proposed new army and the first time he heard himself mentioned as its commander.

Looking backward, historians and others have wondered how and why the assignment came to Pope, although no records, periodicals, memoirs, letters, or other historical sources for the year show surprise on the part of politicians, soldiers, or the general public, all of whom seem to have taken the appointment without particular comment. Lincoln must have made up his mind before he left Washington or Stanton would not have had the authority to make such an offer while the president was away. Pope's father-in-law had something to do with it. Stanton's telegram to Pope opened with the sentence, "I am glad to hear from Mr. Horton that you are in St. Louis today."[3]

Chase must have had a hand in it, perhaps for his own purposes. In 1862 Chase was the real secretary of war through his own assertiveness; and Stanton, something of an outsider in the cabinet and a former severe critic of Lincoln, looked to Chase for advice, took it, and at times accepted Chase's military recommendations. While Pope remained in Washington in June and July Chase very publicly took the young general under his wing as protégé. Neither Lincoln, Stanton, nor Chase seems to have asked any military opinion of Pope. Lincoln and Stanton apparently still believed in their own intuitive wisdom. Halleck grumbled at losing a top subordinate but no one asked what he thought of Pope or told him why Pope was going to Washington. Pope himself never seems to have asked other officers what they thought of the idea, although he must have talked Stanton's offer over with his father-in-law and probably with Chase. Pope had his own good opinion of himself and felt able to handle any assignment if he wanted to accept it.

Writing twenty-five years later, he remembered that officers in St. Louis advised him against going to Washington to get embroiled in eastern operations,[4] but the advice seemingly came unasked, and his advisers had no knowledge of the specific assignment.

In June 1862, Pope was as good a choice for this auxiliary command as any other Union officer, though Lincoln has been criticized for his choice. In the West there were only a few generals who had successfully commanded an independent army. Grant was the foremost in this regard, but Lincoln did not know him. In the East the experienced generals were all connected with the Army of the Potomac, and it would have been difficult to have chosen one of these officers to command the newly formed army. Lincoln needed someone he knew, could rely on, and who would fight; Pope met these requirements. Even with the exciting news from Memphis, New Orleans, and McClellan's peninsular campaign, the public had not had time to forget Pope. Stanton's offer came only twenty-two days after Pope's army led the way into Corinth, seventy-seven days after Island No. 10 fell, and only one hundred days after the seizure of New Madrid.

Though avowed Democrat McClellan and his hand-picked Democratic corps commanders might take Richmond and give the Union a victory earned by Democrats, Pope had one asset that most generals did not; he was an avowed Republican. This almost certainly made him Lincoln's first choice in the tangled political scene of 1862. Whoever took the assignment automatically became McClellan's foil. Pope already disliked McClellan, whom Lincoln promoted over Pope's head in 1861. The chance to become the Republican national hero pushed forward to challenge McClellan may have been an unconscious element in Pope's final decision. On June 25 Pope spoke to the House of Representatives, probably following an invitation arranged by his father-in-law. With no pretense at discretion and little humility, Pope described his western campaigns, freely criticized western commanders, emphasized that slavery must go, declared the war in the West at an end, and undercut McClellan by saying that experience at Corinth showed that Confederate forces defending Richmond could not amount to more than half the numbers being used in current estimates. He charmed his largely Republican audience, who also probably liked the appearance of this young, portly, handsome man with black hair and black beard, dressed in a well-cut uniform tailored in New York. A New York reporter commented, "The House was struck with Pope's frankness and ability, which probably assures him a command in the East."[5]

Lincoln had been at West Point conferring with retired General Scott but returned to Washington on the day that Pope spoke. Lincoln and Stanton now called Pope to another meeting in which they expected Pope to give his answer. They explained once more that Pope and the army would have two objectives: to catch Jackson if possible, but at least to keep him away from Washington and Richmond; and to help McClellan by drawing Confederate forces away from Richmond. Threatening the Virginia towns of Gordonsville and Charlottesville would, they thought, best accomplish the second objective. Pope did not like the plan. It called for cooperation with McClellan, who was not likely to cooperate with Pope. If the Confederates defeated McClellan, Pope would be left in the field, alone, open to attack by the whole Confederate Army. Also, Pope was a westerner taking over an eastern command made up of easterners whom he had never seen and whom he had had no hand in choosing. Seeing the assignment as a "forlorn hope," he told Lincoln and Stanton that he would prefer not to accept it.

They did not give a direct order, but applied patriotic pressure by suggesting that in the public interest Pope had a duty to undertake the job. This was no longer the old friend in Illinois, but President Lincoln, Commander-in-Chief, talking to a subordinate. Pope accepted.[6]

On the next day, Lincoln wrote the order constituting the Army of Virginia, which gave Pope command of First Corps under Fremont, Second Corps under Banks, Third Corps under McDowell, the forces under General Samuel D. Sturgis at Alexandria, and the various outposts making up the defenses of Washington.

The second paragraph of the order outlined a mission much enlarged from the one explained to Pope: "The Army of Virginia shall operate in such manner as, while protecting western Virginia and the nation's capital from danger or insult it shall in the speediest manner attack and overcome the rebel forces under Jackson and Ewell, threaten the enemy in the direction of Charlottesville, and render the most effective aid to relieve General McClellan and capture Richmond."[7] On the same day as the order, the Confederates made its execution urgent when they attacked McClellan's forces at Mechanicsville instead of waiting for McClellan to complete his final preparations for the attack on the Confederate capital as he had expected.

McClellan, not consulted, shortly heard about Pope's assignment and resented it. He saw this as a slight to him and proof that Lincoln would not trust him. He saw Pope as a direct threat to his command. McClellan would not admit that he needed any help in taking Richmond, even if Lincoln's order very publicly said that he did, and McClellan had no intention of sharing glory with a Republican.

Whatever McClellan might think, Pope had his assigned duties. Sound military practice called for first making an estimate of the situation. To Pope this was an army thrust upon him, an army of enlisted strangers and foolish corps commanders all of whom outranked him, an army in which two of the three corps and all three of the corps commanders had suffered defeats that left them bruised. Pope assumed command on June 27. Fremont resigned at once, refusing to serve under a former subordinate.[8] Pope should have picked Fremont's replacement, but Stanton named Franz Sigel to command First Corps.[9] Pope knew Sigel as a skulker in Missouri in 1861, but also realized that in 1862 Sigel was untouchable as a darling of German-Americans who voted almost solidly Republican.

Pope inherited another untouchable: the commander of Second Corps, Republican Nathaniel P. Banks, a civilian in uniform, once governor of Massachusetts, once Speaker of the House, whose removal would bring thundering protest from New England Republicans. Commander of Third Corps, Irwin McDowell, was chiefly known as the general who lost the Battle of Bull Run in 1861.

On paper Pope had about 43,500 troops including 5,000 cavalry. First Corps with about 13,500 troops and Seconds Corps with about 10,000 were off in the Shenandoah Valley. Third Corps with about 20,000 troops occupied a stretch in northern Virginia between Manassas and Fredericksburg.[10] Pope had to bring these separate units together to fuse them into an army. Pope saw that events at Richmond had already changed his field situation. He reasoned that Jackson and Ewell must be at Richmond taking part in the city's defense, which meant that the Shenandoah Valley must be open. If he could get his army together and moving, Pope could almost have a free hand in the Valley and could walk into Gordonsville and Charlottesville as easily as he walked into New Madrid in March.

Pope also knew he was the Republican general upon whom Lincoln and the party depended to give force to their political moves. The Union had to show that the rebel cause was hopeless or face intervention by Great Britain and France to reopen the flow of cotton. Lincoln wanted to issue an Emancipation Proclamation but needed a victory to support it. Someone had to stop McClellan before he became a political threat to the president; a Republican victory might do it. Republicans and Democrats would fight the coming national election in November on the necessity of the war and the Republican handling of it.[11] In the background, dimly, Salmon P. Chase may have been counting on Pope and the Republican army to further some scheme of his own that could use the party as its cover.

Although he knew part of the political tangle, Pope's first concern was organization. On June 28 he ordered First and Second Corps to start marching eastward over the mountains to Front Royal, Virginia, and ordered one division of Third Corps to march from Manassas to Warrenton.[12] His army would form a line between Sperryville and Warrenton, then move south. Pope was still sending orders out by telegraph from his command post at the War Department on Pennsylvania Avenue. He planned to join his army soon, but when the Confederates attacked McClellan, Pope was tied to Washington; Lincoln would not let him leave.

For all his reading and order writing, Lincoln did not have enough technical military knowledge to understand McClellan's almost hourly dispatches from Richmond. The president wanted an adviser and chose Pope. All during the Seven Days' Battles Pope sat at Lincoln's side in the military telegraph office explaining to the president what McClellan's dispatches meant. At the same time, Pope had to concentrate his army and direct the first phase of its campaign by telegraph. Sitting at Lincoln's side gave Pope a chance to cut down McClellan and practically made him an off-stage battle participant. Pope warned Lincoln that McClellan would make a terrible mistake by changing his base.[13] There is no record of any other unkind remarks about Little Mac during this period,

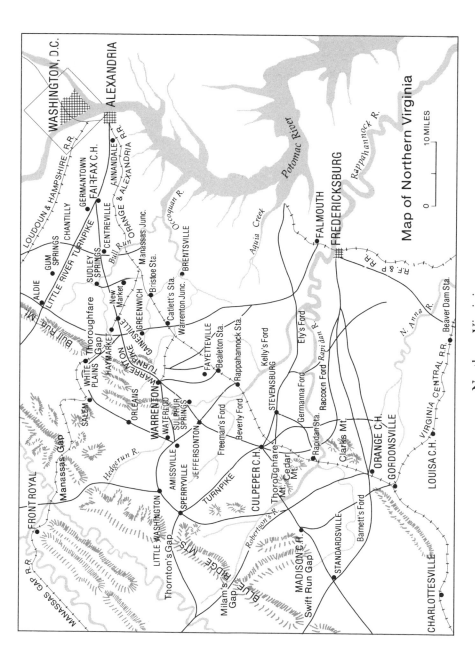

Northern Virginia

but a rival with almost exclusive access to the president's military ear would have been foolish to fumble such a chance.

As early as the Battle of Gaines's Mill on June 27, McClellan's dispatches hinted that he planned to shift his base from White House Landing on the York River to Harrison's Landing on the James, withdraw from Richmond, and wait for reinforcements. Pope advised Lincoln not to allow the movement.[14] If McClellan moved his army to this point twenty-five miles southeast of Richmond, any relieving force would have to fight its way through the whole army of northern Virginia to reach McClellan. Lincoln accepted Pope's advice, but left McClellan the choice of acting on it: "Save your Army at all events . . . General Pope thinks if you fall back it would be much better toward York River than toward the James."[15] McClellan would inevitably blame Pope for meddling and knew that while he fought, Pope sat at Lincoln's side as a bullet-proof critic. There would be consequences.

On the day Lincoln sent this wire, Pope attended a cabinet meeting at Lincoln's invitation. All the members got a favorable impression of the bearded young general who looked so confident and answered questions with such assurance. By now Lincoln and his cabinet knew that McClellan saw himself in danger, real or imagined, and might withdraw his huge army to a cul-de-sac south of Richmond. Someone asked Pope if he could take his army south on a relief expedition. Then McClellan could resume his attack on Richmond from the east; Pope could attack from the west; Richmond would fall. This meant giving the Army of Virginia a mission to attack instead of a mission to feint, threaten, and defend. Pope answered forthrightly that he would attack the enemy when and where ordered, but in this situation McClellan must have orders to attack the enemy at the same time. Otherwise, Pope said, McClellan could let the Army of the Potomac stand by and watch the Army of Virginia be sacrificed.[16] In his usual incautious way Pope made no secret of his mistrust of McClellan, and even though cabinet meetings were supposed to be confidential, Pope's comments traveled along the grapevine to McClellan.

The Seven Days' Battles ended on July 1. McClellan did not take Richmond and in spite of all advice took his army into camp at Harrison's Landing on July 2. There he sulked in his riverboat on the James while wiring Lincoln for immense numbers of reinforcements that the Union could not have furnished even if McClellan had really needed them.

At this point Pope's real mission boiled down to defending Washington after he got his army together, but Lincoln and Stanton, concerned about the Army of the Potomac, let Pope go on planning to take his army south. On July 4 Pope accordingly wrote McClellan a letter outlining what he proposed for the Army of Virginia's operations, saying "it is my earnest wish to cooperate in the heartiest and most energetic manner with you."[17] McClellan sent Pope a vague, chilly reply that said nothing about cooperation and only promised: "As soon as Burnside arrives, I will feel the force of the enemy and ascertain his exact position. If I learn that he has moved on you I will move to Richmond and endeavor to take it."[18] To Pope, that ended it. McClellan as much as admitted that Pope's army was meant to take the full Confederate attack while McClellan slipped unopposed into Richmond.

Being left to face the whole Confederate Army was Pope's nightmare. Lee, with 85,000 troops, would have two to one odds in his favor when attacking Pope's army of 43,500. As Pope wrote later, allowing McClellan's change of base lay at the root of everything.

> By this movement the whole of the enemy would be interposed between his army and mine, and . . . they would then be at liberty to strike in either direction as they might consider it most advantageous. . . .
>
> It would be impossible to send any of the forces under my command to re-enforce General McClellan without rendering it certain that the enemy, even in the worst case of themselves, would have the privilege and power of exchanging Richmond for Washington City; to them the loss of Richmond would be trifling, whilst the loss of Washington to us would be conclusive, or nearly so, in its results upon this war.[19]

Knowing that McClellan would never cooperate with him, Pope again asked to be relieved of his command and sent back to the West; Lincoln refused. Pope sat down to his plans again "with grave forebodings of the result."[20] At the moment McClellan was not fighting, but McClellan would fight again, Pope thought, and Pope would keep the Army of Virginia to its original mission: "so operate upon the enemy's lines of communication to the west and northwest as to force him to make such heavy detachments from his main force at Richmond as would enable the Army of the Potomac to withdraw from its position at Harrison's Landing and to take ship for Aquia Creek or for Alexandria."[21]

While McClellan sat at his new base refusing to move without reinforcements, Pope had to sit in his command post on Pennsylvania Avenue as the only top military officer available for consultation in Washington. Lincoln and others visited McClellan to decide what to do with him. Pope saw that only a supreme commander could enforce coordination and cooperation between the Army of the Potomac and the Army of Virginia. The original order constituting the Army of Virginia specified only that "When the Army of the Potomac and the Army of Virginia shall be in position to communicate and directly cooperate at or before Richmond, while so operating together, shall be governed, as in like cases, by the Rules and Articles of War."[22] This probably meant that McClellan, as senior in rank, would command if the two armies met at Richmond; it covered nothing before that.

Pope realized that this was his moment of opportunity. He wanted a supreme commander who would support him and owe him a debt for the recommendation. While McClellan sulked at Harrison's Landing, Pope could move without McClellan's knowledge. Since Lincoln and Stanton seemed inept in handling military affairs, they might think the time right to appoint a new general-in-chief to fill the office left vacant since March of 1862. Pope suggested General Henry Wager Halleck.[23] Halleck's name had come up before,[24] but Pope seems to have been Halleck's major supporter. Lincoln named Halleck General-in-Chief on July 22.[25] This satisfied Pope, but unexpectedly lengthened his captivity in Washington. Halleck moved as sluggishly as McClellan. When Halleck wired Lincoln asking two weeks to wind up affairs in Corinth, Lincoln, who trusted only Pope as a military adviser, told Pope he must stay in Washington until Halleck arrived.[26] Pope decided to enjoy his stay by riding the social merry-go-round of wartime Washington.[27] To mix with men and women of power gave the tingling feeling of also having power. Pope was a social success.[28] He was seen. Above all, he was heard.

On July 8 Pope spoke to a delighted Joint Committee on the

Conduct of the War. Placing himself squarely with the radical Republicans, Pope told the committee that slavery must go at once; that McClellan's Peninsular Campaign was a bad mistake, weakening the defenses of Washington and calling for a difficult and hazardous supply route; that McClellan should never have changed his base to Harrison's Landing; and that now all the administration could do was bring McClellan and his army back to Washington.[29] He said in his roaring voice what his listeners wanted to hear, and he spoke all over town. Lincoln, Pope insisted, should remove McClellan from command at once or Halleck would be forced to do it.[30] McClellan stood out for his "incompetency and indisposition to active movements."[31] Pope's quips might have hit the mark, but were unwise in a city where private comments became public headlines in an instant.

Pope was so indiscreet that it is still a question whether he spoke his own thoughts or, knowingly or unknowingly, spoke after being manipulated. Both Stanton and Chase used Pope as their mouthpiece to test some of their ideas on Lincoln and the public.[32] Chase in particular cultivated the young general, invited Pope and his father-in-law to dinner at Chase's home,[33] and kept writing Pope letters of advice in the field.[34]

Pope needed all the advice he could get. In the confusion about what to do with McClellan and the uncertainty that McClellan might renew his attack, Pope felt he would do best by sticking literally to Lincoln's June 26 order until told otherwise, even if operations at Richmond were in a state of suspense and the Army of Virginia's objective accordingly unclear. Lincoln's order said to threaten Gordonsville. On July 7 Pope ordered General John Hatch, commanding Second Corps Cavalry, to speed off to Culpeper and to send a strong picket force ahead to Orange.[35] Five days later Pope ordered Hatch to seize Gordonsville and Charlottesville.[36] Pope had a swift cavalry raid in mind, but did not make that clear in his order. He would now find the sharp difference between giving commands in the field and sending commands over telegraph wires from a distant headquarters.

Hatch took the time to collect a sizeable striking force including infantry, artillery, and a train of supply wagons. When he finally came in sight of Gordonsville, he found Confederate General Richard Ewell, Stonewall Jackson's right-hand commander, already in possession.[37] Unexpectedly, Ewell was back in the Valley. Pope swore as he read the dispatches and gave Hatch a telegraphic dressing down.[38] Hatch's bungling cost Pope his chance to control Gordonsville and Charlottesville, as well as his chance to cut the Virginia Central Railroad. These would be critical later, but at the time Pope was more upset at finding Ewell back in the Shenandoah Valley. Pope knew that no one had yet decided what to do with McClellan and his army, now in their third week of sitting idly at Harrison's Landing, and yet the raiders of the Shenandoah had returned. Under the circumstances Pope decided not to order his army farther south until he could take the field in person and talk matters over with his three corps commanders, who were almost strangers to him. In the meanwhile he had enough to do tending to details of organizing and administering the Army of Virginia as its three components marched to meet.

Farther south in Virginia the Confederates took advantage of the lull in fighting, as Lincoln, Stanton, McClellan, and even Pope seem to have expected them to do. General Robert E. Lee, now commanding the Army of Northern Virginia, thought about the exchange of Richmond for Washington, as Pope feared, but wanted a more definite picture before committing himself. Even then, however, he felt safe to detach raiding forces to defend Gordonsville. On July 13, one day after Pope ordered Hatch to make his raid, Lee ordered Jackson and Ewell to march to Louisa Court House, guard the Virginia Central Railroad there, occupy Gordonsville, and bar any further Union advance toward Richmond.[39] These veterans reached Gordonsville at least a day ahead of Hatch and then dug in to wait and watch for movement from the north.

In Washington Pope went ahead with his plans. On July 14 he finished the required formality of an address to his troops. Pope, though, had to address his troops by telegraph and printed copies. Pope gave notice that he would wage hard Republican war and not McClellan's kid-glove, Democratic kind. "Let us understand each other," he opened,

> I have come to you from the West, where we have always seen the backs of our enemies, from an army whose business it has been to seek the adversary and to beat him when he was found. Whose policy has been attack and not defense. In but one

instance has the enemy been able to place our Western armies in a defensive attitude. I presume that I have been called here to pursue the same system, and to lead you against the enemy. It is my purpose to do so and that speedily. I am sure you long for the opportunity to win the distinction you are capable of achieving. That opportunity I shall endeavor to give you. Meanwhile, I desire you to dismiss from your minds certain phrases I am sorry to find so much in vogue amongst you. I hear constantly of "taking strong positions and holding them," of "lines of retreat," and of "bases of supplies." Let us discard such ideas. The strongest position a soldier should desire to occupy is one from which he can most easily advance against the enemy. Let us study the probable lines of retreat of our opponents and leave our own to take care of themselves. Let us look before us, and not behind. Success and glory are in the advance, disaster and shame lurk in the rear. Let us act on this understanding, and it is safe to predict that your banner shall be inscribed with many a glorious deed and that your names will be dear to your countrymen forever.[40]

It was not a Napoleonic performance and probably left no traces with his soldiers, but the address did go out of its way to give McClellan a jab by quoting some of his much-used phrases. Pope also took a new tone: the Republican tone adopted after the Seven Days' Battles. At first Lincoln wanted a tone of persuasion and conciliation, but as the war went on longer, Lincoln wanted a fight to the death. Reporters tossed it faint praise,[41] and the address drew criticism from others on the grounds of needlessly irritating McClellan, needlessly comparing western successes with eastern failures, and generally carrying political overtones. Although Pope accepted responsibility for the whole address, Stanton in fact dictated the argumentative passages and was using Pope's address as a trial balloon to test public reaction.[42]

The address also resurrected an ancient military joke. Pope was supposed to have begun his address with the heading, "Headquarters in the Saddle." Lee was then supposed to have said, "If so, his headquarters are where his hindquarters ought to be." In 1887 Pope wrote of this with unexpected good humor:

I think it due to army tradition, and to the comfort of those who have so often repeated this ancient joke in the days long before the civil war, that these later wits should not be allowed with impunity to poach on this well-tilled manor. This venerable joke I first heard when a cadet at West Point, and it was then told of that gallant soldier and gentleman, General W. J. Worth, and I presume it could be easily traced back to the Crusades and beyond. Certainly I never used this expression or wrote or dictated it, nor does any such expression occur in any order of mine; and as it has perhaps served its time and effected its purpose, it ought to be retired.[43]

The 1862 revival of this timeless nonsense is traceable to the work of some *Richmond Inquirer* wordsmith around July 29. In more recent days, *Dere Mable* of World War I and *See Here, Private Hargrove* of World War II have lifted the same kind of military antique from the mothballs.

Pope followed his address with a series of general orders governing conduct of troops in the field. These would remind Southerners that by starting a war they submitted to the laws of war. General Orders five and six, dated July 18, ordered the Army of Virginia to live off the land, requisition supplies locally, and pay with treasury vouchers.[44] General Order seven, dated July 20, carried over to Virginia Pope's Missouri system of fines, indemnities, and forced service for civilians living within five miles of communications cut by guerrillas or houses from which anyone fired on Union soldiers.[45] General Order eleven, dated July 23, allowed commanders to deport to Confederate territory any male who refused to take an oath of allegiance to the Union. Violating the oath, or returning within the Union lines after deportation, meant treatment as a spy, for which the penalty could be death.[46]

Lincoln approved;[47] the newspapers approved;[48] Confederates did not. Although Pope wrote correctly that such measures were "common in the history of warfare,"[49] a Richmond newspaper called them "barbarous."[50] Lee called Pope a "miscreant"[51] and told Jackson, "I want Pope suppressed."[52] President Jefferson Davis threatened to treat all Pope's officers and men as criminals and not as lawful combatants under the rules of war.[53] The hullabaloo faded away shortly. Even Jefferson Davis conceded that Pope's orders complied with the laws of war; the Confederates would treat captured soldiers of the Army of Virginia as prisoners of war, not as felons to put in irons. Pope faced the music alone, however. There is a strong suspicion that Stanton took part in drafting these orders and Pope's address, and used the orders as another trial balloon.

As July went on Pope had reason to be increasingly upset. Lincoln still held him in Washington. Pope had swallowed all the criticism for an address and orders partly written by others and approved by Lincoln. And on July 19 his only child died in St. Louis. On July 22 Pope had reason to feel better. Halleck reached Washington and spent the next day meeting with Lincoln, Stanton, and Pope to discuss the question of McClellan.[54] Pope thought that Halleck's coming would free him automatically to take the field, but the new general-in-chief wanted to talk to McClellan in person and in Halleck's absence Lincoln still wanted Pope in Washington.

Halleck sailed to Harrison's Landing to talk with McClellan from July 24 to 27. Nearly four weeks after withdrawing from Richmond McClellan still believed that Lee had 200,000 troops. He would not resume his attack against Richmond unless Halleck would send 25,000–50,000 reinforcements. Halleck shrugged his shoulders and returned to Washington feeling that he had no choice but to bring the Army of the Potomac back to join the Army of Virginia.

Pope was getting further criticism, this time for dallying at the War Department while commanding an army long distance.[55] Feeling himself free after Halleck returned, Pope began taking steps to join his army even before Lincoln, Stanton, and Halleck reached a final decision about McClellan. Pope did meet with Halleck, however, to decide on Pope's mission when he went out. As Pope remembered twenty-five years later, they agreed that if Lincoln ordered McClellan's army back, Pope's army would guard the approaches to Washington and if attacked would fight a delaying action to give McClellan plenty of time. If the enemy did not move north in any force, Pope would threaten enemy communications at Gordonsville and Charlottesville to draw the enemy away from Richmond and McClellan's army.

The Army of the Potomac would disembark at a point on the Rappahannock River and march to join Pope. At that time the question of command would come up. Pope assumed that Halleck would then take the field in person as supreme commander and, presumably, lead the two armies in a consolidated campaign for Richmond. What would happen if McClellan's troops joined Pope but Halleck stayed in Washington was left open; that unanswered question led to trouble both about command and the strengthened army's final mission.

Halleck ordered that Pope must keep communications open with Fredericksburg at all times and at all costs to ensure the meeting of the armies.[56] The Army of Virginia would leave Warrenton with a mission to defend and delay until the Army of the Potomac could join it. Lincoln's order of June 26 was still in force, however, unrevoked and unchanged, even though its underlying assumptions had undergone violent change. It still read, "The Army of Virginia . . . shall in the speediest manner attack and overcome the rebel forces under Jackson and Ewell."[57] This would cause more trouble in trying to fix the Army's mission, its proper deployment, and its attitude toward the enemy. Although Pope could not know it, Lee had already decided to move on Washington with the whole Army of Northern Virginia, guaranteeing that Pope would march into his nightmare unsupported. On July 27 Lee strengthened the forces of Jackson and Ewell by sending additional troops as his first step in an unexpected Confederate initiative.[58]

Finally on July 29, 1862, General John Pope left the fantasy land of Washington and advising president and the secretary of war while commanding an army miles away in Virginia. Leaving Washington "on an extra train, handsomely decorated with flags,"[59] Pope embarked for Warrenton, Virginia, to meet his corps commanders and to see his army for the first time.

NOTES

1. Stanton to Pope, June 19, 1862, OR XVII, part 2:17.
2. John Pope, "The Second Battle of Bull Run," in Robert Underwood Johnson and Clarence Clough Buel, eds., *Battles and Leaders of the Civil War,* 4 vols. (New York, 1887), 2:449–50.
3. See note 1.
4. Pope, 2:449.
5. *New York Daily Tribune,* June 26, 1862.
6. John Pope. "The Second Battle of Bull Run," *Battles and Leaders,* 2:450.
7. Order Constituting the Army of Virginia, Executive Mansion, June 26, 1862, OR XII, part 3:435.
8. GO 1, Army of Virginia, June 27, 1862, OR XII, part 3:346. Fremont to Stanton, June 27, 1862, OR XII, part 3:437–38; Stanton to Fremont, June 27, 1862, OR XII, part 3:438.

9. See Sigel to Pope, June 29, 1862, OR XII, part 3:440.

10. Returns, June, 1862, OR XII, part 3:448.

11. See J. G. Randall and David Donald, *The Civil War and Reconstruction,* 2d ed. (Lexington, Mass., 1969), for full treatment of these political concerns.

12. Pope to Schenck, June 28, 1862, OR XII, part 3:441; Pope to Banks, June 28, 1862, OR XII, part 3:349; Pope to McDowell, July 3, 1862, OR XII, part 3:450.

13. Pope, 2:452–54.

14. Ibid.

15. Lincoln to McClellan, June 28, 1862, OR XI, part 3:269.

16. See T. Harry Williams, *Lincoln and His Generals* (New York, 1952), 124.

17. Pope to McClellan, July 4, 1862, OR XI, part 3:295.

18. McClellan to Pope, July 7, 1862, OR XI, part 3:306. Burnside was ordered to withdraw his corps from North Carolina and transport it to Fort Monroe to reinforce McClellan.

19. Pope, Final Report, Jan. 27, 1863, OR XII, part 2:20, 22.

20. Ibid., 22.

21. Ibid., 23.

22. See note 7.

23. John T. Morse, Jr., ed., *Diary of Gideon Welles, Secretary of the Navy under Lincoln and Johnson,* 3 vols. (Boston, 1911), 1:108.

24. See Williams, 135.

25. Ibid.

26. See Pope to McDowell, July 20, 1862, OR XII, part 3:487.

27. See Margaret Leech, *Reveille in Washington* (New York, 1941).

28. See Williams, 122.

29. Reports of the Joint Committee on the Conduct of the War, 37th Cong., 3d Sess., 1863, 1:276–82.

30. David Donald, ed., *Inside Lincoln's Cabinet: The Civil War Diaries of Salmon P. Chase* (New York, 1954), 97–98.

31. Ibid.

32. Ibid., 98.

33. Ibid., 96–97.

34. Ibid., 103, 111.

35. Pope to Banks, July 7, 1862, OR XI, part 3:458.

36. Col. George Ruggles to Banks, July 12, 1862, OR XI, part 3:457.

37. Banks to Pope, July 18, 1862, OR XI, part 3:481.

38. Pope to Banks, July 19, 1862, OR XI, part 3:486.

39. GO 150, Army of Northern Virginia, July 13, 1862, OR XI, part 3:915.

40. Address to the Army of Virginia, July 14, 1862, OR XI, part 3:473.

41. See *New York Daily Tribune,* July 15, 1862, "it seemed Pope was contemplating independent offensive action instead of coordinated action with McClellan." See also *Philadelphia Public Ledger,* July 18, 1862, "It is bad practice for a general to announce what he is going to do to the enemy before he does it."

42. Jacob D. Cox, *Military Reminiscences of the Civil War*, 2 vols. (New York, 1900), 1:222. Cox was Pope's friend and subordinate. Meeting Pope after the war, he asked about this.

43. Pope, 2:494.

44. GO 5, Army of Virginia, July 18, 1862 (Infantry), OR XII, part 2:50; GO 6, Army of Virginia, (Cavalry), Ibid.

45. GO 7, Army of Virginia, July 20, 1862, OR XII, part 2:51.

46. GO 11, Army of Virginia, July 23, 1862, OR XII, part 2:52.

47. See Donald, 95.

48. See *Boston Evening Transcript*, July 21, 1862; *New York Daily Tribune*, July 19, 1862; *Chicago Tribune*, Aug. 2, 1862.

49. Pope, Final Report, OR XII, part 2:23.

50. *Chicago Tribune*, July 31, 1862, quoting *Richmond Dispatch*, July 2, 1862.

51. Lee to George Randolph, July 28, 1862, OR XI, part 2:916.

52. Lee to Jackson, July 27, 1862, OR XII, part 3:918-19.

53. Davis to Lee, July 31, 1862, OR, Series II, part 4:830-31; Lee to Gen. Commanding U.S. Army, Aug. 2, 1862, OR, Series II, part 4:329-30; and see Halleck to Lee, Aug. 9, 1862, OR, Series II, part 4:362.

54. Pope to McDowell, July 23, 1862, OR XII, part 3:500.

55. See *New York Daily Tribune*, July 19, 1862; see also Maj. Gen. John E. Wool to Pope, July 20, 1862, OR XI, part 3:488.

56. Pope, 2:458.

57. See note 7.

58. Lee to Jackson, July 27, 1862, OR XII, part 3:918.

59. *Boston Evening Transcript*, July 31, 1862.

Lucretia Backus Pope, mother. (Cour-
tesy of the Illinois State Historical
Library, Springfield)

Judge Nathaniel Pope, father. (Cour-
tesy of the Illinois State Historical
Library, Springfield)

Major General John Pope. This engraving was made from a photo taken by
Brady in July 1862 while Pope was in Washington.

Clara Horton Pope, wife, at 47. (Special Collections Division, U.S. Military Academy Library)

Major General Fitz John Porter. (Library of Congress)

Pope toward the end of his military career. (Special Collections Division, U.S. Military Academy Library)

Pope at 60. (National Archives photo no. 111-BA-230)

Carondelet running batteries. (*Frank Leslie's Illustrated Newspaper,* April 26, 1862, p. 385, Minnesota Historical Society)

Night Expedition. (*Frank Leslie's Illustrated Newspaper,* April 26, 1862, p. 408, Minnesota Historical Society)

Confederates evacuating Corinth. (*Harper's Weekly,* June 21, 1862, p. 184, Minnesota Historical Society)

Battle of Cedar Mountain. (*Frank Leslie's Illustrated Newspaper,* August 30, 1862, p. 356, Minnesota Historical Society)

Chapter Nine

PROBES

WHEN POPE'S BRIGHTLY DECORATED special train came to a stop at the Orange and Alexandria Railroad station at Warrenton Junction, the general got off to meet his army for the first time and to take personal charge of its movements. He was then forty years old, stout, of medium height, with black hair getting thin on top and with a black, bushy beard. At times he needed glasses. He wore well-tailored uniforms and smoked big, black cigars; he rose early. Observers commented that he looked young and alert, had good manners, a good memory, particularly for topography, and endless curiosity. As his chief topographer found, Pope proved "a much cleverer man than I first took him for." Others found Pope "a keen, cool man of the world," "irascible and impulsive in his judgments of men, but in his pleasant moods jolly, humorous, and clever in conversation," "an indefatigable worker," and even "a military genius."[1]

He believed "in aggressive warfare continually, with large bodies of cavalry offending the enemy far in advance, with his main army strongly posted to support the advance."[2] Pope's army was having a difficult time following this theory of warfare. The Army of Virginia was already off to a bad start because of telegraphic orders. Misinterpreting what Pope meant, General Hatch, commanding Second Corps Cavalry, followed up a bad first move with a bad second move when he failed again in a half-hearted raid against Charlottesville.[3] Pope knew that he could clear up these problems of misinterpretation by issuing orders in person. He also knew that it took a commander's personal appearance to inspire the will to fight. Even in ideal conditions an army became a fighting unit in harmonious movement only after long service as a unit, and Pope knew that in August 1862 he would not have much time to get to know his army; he had to put it together, make last minute adjustments, and set it marching against the enemy, all at once.

The three corps were trudging to join each other at Pope's concentration point, Sperryville, which Pope considered the gateway to the Shenandoah Valley[4] and which Pope had to control to seal off the Valley. The army would then move to Pope's intended base at Culpeper, located on the Orange and Alexandria Railroad and the army's lifeline to the supply depots at Manassas Junction.

From July 30 to August 6 Pope spent his time looking over his troops and getting acquainted with his top subordinates while the army drew together. This one-week lull also gave him the chance to put into effect the cavalry reform that he contributed to Civil War tactics. The experiment in Mississippi matured in Virginia.[5] Pope's Army of Virginia inherited the old scheme of assigning cavalry detachments to corps, brigades, and smaller units, and giving full control to those unit commanders, subject only to the orders of a corps cavalry commander who, in spite of his title, coordinated but could not command. Orders and reports went down and up the chain of command, always through channels, with results like Hatch's raids.[6]

Pope's new system gave command of all cavalry units within a corps to a chief of corps cavalry[7] and gathered together all cavalry units into a single unit called corps cavalry.[8] Only Pope as commanding general and his three corps commanders could give orders to the cavalry. General Joseph Hooker, who served as Pope's subordinate in this campaign, later created a separate cavalry corps when he commanded the Army of the Potomac.[9] Pope would find out shortly whether his method brought the same good results as General Jeb Stuart's separate cavalry command in the Army of Northern Virginia.

Long before Pope reached his army the Confederates were ready for him. Military intelligence in Richmond had no trouble getting news from Washington, and as early as June 29 announced Pope's appointment to command the Army of Virginia.[10] Richmond newspapers followed the announcement by printing in full Pope's address to his army and his orders for conduct in the field that differed so much from McClellan's.

This publicity, along with indignant editorials, built Pope up in advance as a despotic braggart sent to ravage the South, which may help explain the fury of Confederate attacks on his army. General James Longstreet remembered the effect on Lee of the address and orders:

> Lee had not known Pope intimately, but accepted the popular opinion of him as a boastful man, quite ambitious to accomplish great results, but unwilling to study closely and properly the means necessary to gratify his desires in that direction. . . .
>
> When General Lee heard of these strange utterances his estimate of Pope was considerably lessened. The high-sounding words seemed to come from a commander inexperienced in warfare. For centuries there has been among soldiers a maxim: "Don't despise your enemy." General Pope's words would seem to indicate great contempt for the enemy.

Lee assumed such concern over Pope's affront to slave owners' concepts of chivalry that on July 27, while Pope was still in Washington, Lee wrote Jackson, "I want Pope to be suppressed."[11]

As soon as he thought Richmond safe from attack, Lee sent Jackson and Ewell, reinforced by A. P. Hill, back into the Shenandoah Valley to start suppressing Pope. The Confederates took their time watching the Army of Virginia, gathering information about it, and waiting for a move into some position where they could pounce with advantage. At that time Pope could not know quite what to expect from the enemy because Lee was not well known in the North and had exercised command of the Army of Northern Virginia only after June 30 when he took over from wounded General Joseph E. Johnston. Lee was getting ready to show Pope and the other Union generals what to expect.

While two armies groped their way toward each other at the foot of the Blue Ridge, the McClellan drama went into another act. McClellan had the same reaction to Halleck's appointment that he did to Pope's: he was furious; it was a slap in the face.[12] Halleck, once McClellan's subordinate, was now going to take McClellan's old place as general-in-chief. When Halleck told McClellan that Lincoln approved withdrawing the Army of the Potomac and then transferring it corps by corps to reinforce Pope, McClellan saw the movement as nothing more than a subterfuge to strip him of his command. McClellan's protests notwithstanding, Halleck first ordered Burnside to send his Ninth Corps from Fort Monroe to Aquia Creek to guard the port of debarkation,[13] and then on August 3 ordered the angry McClellan to start embarking his troops on transports carrying them to Aquia Creek.[14]

From the first no one could have expected McClellan to comply cheerfully with an order authorized by Lincoln, issued by Halleck, benefiting Pope, and nullifying McClellan's command. By oversight or design Halleck added a clause practically delivering Pope and his army into McClellan's hands: "the entire execution of the movement is left to your own discretion and judgment."[15] McClellan would use his discretion and judgment to see that his troops stayed with him as long as possible despite the effect on others. In spite of Halleck's friendship with Pope and his probable debt to Pope for his assignment as general-in-chief, Halleck treated McClellan gently. Pope might fall and McClellan might rise again; Halleck meant to be a survivor. His good relations with McClellan in September of 1862 hint that, like Talleyrand, Halleck acted mainly from motives of survival. Others standing back from the Pope-McClellan feud wanted to see how they could profit from Pope's taking over McClellan's troops. Pope would not need to know that he was serving their interests. In Washington where there were few secrets it was no secret that Stanton and Chase would like McClellan dismissed and replaced with a Republican, and it was also no secret that Chase more or less ruled Stanton. What either man had in mind if Lincoln did dismiss McClellan never came out, but in politics in wartime whoever controlled a man who controlled an army was someone to reckon with.

In later years Pope liked to pose as an innocent victim of 1862 politics, almost a bystander, but he tended to gloss over his own part in the Army of the Potomac tangle. He was jealous of McClellan from the first. In 1862 he knowingly took the Washington spotlight as McClellan's up-and-coming rival. He denounced McClellan in public, to the president, to the cabinet, to the House of Representatives, and to the Joint Committee on Conduct of the War, calling McClellan slow and incompetent. In private Pope criticized the entire peninsular campaign, urged Lincoln to dismiss McClellan, and after McClellan withdrew to Harrison's Landing, repeatedly insisted that Lincoln must recall the Army of the Potomac. Pope knew that by the time the recall took place, Pope would be in the field with his Army of Virginia asking for reinforcements that Halleck had promised. Reinforcements could come only from the Army of the Potomac.

Although Pope never asked outright to command that army, he did not oppose having command thrust upon him corps by corps through reinforcements. Like many others, he would accept indirectly what might not be good form to accept directly. No one knows if Pope planned this, taking a gigantic gamble that his plan would work, or if he acted under the guidance of someone in Washington's inner circle. In any case, when Lincoln and Halleck ordered McClellan's army back, Pope found hordes of soldiers coming after him. Pope had seconded the withdrawal, which intensified the feud with McClellan at a time when McClellan controlled the reinforcements essential to Pope's army.

On August 6 Pope set his columns marching southeast toward Culpeper.[16] He was going out, as he said, to cover the approaches to Washington, to deny the enemy access to the Shenandoah Valley, and to entice Confederate forces away from Richmond where they might threaten McClellan's embarking army.[17]

As General Longstreet recalled, Lee's plan centered on lifting the pressure against Richmond by forcing McClellan's withdrawal, which he hoped to do by threatening Washington in a sweep northwest. Lee "had also in view the Army of Virginia as the first obstacle in the way of relief to Richmond—an obstacle to be removed, if possible, before it could be greatly reenforced from other commands."[18]

As the Army of Virginia moved south, Pope wanted to probe enemy country to seek out Jackson. Pope would move as freely as he could while obeying Halleck's order to keep communications open with Fredericksburg, an order which, Pope said, was the same as sending him out to fight with one leg tied.[19] At the same time Jackson's forces left Gordonsville and began moving north to find Pope.

By August 7 Pope had his army marching in a column twenty miles long that stretched from Sperryville to Culpeper. Pope and First Corps were still at Sperryville. The Second Corps, which was in the advance, had reached Culpeper, and the cavalry of the Third Corps under General Bayard was ahead of them in the vicinity of Rapidan Station. The cavalry were being pressed back by Jackson's vanguard. To support them Banks sent General Crawford's brigade forward on the road to Rapidan Station. Meanwhile Pope, while reviewing Sigel's troops, was informed that some of the enemy had crossed the Rapidan River moving north. He immediately jumped on his horse and rode to the head of his column at Culpeper.[20]

From headquarters at Culpeper Pope sent out orders hurrying his outlying troops to him. Scouts reported Jackson with roughly 22,000 troops: Jackson's division of 8,000; Ewell's of 6,000; and a mixed force of another 8,000 made up of A. P. Hill's division and the Second Brigade, Louisiana Volunteers. Pope's army had a paper strength of 43,500.

Jackson was carrying direct orders to attack Pope,[21] and by August 8, only two days on the march, forward elements of Pope's army met Jackson's troops. Pope wired Sigel to hurry First Corps from Sperryville. He also pulled General Rufus King with his First Division of Third Corps from Fredericksburg, where the division guarded communications and the port of Aquia Creek until Burnside arrived with his Ninth Corps to take over that assignment.[22] On the next morning, still waiting for Sigel and First Corps to reach Culpeper, Pope formed his troops in lines of battle but did not plan to attack until First Corps arrived and until he could see what the Confederates would do. An attack on his left would threaten his communications with Fredericksburg. At 9:25 A.M. Pope decided to move the remainder of the Second Corps forward south of Culpeper, still in line of battle but in holding position until First Corps reached the army.

At that time he sent the following verbal order through his aide, Colonel Louis H. Marshall: "General Banks to move to the front immediately, assume command of all forces in the front, deploy his skirmishers if enemy advances, and attack him immediately as he approaches and be reinforced from here."[23] Taking the precaution to have Colonel Marshall write this order down, General Banks assumed command. He had most of the forward troops in line by noon. General Benjamin Roberts, chief of cavalry and inspector general of the Army of Virginia, helped him pick his ground and lay out his lines. While doing so he reminded Banks that General Pope wanted a holding action and no more.[24] Assuming that he had made all preparations necessary, Pope spent the day in or near his headquarters tent.

Pope's soldiers spent four hours watching Jackson's troops file into battle positions opposite them. A desultory artillery duel took place from noon until about 4 P.M. Banks reached the field at about 1:00. That day each commander suffered from the same kind of delusion. Jackson thought he faced only Banks's Second Corps with its estimated strength of no more than 14,000. Banks thought that he faced only one division, Jackson's, with its reported strength of 8,000. Relying on overstated morning reports, Banks also thought that Second Corps had 14,000 effectives ready for duty. Deluded and misinformed, each commander believed that he had numerical superiority over the other and itched to exploit his advantage before reinforcements ended it. At 5:00 Banks could not hold himself back and ordered an attack on the Confederate left and center that had shock effect enough to roll the Confederate line back for a mile. Jackson called up one of his reserve divisions, rallied his troops, and began to pound Banks's right flank. What followed was a bloody hand-to-hand struggle in which the Confederates, who now outnumbered Banks two to one, got the upper hand and kept pressing Second Corps back. By then Banks realized that he risked being overwhelmed and was trying to withdraw. Pope and McDowell were sitting in front of Pope's headquarters tent in late afternoon smoking and chatting, when Pope heard the boom of artillery getting louder and realized that this was not the sound of a holding action but that of a general engagement. Someone had disobeyed orders.[25]

Speeding into action, Pope told McDowell to get Ricketts's division, then four miles north of the battlefield, to the front. He also ordered Sigel to hurry the First Corps forward to the fighting. Having given these orders Pope galloped to the battlefield where he met Banks. In a short time the reserves came up and the First Corps arrived; the Union line held. Pope came under heavy enemy fire and barely escaped being taken. Just as the firing died away, General George Gordon of Second Corps came up to Pope and said, "General Pope, this battle should not have been fought, Sir!" "I never ordered it fought, Sir!" Pope replied. Banks was standing within hearing distance.[26] Pope reported to Halleck: "The fight of Saturday was precipitated by Banks, who attacked instead of waiting, as I directed him, until the Corps of Sigel was rested after its forced march."[27] In his later official report Pope wrote: "I directed him

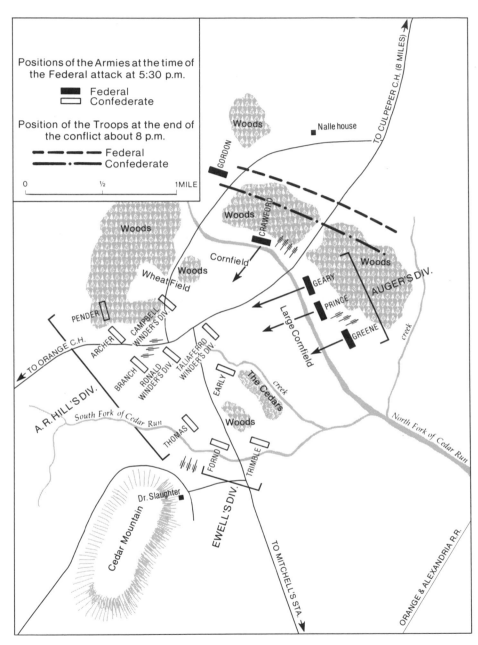

Positions of the Armies at the time of
the Federal attack at 5:30 p.m.

■ Federal
☐ Confederate

Position of the Troops at the end of
the conflict about 8 p.m.

— — — Federal
—·—·— Confederate

0   ½   1 MILE

TO CULPEPER C.H. (8 MILES)

Woods

Nalle house

GORDON

Woods

CRAWFORD

Woods

Cornfield

Woods

AUGER'S DIV.

WheatField

Woods

GEARY

PENDER

PRINCE

Large Cornfield

GREENE

ARCHER

CAMPBELL

WINDER'S DIV.

creek

TO ORANGE C.H.

TALIAFERRO

WINDER'S DIV.

BRANCH

RONALD

WINDER'S DIV.

EARLY

The Cedars

creek

A. R. HILL'S DIV.

South Fork of Cedar Run

NORTH Fork of Cedar Run

THOMAS

Woods

FORNO

TRIMBLE

EWELL'S DIV.

Dr. Slaughter

Cedar Mountain

TO MITCHELL'S STA.

ORANGE & ALEXANDRIA R.R.

Battle of Cedar Mountain, August 9, 1862

[Banks], when he went forward from Culpeper Court House, that if the enemy advanced to attack him in the strong position which I had instructed him to take up, he should push his skirmishers well to the front and notify me immediately."[28]

This was the Battle of Cedar Mountain. The Army of Virginia pushed Stonewall Jackson back at a cost of 2,381 Union casualties to 1,365 for the Confederates.[29] Second Corps took such a whipping that Pope ruled it out as a combat unit and assigned it to rear guard and supply duties.[30] As a Republican with high connections Banks was untouchable, and Pope could only send him to the rear; He would bungle again in 1863 and 1864. Banks's eagerness reduced Pope's effectives to no more than 30,000 until reinforcements came from the Army of the Potomac. Worse, it threw the whole campaign off-balance and ruined Pope's one real chance to catch Jackson. If Banks had waited for First Corps his forces would outnumber Jackson's. Since the struggle on August 9 showed that each side had about the same fighting ability, numbers would seem decisive.

Pope liked to clear himself of defeats and reverses by blaming others, but in this case he was justified in blaming Banks for advancing over a mile and attacking the enemy in his position. There was nothing in Pope's order that called for such action. Pope's style of command in this battle needed review. It may have been protocol for the commanding general to give a subordinate his orders and command in the field, but it was unwise not to have been on the field himself rather than at Culpeper seven miles away. Pope did not seem to grasp this fact of command since he repeated the same procedure at Second Bull Run leaving an ineffective commander to carry out important actions.

Both Pope and Jackson treated the affair at Cedar Mountain as a draw. Neither wanted to reopen the battle: Pope because of casualty losses, Jackson because he saw Pope reinforced. On August 11 Jackson took his force across the Rapidan, marching south.[31] Pope followed slowly, watching but not provoking action. Marching promptly along both sides of the Rappahannock from Fredericksburg, General Rufus King's First Division Third Corps arrived on the evening of August 11.[32] Three days later two divisions of Burnside's Ninth Corps, totaling 8,000 under Generals Isaac I. Stevens and Jesse L. Reno, also came from Fredericksburg.[33]

Pope was relying mainly on the Army of the Potomac for

reinforcements, however, and General McClellan was shuffling. No Army of the Potomac troops left Harrison's Landing before August 14.[34] None could debark at Aquia Creek for some days after that and it was still a long march to Pope. While awaiting reinforcements, Pope established a line along the Rapidan River, still probing. On August 16 he ordered a cavalry raid on Louisa Court House, not fifty miles from Richmond. His raiders found the headquarters of General Jeb Stuart, cavalry commander of the Army of Northern Virginia, nearly caught Stuart, and brought Pope a letter written two days earlier by Lee to Stuart. Lee's letter outlined the present deployment of Lee's forces and stressed Lee's iron resolve to crush Pope before McClellan's army joined him.[35]

Pope now felt the tautness in his throat that came from knowing he raced against time. Lee reasoned that the Army of the Potomac would return north since no reinforcements were going to McClellan at Harrison's Landing. Richmond was safe for the time being and Lee could throw the whole Army of Northern Virginia against Pope. Pope took proper action. Under mounting pressure from the Confederates, who were now reinforcing Jackson in large numbers, Pope withdrew his entire army to the north side of the Rappahannock River on August 18 and 19. On the following day the enemy attacked in force and tried to make a crossing of the river at several places but was repulsed.[36]

Lincoln was getting edgy: "President uneasy about Pope," Chase wrote in his diary on August 19.[37] Pope was getting edgy about reinforcements, and on the same day he wrote Halleck that he thought the Rappahannock line too far forward to hold unless he was reinforced at once.[38] Halleck answered with what seemed a solid promise: "Dispute every inch of ground and fight like the devil until we can re-enforce you. Forty eight hours more and we can make you strong enough."[39]

By August 21 Pope could see that the Confederates had now begun to look upriver for places to outflank his right; frontal attacks were getting nowhere. Pope's holding action became a wearisome deadlock in which two armies underwent a daily grinding of attack and counterattack to the background music of artillery fire. The outnumbered Army of Virginia had no time to rest. Both sides tried reconnaissances and raids. A raid by Stuart, who was famous for them, let him repay Pope when his soldiers found

Pope's tent, grabbed one of Pope's dress uniforms, which Stuart sent to Richmond for display as a trophy, and captured what Stuart claimed was Pope's dispatch book. Although Pope tried to slough it off, Stuart's raid bruised his dignity and Pope wrote sourly of "the success of this small cavalry party of the enemy" as "very trifling and attended with little damage."[40]

On August 23 Pope got further reinforcements. General John F. Reynolds reached Kelly's Ford with his 6,000 Pennsylvania Reserves. General Phil Kearny arrived at Warrenton on August 25 with the 7,500 troops of the First Division, Third Corps, Army of the Potomac.[41] Knowing that he had these troops to back him up, Pope was able to swing his army westward trying to catch Stuart, but Stuart was able to escape.

Stuart had raided Pope's rear trying to burn a critical bridge on the Orange and Alexandria Railroad, Pope's lifeline. Knowing when he left Warrenton that he might face the whole Army of Northern Virginia, Pope took steps to secure his depots at Alexandria and Manassas Junction as well as every inch of the line between his depots and the army. Curiously, the railroad that gave mobility in warfare almost immediately immobilized large numbers of troops needed to guard it. As early as August 13, Pope met railroad troubles when Union generals at Alexandria commandeered trains and took away the transport needed to bring General Jacob Cox's Kanawha Division to join Pope.[42] Although Halleck should not have let an army enter the field without absolute control of necessary communications in the rear, it was not until August 18 that Pope got Halleck's permission to appoint railroad expert Colonel Herman Haupt commander of all the railroads in Army of Virginia territory. All movements of troops and supplies needed his authority.[43]

In spite of this, rear guard and railroad troubles continued to pop up. On August 22 General Samuel Sturgis at Alexandria took over a train in spite of Pope's order giving Haupt control, snarling, "I don't care for John Pope a pinch of owl's dung."[44] Until Haupt intervened Sturgis's probably drunken act resulted in delaying 10,000 troops waiting to join the Army of Virginia.[45] At another time Haupt found the commanding general of the Second Division, Third Corps, Army of the Potomac, missing when his troops started to board their trains. Knowing his generals, Colonel Haupt went straight to the Willard's Hotel bar in Washington where he found Major General Joseph Hooker.[46] In a comment applying to all Union and Confederate armies the assistant secretary of war said to Haupt, "Be patient as possible with the generals. Some of them will trouble you more than they will the enemy."[47]

While these acts might rouse Pope's violent temper, he began to worry more about a rumor that started circulating on August 22: the Confederates planned to attack Pope's supply depot at Manassas Junction. Even Halleck heard this rumor in Washington and sent Pope the superfluous, fluttery advice, "The enemy is concentrating, it seems, near Manassas and Bull Run. You must look out for this and immediately break it up, for your supplies must come from Washington, and you must move back in this direction if compelled to retreat. Do not let him separate you from Alexandria."[48] Pope was already taking steps.

On the same day Pope wired irascible General Sturgis at Alexandria to post guards all along the thirty-five-mile stretch of railroad between Alexandria and Catlett's Station and to take personal charge of the posting.[49] Pope relied mainly on reinforcements coming to him by way of Alexandria; these would guard his rear and right flank. He wrote later, "I also sent orders to the Colonel commanding at Manassas Junction for the first division that reached there from Alexandria to halt and take post in the works of that place, and directed him also to push forward all his cavalry in the direction of Thoroughfare Gap to watch any movements the enemy might make from that direction."[50]

Colonel L. B. Pierce commanding at Manassas Junction wired his chief, General Sturgis, the following day,

> From all I can learn there will be an effort made tonight to burn the commissary stores at this place. . . . The enemy at Catlett's are not guerrillas, but from the main body of the enemy. . . . They are crossing the Rapidan from somewhere above in considerable force, . . . and design coming down through Thoroughfare Gap and Warrenton for the purpose of either flanking Pope or making a raid of some kind. All the military roads are open at this point, and nothing can prevent such a disaster.[51]

General Sturgis never forwarded this information to Pope, and saw no need to strengthen Colonel Pierce's forces at Manassas Junction. On his part, Pope sent no one back to check on whether General

Sturgis posted his railroad guards or whether Colonel Pierce got any troops to post at Manassas Junction or sent anyone to watch Thoroughfare Gap.

On August 23 Confederate attack was still only a rumor, but the Manassas Junction supply depots offered such a critical target that caution called for treating the rumor as true. Pope certainly saw that Thoroughfare Gap opened from a valley giving beautiful cover to a flanking movement around his right and that open roads led from Thoroughfare Gap to Manassas Junction. On the next day Confederate planners were taking these facts into account.

NOTES

1. George H. Gordon, *Brook Farm to Cedar Mountain* (Boston, 1883), 310; Cecil D. Eby, Jr., ed., *A Virginia Yankee in the Civil War: The Diaries of David Hunter Strother* (Chapel Hill, N.C., 1961), 64–65, 68, 72–75; Douglas Southall Freeman, *Lee's Lieutenants: A Study in Command*, 3 vols. (New York, 1942), 2:72.
2. Eby, 72.
3. Pope, Final Report, OR XII, part 2:24.
4. Eby, 66.
5. See discussion of Pope's experiments with corps cavalry on pp. 87–88, 110.
6. See note 3.
7. SO 31, Army of Virginia, Aug. 2, 1862, OR XII, part 3:525–26.
8. SO 45, Army of Virginia, Aug. 16, 1862, OR XII, part 3:581.
9. Thomas F. Thiele, *The Evolution of Cavalry in the American Civil War* (Ph.D. diss., University of Michigan, 1951), 102.
10. James Longstreet, "Our March against Pope," in Robert Underwood Johnson and Clarence Clough Buel, eds. *Battles and Leaders of the Civil War*, 4 vols. (New York, 1887), 2:513.
11. Ibid., 2:513–14; Lee to Jackson, July 27, 1862, OR XII, part 3:919.
12. McClellan to S. L. M. Barlow, July 23, 1862, Henry E. Huntington Library and Art Gallery, San Marino, Calif.
13. Halleck to Burnside, Aug. 1, 1862, OR XII, part 3:524.
14. Halleck to McClellan, Aug. 3, 1862, OR XII, part 1:80.
15. Ibid.
16. Pope, Final Report, OR XII, part 2:24.
17. Ibid.
18. See note 10.
19. Gen. John Pope, "The Second Battle of Bull Run," in *Battles and Leaders*, 2:458.
20. See note 16.
21. Lee to Jackson, July 27, 1862, OR XII, part 3:918–19.

22. Ruggles to Sigel, Aug. 8, 1862, OR XII, part 3:547; Pope to King, Aug. 8, 1862, OR XII, part 3:548; Burnside to Halleck, Aug. 4, 1862, OR XII, part 3:528.

23. John Codman Ropes, *The Army under Pope,* Campaigns of the Civil War Series (New York, 1881), 20.

24. Pope, Final Report, OR XII, part 2:26.

25. Ibid.; Eby, 75; Captain C. H. Morgan to Sigel, Aug. 9, 1862; Sigel Papers, New York Historical Society, New York.

26. Gordon, 315.

27. Pope to Halleck, Aug. 11, 1862, OR XII, part 2:133.

28. Pope, Final Report, OR XII, part 2:26. For a recent discussion of the battle, see *Lee Takes Command: Time-Life History of the Civil War* (Alexandria, Va., 1984), 99–109. This biography will not cover details of battles except as they relate to Pope in person or show problems handled by Pope in person.

29. "The Opposing Forces at Cedar Mountain, Virg., Aug. 9, 1862," in *Battles and Leaders,* 2:495–96.

30. Ropes, 28–30.

31. Ibid., 31.

32. Pope, Final Report, OR XII, part 2:27.

33. Ibid., 28.

34. "Report of Maj. Gen. George B. McClellan," H. Ex. Doc. 15, 38th Cong., 1st Sess., 1864, 148.

35. Pope, Final Report, OR XII, part 2:29.

36. Ibid.

37. David Donald, ed., *Inside Lincoln's Cabinet: The Civil War Diaries of Salmon P. Chase* (New York, 1954), 115.

38. Pope to Halleck, Aug. 19, 1862, OR XII, part 3:601; Pope to Halleck, Aug. 20, 1862, OR XII, part 3:603.

39. Halleck to Pope, Aug. 21, 1862, OR XII, part 2:57.

40. Pope, Final Report, OR XII, part 2:31.

41. Report of Gen. Reynolds, OR XII, part 2:392; Kearny to Pope, Aug. 21, 1862, OR XII, part 3:614.

42. Ruggles to Cox, Aug. 13, 1862, OR XII, part 3:570.

43. GO 22, Army of Virginia, Aug. 18, 1862, OR XII, part 3:598.

44. Herman Haupt, *Reminiscences of General Herman Haupt* (Milwaukee, 1901), 80.

45. Ibid., 83.

46. Ibid., 90.

47. Ibid.

48. Halleck to Pope, Aug. 22, 1862, OR XII, part 2:625.

49. Pope, Final Report, OR XII, part 2:33.

50. Ibid.

51. Pierce to Sturgis, Aug. 23, 1863, OR XII, part 3:632.

Chapter Ten

TENSION

POPE HELD LEE SOUTH OF THE Rappahannock so ably and so long that members of Lee's staff were reported to admit that Pope outgeneraled them,[1] but as Lee kept moving west, Pope had to keep extending his right and weakening his tie with Fredericksburg on his left. He wanted to cut the leg-irons that bound him to Fredericksburg anyway, and be free to maneuver, attack, or defend as the situation shifted. When Pope learned that Second and Sixth Corps, Army of the Potomac, landed at Alexandria and would join him from there instead of Aquia Creek,[2] he felt that Fredericksburg had served its purpose in guarding the Aquia Creek port of debarkation. He could ignore Halleck's order and begin a series of movements to battle and, he hoped, catch the enemy.

At the same time Lee and Jackson were meeting at Jeffersonton not ten miles away to go over their campaign and to plan how to overcome their stalemate. Frontal attacks had not done it. Trickery might. On August 24 they agreed to try a "bird with broken wing" trick. Jackson would march his division west, outflank Pope's right, and head north. For one day Longstreet would hold his division at the Rappahannock, making noise and keeping Pope busy. Once north, Jackson would swing east to attack the Manassas supply depots in Pope's rear, and Longstreet would start his division north over Jackson's route to meet Jackson. Pope would almost certainly move to chase Jackson, who would withdraw west as if in retreat and would invite Pope's attack. When Pope attacked, the two divisions of Jackson and Longstreet would join and the reunited Army of Northern Virginia would crush Pope.

Pope's psychological makeup was basic to the plan. In Lee's

evaluation Pope underrated Confederate troops and was over-confident, overhasty, likely to snap at bait without seeing it as bait. Lee also knew that Pope had his troubles handling a makeshift, two-month-old army. Reinforcements were coming, but they could cause as much confusion as strength. Jackson liked Lee's plan. Although it called for splitting forces in the face of the enemy, a practice denounced in all military textbooks, success in revolution called for taking great risks. If Pope saw through the scheme he could overwhelm Longstreet in front of him and then turn to Jackson or overwhelm Jackson and then take care of Longstreet, or he could retire to the defenses of Washington to regroup and repair his supply system. Lee and Jackson took those chances, almost staking the whole Confederate cause on their judgment.

On August 25 Jackson and his troops began their march upcountry through Amissville, Orlean, Salem, White Plains, Thoroughfare Gap, and Haymarket. Pope received news that scouts had watched a Confederate force of about 20,000 march uphill and around Pope's right flank on the way to Amissville and probably Front Royal. Pope relayed this news to Halleck[3] and warned the Union commander at Winchester to keep close watch on Front Royal.[4] For the moment Pope thought little of this. Perhaps they were going off on a raid or formed the advance guard of a march by the whole Confederate Army of Northern Virginia into the Shenandoah Valley by way of Luray and Front Royal.[5] Despite past orders to secure his rear, Pope felt no alarm.[6]

On August 25 Pope was thinking more about the vagueness of his position and his lack of direction from Washington. He wanted to attack but had not yet received his promised reinforcements. If he did attack, he wondered what troops he actually commanded and what his mission should be. He complained to Halleck,

> Please let me know, if it can be done, what is to be my own command, and if I am to act independently against the enemy. I certainly understood that as soon as the whole of our forces were concentrated you designed to take command in person, and that when everything was ready we were to move forward in concert. . . . The troops arriving here come in fragments. Am I to assign them to brigades and corps? I would suppose not, as several of the new regiments coming have been assigned to army corps directly from your office. In case I commence offensive operations, I

must know what forces I am to take, and what you wish left, and what connexion must be kept up with Burnside. . . . It has been my purpose to conform my operations to your plans, yet I was not informed when McClellan evacuated Harrison's Landing, so that I might know what to expect in that direction. I understood that this Army was to maintain the line of the Rappahannock until all the forces from the peninsula had united behind that river. I have done so. I understood distinctly that I was not to hazard anything except for this purpose, as delay was what was wanted.[7]

On the evening of the same day he sent his regular dispatch to Halleck, by now showing weariness with his command:

McDowell's is the only corps that is at all reliable that I have. Sigel, as you know, is perfectly unreliable, and I suggest some officer of superior rank be sent to command his army corps. . . . Banks's corps is very weak . . . much demoralized . . . must be left somewhere in the rear to be set up again. Sigel's corps, although composed of some of the best fighting material we have, will never do much service under that officer.[8]

Halleck replied to Pope's queries on the next day, but did not answer them. Hiding behind vague generalities and evasion, Halleck wrote, "The main object has been accomplished in getting troops from the Peninsula." As to his failure to report McClellan's quitting Harrison's Landing, "Just think of the immense amount of telegraphing I have to do and then say whether I can be expected to give you the details of the movement of others." As to Pope's next move, perhaps Pope should attack, perhaps not: "If possible to attack the enemy in flank do so, but the main object is to ascertain his position. Make cavalry excursions for that purpose, especially toward Front Royal."[9]

After this Pope must have written Halleck off. Pope did have good news to offset Halleck's letter: General Samuel P. Heintzelman, commanding Third Corps, Army of the Potomac; General Joseph Hooker with Second Division, Third Corps, Army of the Potomac; and General Abraham S. Piatt with one brigade of Sturgis's Reserve Division were at Warrenton Junction; and General Fitz John Porter with his crack Fifth Corps, Army of the Potomac, was at Bealeton.[10] These units added 20,000 combat-ready troops. Pope was still waiting for the promised Second and Sixth Corps, Army of the Potomac.[11]

By this time Pope had had to shift the east-west axis of his army to a north-south one to meet Lee's continuous moves west along the Rappahannock. McDowell's Third Corps held the right wing nearest Jackson's march route; Sigel's First Corps, the center; and Banks's wounded Second Corps, the left. McDowell and Sigel watched Jackson's uphill march and gave it more weight than Pope did. By August 26 McDowell knew from reports of his chief of cavalry that Jackson was not going to Front Royal but turned east and was coming down from White Plains and Thoroughfare Gap on the line of the Manassas Gap Railroad. Ricketts, the commanding general of the Second Division, Third Corps, holding the extreme right, was warned.[12] A regiment of Pennsylvania cavalry actually watched Thoroughfare Gap but on seeing Jackson's force wheeled back and rode away without reporting anything.[13] No one reported any of this to Pope. By that afternoon all of Jackson's troops had cleared Thoroughfare Gap. Longstreet's soldiers had started north.

While the Confederates were starting to carry out Lee's plan, an enemy within was starting to undermine Pope. High-ranking officers of the Army of the Potomac, Democrats, handpicked by McClellan and loyal to him, detested their assignment to the Army of Virginia and seemingly resolved to do nothing to help carry out its objectives. General Fitz John Porter commanding Fifth Corps, Army of the Potomac, headed this group. He was McClellan's closest personal friend and was of all officers the most exasperated to find himself assigned to serve McClellan's rival. Porter commanded his Fifth Corps ably during the Seven Days' Battles. He wanted the Army of the Potomac to fight again and looked at the transfer of Army of the Potomac units to Pope as nothing but a Republican way to ease McClellan out of his command. To Porter, criticism of McClellan was criticism of Porter. Porter was also a friend and correspondent of another general who had reason to be grateful to McClellan, General Ambrose E. Burnside, rescued from bankruptcy by McClellan in the 1850s.

Almost as soon as Porter reached Bealeton he wrote Burnside: "Everything here is at sixes and sevens, and I find I am to take care of myself in every respect. Our line of communication has taken care of itself, in compliance with orders. The army has not three days' provisions. The enemy captured all of Pope's and others' clothing and from McDowell the same including liquors."[14] His reference to the line of communications echoed Pope's address to his army; that to McDowell referred to his reputation as a hard drinker.

Some of Pope's advisers had foreseen this kind of silent sabotage. A colonel happened to overhear a heated discussion among general officers of the Army of Virginia: "At this meeting of the Generals I was struck with the earnestness with which General Kearny was trying to impress upon Pope the utter futility of hoping for any help from the Fifth Corps of the Army of the Potomac. He was perfectly fierce in his denunciation of what he called the spirit of McClellanism pervading officers in high command in that Army."[15] Kearny was talking directly to Pope and delivered a clear warning.

At 8 P.M. on August 26, Pope learned that the enemy had struck his rear and cut his telegraph line, cut the Orange and Alexandria Railroad line at Bristoe Station, ending his communications with Washington.[16] A little later he learned that Jackson commanded the raid and had gone on from Bristoe Station to Manassas Junction where he destroyed Pope's supplies and supply depots.[17] This could only mean that Halleck had failed him and that his subordinates had failed to carry out orders to guard Manassas Junction. Pope wrote later,

> The moment our communications were interrupted at Kettle Run I was satisfied that the troops which had been promised me from the direction of Washington had made no considerable progress. Had Franklin been even at Centreville on the 26th, or had Cox and Sturgis been as far west as Bull Run on that day, the movement of Jackson through Thoroughfare Gap upon the railroad at Manassas would have been utterly impracticable. So confidently did I expect, from the assurance which I had time and again received, that these troops would be in position . . . that Jackson's movement towards White Plains, and in the direction of Thoroughfare Gap, had caused but little uneasiness.[18]

Pope deduced that Lee split his forces and that Jackson's hit at Manassas Junction was more than a raid. Pope must also have realized too late that Lee tricked him. Enemy forces across the

Rappahannock had held him back with empty shows of force. It was time for a quick decision. He wrote later, "I determined . . . at once to abandon the line of the Rappahannock, and throw my whole force in the direction of Gainesville and Manassas Junction, to crush the enemy, who had passed through Thoroughfare Gap, and to interpose between the Army of General Lee and Bull Run."[19]

That was the turning point in Pope's campaign. He leaped to the attack, setting aside his mission to hold and defend. Although Pope acted as any good general should when he saw a chance to destroy the enemy, he stood unsupported without his promised reinforcements, with an army exhausted from two weeks' steady fighting, with his lifeline to Washington cut and his ammunition, food, and supplies running out at an alarming speed. He seems to have thought that his army could take a position between Washington and Jackson's army. This would let rear elements of his army try to reopen communications with the capital while forward elements fell on Jackson. It was a gamble and its success rested on whether Jackson was where Pope thought he was and, furthermore, if he would stay there. By midnight Pope knew that another enemy force was in camp at White Plains just west of Thoroughfare Gap. He wired McDowell, "Whether his whole force, or the larger part of it, has gone around is a question which we must settle immediately."[20] Pope's next moves show that he concluded that Longstreet had not yet joined Jackson. Pope was now in the same position that Lee was in earlier: he must keep one division from reinforcing another. He chose to catch Jackson.

On the morning of August 27, Pope issued orders for a great encircling movement to trap Jackson south of the Warrenton Turnpike between Gainesville and Manassas Junction. McDowell would march First and Third Corps along the Warrenton Turnpike from Warrenton to Gainesville. Heintzelman would march Third Corps, Army of the Potomac, and the First Division of Ninth Corps from Catlett's Station to Greenwich. Porter would wait at Warrenton Junction until Banks relieved him with Second Corps and would then march his Fifth Corps, Army of the Potomac, toward Greenwich and Gainesville to support the right wing.[21] Pope rode along the Orange and Alexandria Railroad from Warrenton Junction to Manassas Junction with Hooker's Second Division, Third Corps, Army of the Potomac. In the afternoon this division caught up

with Jackson's rear guard commanded by Ewell and got into a fight
known as the Battle of Kettle Run, resulting in 300 casualties for
each side. Hooker was running low on ammunition and let Ewell
withdraw without pursuit.[22] Pope's plan to trap Jackson assumed
that Jackson would stay somewhere near Manassas Junction, but at
3 A.M. Jackson marched all three of his columns almost due north
to a meeting place at Sudley Springs, north of the Warrenton
Turnpike.[23]

Porter tipped his hand again in a private letter to Burnside
written on August 27, enclosing Pope's orders of the day:

> I send you the last order from General Pope, which indicates
> the future as well as the present. Wagons are rolling along rapidly
> to the rear, as if a mighty force was propelling them. I see no
> cause for alarm, though I think this order may cause it. . . . I find
> a vast difference between these troops and ours, but I suppose
> they were new as today they burnt their clothes, etc., when there
> was not the least cause. I hear that they are much demoralized
> and needed some good troops to give them heart and, I think,
> head. We are working now to get behind Bull Run and I pre-
> sume we will be there in a few days if strategy don't use us up.
> The strategy is magnificent and tactics in inverse proportion. . . .
> I do not doubt the enemy have large amounts of supplies pro-
> vided for them and I believe they have a contempt for this Army
> of Virginia. I wish myself away from it, with all our old Army of
> the Potomac and so do our companions.
>
> Most of this is private, but if you can get me away, please.
> Make what use of this you choose, so it does good.[24]

That same evening Pope sent Porter an order from Bristoe
Station: "The major general commanding directs that you start at
one o'clock tonight and come forward with your whole corps . . . so
as to be here at daylight tomorrow morning. . . . It is necessary by
all accounts that you should be here by daylight."[25] A captain
delivered this in person and remembered that Porter took the
order, read it, and handed it to a general near him, saying,
"Gentlemen, there is something for you to sleep on." In the captain's
presence Porter then coolly ordered his division commanders to
start marching at 3 A.M.[26] Fifth Corps, Army of the Potomac,
started its march at 4 and did not reach Bristoe Station until
10:30.[27] Pope meant Porter to save Hooker from annihilation if

Jackson turned west, but Jackson did not turn. Pope apparently chose to overlook Porter's outright insubordination. If Jackson had in fact annihilated Hooker, Porter would have faced serious trouble.

On the same day McClellan resurfaced in Washington circles. He had reached Alexandria the day before and was now living on his steamer. Since Jackson had cut Pope's communications with the capital, Lincoln was concerned about what was going on in Virginia and turned to McClellan as an old friend, wiring, "What news from the front?"[28] McClellan supplied his information and in return finagled the post of military adviser to Lincoln. From now on McClellan would interpret Pope's moves to Lincoln as Pope had formerly interpreted those of McClellan. McClellan was not going to help Pope any more than he was forced to. Second and Sixth Corps, Army of the Potomac, sat in Alexandria with their 19,000 troops awaiting orders assigning them to the Army of Virginia. McClellan knew that Halleck had promised them to Pope, that Pope was relying on them, and that Pope might be in trouble. After three days of all the delaying moves that McClellan could invent, including asking time to get cavalry and artillery for Franklin, suggesting that Franklin would serve better by staying near Washington to defend the capital, and ignoring direct orders from his general-in-chief, Halleck, McClellan finally ordered Franklin to march on August 29.[29] Second Corps, Army of the Potomac, was still in Alexandria.

Colonel Haupt remembered making a call on McClellan aboard McClellan's private steamer at Alexandria. He explained to McClellan that because of Jackson's Manassas Junction raid Pope now lacked rations and forage, and asked McClellan's help in getting such supplies to Pope.

> I explained my plans for giving them relief, but a strong force was necessary to protect the trains. General McClellan listened, and, when I ceased, remarked that he could not approve the plan, that it would be attended with risk.
>
> I reminded the general that military operations were usually attended with risk but that I did not consider the risk in this case excessive. My representations and arguments availed nothing, the general would not give his consent, or assume any responsibility, and would give no orders, instructions or suggestions of any kind.[30]

As he rode off to continue his chase of Jackson, Pope had enemies in Washington and in his own army as deadly as those he faced in the field.

NOTES

1. See the *Washington Star,* Aug. 26, 1862, reporting Confederate staff meeting of Aug. 21, 1862, to decide "where the blame should rest in being outgeneraled by Pope."
2. Halleck to Pope, Aug. 26, 1862, OR XII, part 3:666.
3. Pope to Halleck, Aug. 25, 1862, OR XII, part 3:653.
4. Pope to Gen. Julius White, Aug. 25, 1862, OR XII, part 3:665.
5. Pope, Final Report, OR XII, part 2:34; Pope to McDowell, Aug. 25, 1862, OR XII, part 2:67.
6. See Pope, Final Report, OR XII, part 2:33-34. Haupt to put a strong division into Manassas Junction works; Halleck asked to speed Sixth Corps, Army of the Potomac, to Gainesville; Pierce to halt first division arriving at Manassas Junction from Alexandria; Sturgis to guard railroad line from Manassas Junction to Catlett's Station; Kearny to place guards in rear from Warrenton to Alexandria; Sixth Corps, Army of the Potomac, expected to be near Gainesville and Reserve and Kanawha Divisions expected to be at Warrenton Junction.
7. Pope to Halleck, Aug. 25, 1862, OR XII, part 2:65-66.
8. Pope to Halleck, Aug. 25, 1862, OR XII, part 3:653.
9. Halleck to Pope, Aug. 26, 1862, OR XII, part 3:666.
10. Pope, Final Report, OR XII, part 2:34-35.
11. See note 9.
12. Gen. John Buford to McDowell, Aug. 25, 1862, OR XII, part 3:657; Col. Edward Schriver to Ricketts, Aug. 26, 1862, OR XII, part 3:669.
13. Unidentified scout to Schriver, Aug. 26, 1862, OR XII, part 3:671.
14. Porter to Burnside, Aug. 27, 1862, OR XII, part 3:699.
15. Col. Daniel Leasure, "Personal Observations and Experience in the Pope Campaign in Virginia," (Paper read before the Minnesota Commandery of the Military Order of the Loyal Legion of the United States, St. Paul, 1887), 144-48.
16. Haupt to Halleck, Aug. 26, 1862, OR XII, part 3:680.
17. B. H. Morse to Stanton, Aug. 27, 1862, OR XII, part 3:696.
18. Pope, Final Report, OR XII, part 2:34.
19. Ibid.
20. Pope to McDowell, Aug. 26, 1862, OR XII, part 2:70.
21. GO (unnumbered), Army of Virginia, Aug. 27, 1862, OR XII, part 2:70.
22. Pope, Final Report, OR XII, part 2:35.
23. Ibid., 39.

24. Porter to Burnside, Aug. 27, 1862, OR XII, part 3:699.
25. Pope to Porter, Aug. 27, 1862, OR XII, part 2:71.
26. Captain DeKay, testifying at Porter trial, OR XII, part 2, supp.:681.
27. Ibid.
28. Lincoln to McClellan, Aug. 27, 1862, OR XII, part 3:692. Lincoln also wired Burnside asking, "Any news from General Pope?" Lincoln to Burnside, Aug. 28, 1862, OR XII, part 3:715.
29. Halleck to Franklin, Aug. 26, 1862, OR XII, part 3:676; Franklin to Capt. F. Sparrow Purdy, Aug. 26, 1862, OR XII, part 3:676; McClellan to Halleck, Aug. 27, 1862, OR XII, part 3:689; Halleck to Franklin, Aug. 28, 1862, OR XII, part 3:707; McClellan to Halleck, Aug. 28, 1862, OR XII, part 3:709; Halleck to McClellan, Aug. 28, 1862, OR XII, part 3:710; McClellan to Halleck, Aug. 28, 1862, OR XII, part 3:710.
30. Herman Haupt, *Reminiscences of General Herman Haupt* (Milwaukee, 1901), 98.

Chapter Eleven

CLASH

GENERAL POPE THOUGHT THAT he had trapped Jackson south of the Warrenton Turnpike, that Longstreet was far away, and that the Army of Virginia now faced a simple matter of disarming a smaller enemy force. Pope's orders for August 28 directed all units to rush to Manassas Junction. "If you will march at the earliest dawn of day," Pope wrote McDowell, "we will bag the whole crowd."[1] What the various regiments, brigades, and corps would do when they reached Manassas Junction was left open.

McDowell now commanded Sigel's First Corps as well as his own Third Corps. On the evening of August 27, he ordered elements of both to ride out to Thoroughfare Gap the next day to meet Longstreet and if possible hold him back, but when he got Pope's order to march to Manassas Junction he cancelled his own order without telling Pope what he had planned.[2]

On the morning of August 28, Pope set out with a column led by the First Division, Third Corps, Army of the Potomac, and the First Division, Ninth Corps. They marched from Bristoe Station along the Orange and Alexandria Railroad line through a country bare of enemy troops until they reached Manassas Junction. The Junction was wrecked, but Jackson had gone;[3] they must look elsewhere.

During the morning's marches other units on other routes met the enemy, even engaged the enemy, but none reported anything to Pope. The Pennsylvania Reserves, for example, found an enemy detachment east of the Warrenton Turnpike near Gainesville, exchanged a few shots, and let the Confederates withdraw without identifying or following them.[4] McDowell reversed himself and sent the Second Division, Third Corps, and all of the Army of Virginia's cavalry west of the Bull Run Mountains where they actually met and fought Longstreet west of Thoroughfare Gap.[5] McDowell knew this and reported nothing to Pope. First Corps came under fire about two miles southeast of Gainesville as the corps marched toward Manassas Junction. Sigel got ready to engage the enemy in regular line of battle and then disengaged when McDowell ordered them to keep marching to Manassas Junction. Again, no one identified the Confederate unit or tried to keep in touch with it.[6]

Not knowing any of this, Pope issued new orders at Manassas Junction. Second Corps would have supply and transport duty; Fifth Corps, Army of the Potomac, would stay in reserve at Manassas Junction; all the rest of the Army of Virginia would "move forward upon Centreville" again without specific orders about what to do on arrival.[7] Some time later Pope gave McDowell an order to intercept Jackson at Gum Spring. Then, changing his mind, he sent McDowell a second order: "I sent you a dispatch a few minutes ago directing you to move on Gum Spring. . . . I do not wish you to carry out the order to proceed to Gum Spring if you consider it hazardous. . . . Give me your views fully, you know the country better than I do."[8] What most of his army did for the rest of this frustrating day took place out of Pope's sight and went unreported except for bits and pieces relayed to him in the evening.

McDowell sent King's First Division, Third Corps, and the Pennsylvania Reserves along the Warrenton Turnpike toward Centreville. He then left the field to ask Pope what he meant in his second Gum Spring order, but spent the rest of the day and most of the night vainly trying to find Pope while Pope in turn looked for McDowell and swore that he could never find the man when he needed him.[9] If the two had met, McDowell would certainly have told Pope about Second Division, Third Corps, and all the cavalry then in action against Longstreet at Thoroughfare Gap.

Sigel's First Corps going north on the Sudley Springs road unexpectedly collided with a Confederate force near the Warrenton Pike and got into lively action. Until the darkness ended the engagement First Corps artillery kept forcing the enemy back. First Corps, holding its ground, spent the night at the scene.[10]

Jackson appeared to be retreating but in fact had his troops hidden in the woods north of the Warrenton Turnpike and behind an unfinished railroad embankment that ran from Sudley Springs to the main Manassas Gap Railroad line at Gainesville. When he saw Union soldiers marching for Centreville, Jackson began to worry that Pope might cross Bull Run, regroup, reopen communications with Washington, and then turn south, which would nullify Lee's plan. At about 6 P.M. the First Division, Third Corps, suddenly came under Confederate shelling east of Gainesville and now faced an infantry attack staged by Jackson to look like the defensive action of a rear guard. When the troops became engaged, the little action turned into a knock-down-drag-out battle in which General John Gibbon's Fourth Brigade, First Division, Third Corps took the leading part with distinction but suffered 839 casualties, more than one-third of all engaged. This was the Battle of Groveton, deliberately arranged by Jackson to keep Pope hot on the chase.[11]

Darkness brought quiet and a ripple effect across the field. General King withdrew his First Division, Third Corps, from Groveton, moved toward Gainesville and Manassas, and lost the enemy.[12] The Second Division of Third Corps under General Ricketts, outflanked by the Confederates at Thoroughfare Gap, withdrew to Gainesville. When Ricketts found that King had pulled back still farther, Ricketts withdrew all the way to Bristoe Station to keep from being isolated and also lost the enemy.[13] If McDowell had stayed in the field instead of trying to find Pope, he might have stopped these extreme withdrawals.

At 10 P.M. Pope finally heard about the Battle of Groveton and the other fights his First and Third Corps had had after leaving Manassas Junction. Still convinced that Jackson was in full retreat, Pope now worried about the chance that Jackson might escape through one of the western gaps. He gave further orders for troop deployment and specific orders to General King to hold First Division, Third Corps, in line toward Thoroughfare Gap.[14]

During these disjointed actions Fitz John Porter wrote Burnside two letters. In the first he commented that

all that talk of bagging Jackson, etc., was bosh. That enormous Gap was left open and the enemy jumped through. . . . The enemy have destroyed all our bridges, burned trains, and made this army rush back to look after its line of communications and find our

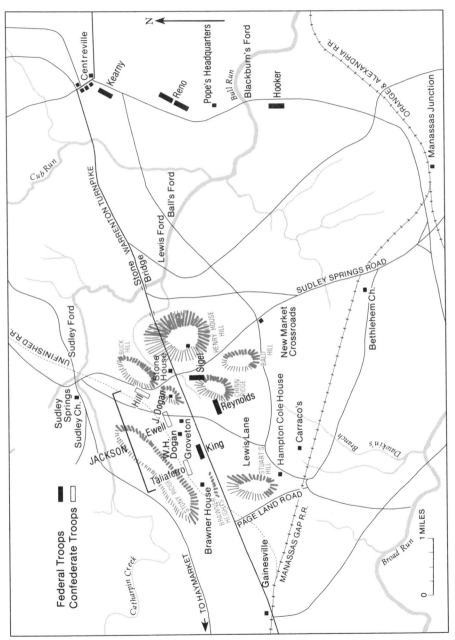

Federal Troops
Confederate Troops

Battle of Groveton, 6–8 P.M., August 28

base of subsistence.... There is a report that Jackson is at Centreville, which you can believe or not.... I expect the next thing will be a raid on our rear by way of Warrenton by Longstreet, who was cut off.[15]

In the second he added,

Banks at Warrenton Junction, McDowell near Gainesville, Heintzelman and Reno at Centreville, where they marched yesterday and Pope went to Centreville with the last two as a bodyguard, at the time not knowing where the enemy was and that Sigel was fighting within eight miles of him and in sight. Comment is unnecessary.... I hope Mac is at work and we will soon get ordered out of this. It would seem from proper statements of the enemy that he was wandering around loose; but I expect they know what they are doing, which is more than anyone here or anywhere knows.[16]

Porter's contempt for Pope was probably as great as Pope's dependence on him to defeat Jackson.

On the next day the Army of Virginia would meet the Confederate Army of Northern Virginia on almost the same ground as that of the first Battle of Bull Run. Pope did not foresee a formal battle but, as his orders show, rather a race to block the escape of a cornered enemy and then a fight to destroy that enemy. Lee, Jackson, and Longstreet, however, carefully planned a textbook battle.[17]

Pope meant to commit nearly all his troops to the battlefield, if not the actual fighting, and at 3 A.M. called in his reserve by wiring Porter to start marching to Centreville "at the first dawn of day" inasmuch as "A severe engagement is likely to take place and your presence is necessary."[18] A little later Pope found that only Sigel's First Corps had stayed in touch with the enemy, which called for rearranging the plan of attack to make First Corps the spearhead. Pope ordered Sigel to attack just after daylight. By 6:30 First Corps had opened fire with all arms. The Confederates returned the fire from what turned out to be the Confederate center.[19] A little later Heintzelman's Third Corps, Army of the Potomac, marched into place at the extreme right. Reno placed his Ninth Corps immediately to the left of Third Corps. Reynolds's Pennsylvania Reserves, who had bivouacked that night just to the left of Sigel's corps, now

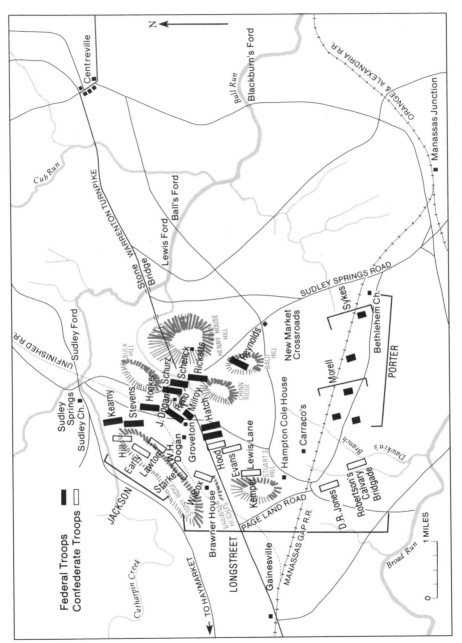

The Field of Second Bull Run, around Sunset, August 29

Federal Troops ■
Confederate Troops □

0   1 MILES

moved forward and formed the extreme left of the Federal forces then engaged.

The battle raged all day between attacks and counterattacks. Sigel, commanding the field, threw regiments and brigades at the Confederates one at a time, not in massed attack, and the piecemeal assaults failed. Pope did not interfere. Union weight was thrown repeatedly at the Confederate left. At one time Union forces managed to push the Confederate left back but could not break it or outflank it. The Confederates regained their lost ground. The unfinished railroad embankment held by Jackson's troops was central to both attack and defense and proved such a strong defensive position that Pope's forces found repeated assaults on it too costly to keep up for long.[20]

Pope took little part in the action. He arrived on the field sometime after noon and for the most part merely watched what was going on without giving further directions. He would have to admit that he had a battle on his hands instead of a chase. By 10 A.M. Porter's Fifth Corps had arrived at Manassas Junction from Bristoe. Here he received an order from Pope telling him to march to Gainesville instead of Centreville.[21] At 11:30 McDowell received a joint order from Pope addressed to both himself and Porter:

> You will please move forward with your joint commands towards Gainesville. . . . Heintzelman, Sigel, and Reno are moving on the Warrenton Turnpike, and must now be not far from Gainesville. I desire that as soon as communication is established between this force and your own, the whole command shall halt. . . .
>
> If any considerable advantages are to be gained by departing from this order, it will not be strictly carried out. One thing must be had in view, that the troops must occupy a position from which they can reach Bull Run tonight or by morning.[22]

Pope had again made himself anything but clear. McDowell decided to talk to Porter. As he remembered, "I rode forward and found General Porter at the head of his corps, on a slight eminence; in front was an open piece of ground, and beyond it the wood skirting the Warrenton road, down which, as we could see from the dust above the trees, the enemy was moving from Gainesville upon Groveton, where the battle was now going on."[23] The time was noon. From where they stood they could see Gainesville in Confederate hands. McDowell told Porter that he interpreted Pope's order as an order to join the attack, since to "move forward . . . towards Gainesville" obviously meant meeting the enemy. As McDowell remembered, he then gave Porter an order to send his Fifth Corps, Army of the Potomac, to attack a Confederate column moving east. McDowell then returned to his own Third Corps and began marching it along the Sudley Road into the developing battle.[24]

Porter, left alone, returned to his corps that he had halted at the edge of a wood two and one-half miles south of the fighting; his corps took cover. He watched Confederate forces maneuver in front of him. Stuart's cavalry raised dust to give the impression of a mighty force. Porter made no effort to identify any enemy unit or to probe the strength of any force ahead of him. Twelve thousand of the best Union soldiers including almost all of the regulars in the Army of Virginia simply sat out the battle "lying idle and exciting disaffection by doubts, sneering criticism, and open abuse of the Commander-in-Chief."[25]

During the afternoon Pope rode along the battle line expecting to see McDowell and Porter hit the Confederate right and wrap it up. At 4:30 P.M. he sent two officers to deliver to Porter the angry order: "Your line of march brings you in on the enemy's right flank. I desire you to push forward into action at once on the enemy's flank, and, if possible, on his rear, keeping your right in communication with General Reynolds. The enemy is massed in the woods but can be shelled out as soon as you can engage their flank."[26] Porter ignored this direct order claiming that it was received too late in the day to carry it out.

At about 5 P.M. McDowell and Third Corps joined in the action. When the firing died away at dusk, Pope held the field and appeared to have won a victory. Still convinced that he was chasing an enemy who was fighting a rear guard action, Pope held his troops in their positions for the night. No scouts or pickets watched the enemy. Pope felt that Porter robbed him of what could have been a historic conquest leading to fame, fortune, and promotion. He wrote bitterly in his official report:

> Nothing was heard of General Porter . . . and his forces took
> no part whatever in the action, but were suffered by him to lie

idle on their arms, within sight and sound of the battle during the whole day. So far as I know, he made no effort whatever to comply with my orders nor to take any part in the action. I do not hesitate to say that if he had discharged his duty as became a soldier under the circumstances, and had made a vigorous attack on the enemy as he was expected and directed to do, at any time up to eight o'clock that night, we should have utterly crushed or captured the larger portion of Jackson's force before he could have been by any possibility re-enforced to have made any effective resistance.[27]

Porter argued later that moving his corps into battle would have meant marching his column past enfilading fire from Longstreet's forces, which Porter said he believed to have reached Jackson before noon. To this Pope could only comment in his reflections twenty-five years later:

> Whatever Porter supposed to be Longstreet's position, however, in no respect touches his obligation to move forward under the circumstances and force Longstreet to develop what he really had, which he (Porter) certainly did not know and had taken no measures to know. The severe fighting on his right, which he heard and interpreted into a defeat for the Union Army, did not permit him to rest idle on the field with his troops in column and with no sufficient effort even to find anything of the field in front of him.
>
> If a mere impression that the enemy is in heavy force and that an attack or further advance might be hazardous is a sufficient reason for a corps commander to keep out of a battle, raging in his hearing, especially when he thinks that his friends are being defeated, it is extremely difficult to see how any army commander would venture to engage in battle at all, unless he could ascertain in advance and keep himself acquainted during the day with the impression of his corps commanders about the propriety of going into battle.[28]

By 7 P.M. Pope knew that Longstreet had joined Jackson and had taken some part in the day's action. Only the advice of Generals Heintzelman, McDowell, and Hooker kept Pope from arresting Porter on the spot.[29] At 8:50 Porter received an icy command:

> GENERAL: Immediately upon receipt of this order, the precise hour of receiving which you will acknowledge, you will

march your command to the field of battle of to-day and report
to me in person for orders.

You are to understand that you are expected to comply strictly
with this order, and to be present on the field within three hours
after its reception, or after daybreak tomorrow morning.[30]

McClellanism had done its work in the field but it still had
work to do in Washington. On August 29, Sixth Corps, Army
of the Potomac, finally left Alexandria to join Pope, only to have
McClellan stop it six miles out, at Annandale, to make sure,
McClellan said, that it could pass Vienna safely. Franklin, the
commanding general, was seen strolling in Alexandria that evening.[31]
Sumner's Second Corps, Army of the Potomac, was now fully
equipped and in Alexandria awaiting marching orders not yet
issued by McClellan.

That day Lincoln wired McClellan, "What news, from the direction of Manassas Junction? What generally?" McClellan replied,

The last news I received from the direction of Manassas Junction was from stragglers, to the effect that the enemy was evacuating Centreville, and retiring towards Thoroughfare Gap. This is
by no means reliable. I am clear that one of two courses should
be adopted; first, to concentrate all our available forces to open
communication with Pope; second, to leave Pope to get out of
his own scrape, and at once to use all our means to make the
capital perfectly safe. No middle course will now answer. Tell me
what you wish me to do.

Lincoln responded, "Yours of to-day just received. I think your first
alternative, to-wit, 'to concentrate all our available forces to open
communication with Pope' is the right one. But I wish not to
control. That I now leave to General Halleck, aided by your
counsels."[32]

Pope knew he was in a scrape because he faced the reunited Army
of Northern Virginia. His own discouraged, tired, hungry army
was fast running out of food and everything else. To retire east
beyond Bull Run to reopen his communications meant a retro-
grade movement that could lose him his army. He had one choice:
fight his way out.

August 30 opened glumly. At 5 A.M. Pope read a dispatch just
received from Franklin saying that McClellan would send him a

supply train from Alexandria if Pope would send back a cavalry escort to guard it. Pope wrote later,

> Such a letter, when we were fighting the enemy, and Alexandria was swarming with troops, needs no comment. . . . It was not until I received this letter that I began to feel discouraged and nearly hopeless of any successful issue to the operations with which I was charged . . . but I determined again to give battle to the enemy on the 30th and at least to lay on such blows as would cripple him as much as possible, and delay as long as practicable any further advance toward the capital. I accordingly prepared to renew the engagement.[33]

Despite his despair, Pope sent Halleck a cheerful wire suitable for newspaper release and not likely to panic Washington: "We fought a terrific battle here yesterday with the combined forces of the enemy, which lasted with continuous fury from day-light until dark, by which time the enemy was driven from the field, which we now occupy. The enemy is still in our front but badly used up. . . . He stood directly on the defensive and every assault was made by ourselves, our troops behaved splendidly."[34]

This time Pope made a definite battle plan after meeting with his corps commanders at 6. It was simple, repeating what developed as the Army of Virginia's plan for the day before: "break the enemy's left," as Sigel remembered hearing Pope say. McDowell would command the field. Porter's Fifth Corps, Army of the Potomac, would lead the attack. Then, in support, from right to left, would be Third Corps, Army of the Potomac; Ninth Corps; First Corps; and, side by side, the two divisions of Third Corps.[35] At the same time Lee was planning to smash Pope's weaker left and had moved part of his army south of the Warrenton Turnpike where the Confederates hid in the woods. By an unexplained error Pope's forces were further weakened when General Griffin, commanding Second Brigade, First Division, Fifth Corps, Army of the Potomac, and General Piatt, commanding Piatt's Brigade, Sturgis's Reserve Division, marched their units off toward Centreville without orders.[36]

After arranging his troops in line of battle Pope realized he could not see an enemy. Generals Heintzelman and McDowell rode out to check and came back to report no enemy in sight and all signs pointing to a headlong retreat. Another commander might have

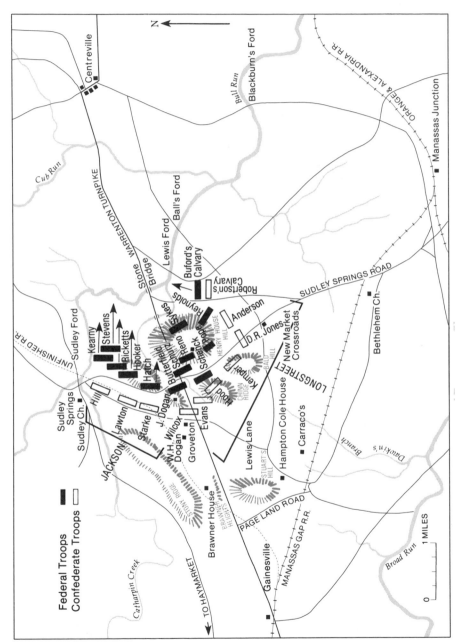

The Field of Second Bull Run, about 6 P.M., August 30

been suspicious. A timeworn precept of war cautioned against giving battle on the enemy's terms, and a lull of this kind could be part of the enemy's terms. Pope nevertheless marched his army ahead and at noon gave Porter a verbal order to start a forward movement after the enemy was spotted. From that moment Pope took little part in the action, following his usual practice, although he certainly kept a sharp eye on the field and probably gave word-of-mouth orders from time to time.

Porter's opening attack around 3 P.M. met such stiff resistance that the corps had to fall back to regroup. The savage battle that developed became a last ditch defense for the Union under relentless pressure from the Confederates on the left. As pressure on his left grew more intense, Pope shifted his headquarters to a landmark of First Bull Run, the Henry House Hill, where he watched the action while under fire. An observer said, "whatever may have been Pope's faults or mistakes, shunning exposure and responsibility on the battlefield was not one of them." An officer remarked, "He was the first general, in chief command, I had ever seen present on the battlefield under fire."[37] At the end of the day neither line had given way although the Confederates had hammered the Union line into the shape of an inverted U. Pope had a close call. By night Lee had had enough and allowed Pope to withdraw to Centreville without pursuit. Pope, not the enemy, was now in retreat. Pope learned Franklin and his corps had just reached Centreville, six miles from the battlefield. Swearing bitterly, Pope ordered Franklin to halt at that point and take charge of the defense works.[38]

After reaching Centreville at around 9 P.M. Pope reported to Halleck, "We have had a terrific battle again to-day. The enemy, largely re-enforced, assaulted our position early to-day. We held our ground firmly until 6 p.m. when the enemy, massing very heavy forces on our left, forced back that wing about half a mile. At dark we held that position. . . . The enemy is badly crippled, and we shall do well enough. Do not be uneasy. We will hold our own here."[39]

Halleck passed this on to Lincoln, who read it early in the morning on August 31. As his secretary, John Hay, remembered, "about 8 o'clock the President came to my room as I was dressing and calling me out he said, "Well, John, we are whipped again, I am afraid. The enemy re-enforced on Pope and drove back his left wing and he has retired to Centreville where he says he will be able to hold his men. I don't like that expression. I don't like to hear him admit that his men need 'holding.' "[40]

On August 31 Pope and his army enjoyed an uneasy day of rest waiting for further Confederate attacks. Retiring to Centreville opened communications with Alexandria. Sumner arrived with Second Corps, Army of the Potomac; thanks to McClellan, two fresh corps reached Pope too late to help in the battle in which their strength would have been decisive. McClellan insisted, "It will be seen that . . . after my arrival at Alexandria, I left nothing in my power undone to forward supplies and reenforcements to General Pope."[41] On the Army of Virginia's day of rest, however, McClellan was writing to Halleck: "I have no confidence in the dispositions made as I gather them. To speak frankly—and the occasion requires it—there appears to be a total absence of brains, and I fear the total destruction of the army. . . . It is my deliberate opinion that the interests of the nation demand that Pope should fall back tonight if possible, and not one moment is to be lost."[42]

For once Pope seemed to agree with McClellan, wiring Halleck:

> Our troops are all here in position, though much used up and worn out. I think it would perhaps have been greatly better if Sumner and Franklin had been here three or four days ago; but you may rely on our giving them as desperate a fight as I can force our men to stand up to.
>
> I should like to know whether you feel secure about Washington, should this army be destroyed. I shall fight it as long as a man will stand up to the work. You must judge what is to be done, having in view the safety of the capital.

Halleck replied as vaguely as Pope could expect: "You have done nobly. Don't yield another inch if you can avoid it. . . . Can't you renew the attack?"[43]

By this time rumors of McClellan's underhandedness began to reach Lincoln. John Hay rode with the president and recalled, "He talked about the state of things by Bull Run and Pope's prospect. The President was very outspoken in regard to McClellan's present conduct. He said it really seemed to him that McClellan wanted Pope defeated. . . . He spoke . . . also of his incomprehensible interference with Franklin's Corps." Later that day Lincoln, Stanton, and Hay ate together. Hay noted, "Stanton was loud about the McC business.

He was unqualifiedly severe upon McClellan. He said after these battles there should be one Court Martial if never any more. He said that nothing but foul play could lose us this battle and that it rested with McClellan and his friends. Stanton seemed to believe very strongly in Pope. So did the President for that matter."[44]

While these discussions went on in Washington, Pope had to deal with the political repercussions of his acts in the field. He did not need to know specifically that Lee would attack again; that would come inevitably. He did know, and had to explain to his corps commanders, that the president would not willingly let the Army of Virginia pull all the way back to Washington until a politically safe moment. An unannounced return could cause panic, would certainly spur Democratic opposition in Congress, and might even tumble the Republican administration that created and sent out this Republican army.[45] For political reasons as well as survival the army must fight again.

On September 1 Pope knew that Confederate forces were massing north of the Warrenton Turnpike to outflank him. Sending two brigades of Sumner's Second Corps, Army of the Potomac, to reconnoiter, Pope sat down to report in full the grievances on which he blamed the sad outcome of his campaign:

> One commander of a corps who was ordered to march from Manassas Junction to join me near Groveton, although he was only 5 miles distant, failed to get up at all, and worse still, fell back to Manassas without a fight and in plain hearing . . . of a furious battle which raged all day. It was only in consequence of my peremptory orders that he joined me next day. . . . Their constant talk, indulged in publicly and in promiscuous company, is that the Army of the Potomac will not fight, that they were demoralized by withdrawal from the Peninsula, etc. . . .
>
> You have hardly an idea of the demoralization among officers of high rank in the Potomac army, arising in all instances from personal feeling in relation to changes of Commander-in-Chief and others. These men are mere tools or parasites, but their example is producing . . . very disastrous results. . . . My advice to you, I give it with freedom, is that . . . you draw back this army to the entrenchments in front of Washington, and set to work in that secure place to reorganize and rearrange it. . . . Where there is no heart in their leaders and every disposition to hang back, much cannot be expected of the men.[46]

Halleck could understand that Pope, as well, had little more fight.

When the reconnaissance party from Second Corps, Army of the Potomac, reported back Pope learned that Jackson now meant to outflank him at Germantown, east of Centreville. Outflanking at that point meant denying access to the Alexandria Turnpike passing through Fairfax and on to Alexandria, the speediest route for the Army of Virginia to take if retiring to the Washington defense perimeter.[47] Pope simply meant to forestall Jackson. General Isaac I. Stevens, commanding Ninth Corps, and General Samuel P. Heintzelman, commanding Third Corps, Army of the Potomac, would march north and hold Jackson off while the rest of the Army of Virginia kept marching toward Washington. Stevens and Heintzelman took off at 1 P.M. and ran into Confederate pickets near Chantilly. Jackson was surprised and caught off-balance before he had fully deployed his troops.

The Battle of Chantilly began at once and lasted all afternoon through a downpour and thunderstorm. The Army of Virginia kept its path open to Washington at a cost of 1,000 more casualties including General Stevens, who seized the colors of his old Seventy-ninth New York Regiment to lead his troops in person, and General Phil Kearny, commanding First Division, Third Corps, Army of the Potomac, who rode into Confederate pickets, refused to stop when challenged, and was shot.[48] The Army of Virginia marched east to camp at Fairfax, not fifteen miles from Washington. The enemy followed.

On September 1 and 2, McClellan took command of the Washington defenses and was told, he said, to take command of the army when it came within those lines, though by whose authority never became clear. On September 1 Lincoln told McClellan he had heard that "the Army of the Potomac was not cheerfully co-operating with and supporting General Pope."[49] A hearty exchange of window-dressing platitudes followed. McClellan wired Porter,

> I ask of you for my sake, that of the country, and of the old Army of the Potomac, that you and all my friends will lend the fullest and most cordial cooperation to General Pope in all operations now going on. The destiny of our country, the honor of our arms, are now at stake, and all depends now upon the cheerful cooperation of all in the field. This week is the crisis of our fate. Say the same thing to my friends in the Army of the

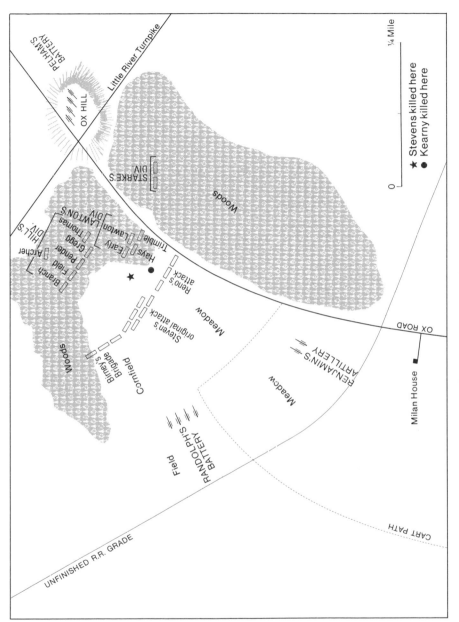

Battle of Chantilly, September 1, 1862

Map labels:

PELHAM'S BATTERY

OX HILL

Little River Turnpike

STARKE'S DIV

Woods

HILL'S DIV

LAWTON'S DIV

Branch

Archer

Field

Pender

Gregg

Thomas

Early

Hays

Trimble

Woods

Reno's attack

Steven's original attack

Meadow

Binney's Brigade

Cornfield

Field

RANDOLPH'S BATTERY

Meadow

BENJAMIN'S ARTILLERY

Milan House

OX ROAD

CART PATH

UNFINISHED R.R. GRADE

★ Stevens killed here

● Kearny killed here

0 ¼ Mile

Potomac and that the last request I have to make to them is that, for their country's sake, they will extend to General Pope the same support they ever have to me. I am in charge of the defense of Washington, and am doing all I can to render your retreat safe, should that become necessary.

Porter replied, "You may rest assured that all your friends, as well as every lover of his country, will ever give, as they have given to General Pope their cordial cooperation and constant support in the execution of all orders and plans. Our killed and wounded troops attest to their devoted duty."[50]

Both letters admitted the existence of an Army of the Potomac clique headed by McClellan, and that its members needed special encouragement to carry out their duties.

Pope was giving Halleck the true, disastrous state of affairs:

As soon as the enemy brings up his forces he will again turn on me. I will give battle when I can, but you should come out and see the troops. They were badly demoralized when they joined me, both officers and men, and there is an intense idea among them that they must get behind the entrenchments. . . . The straggling is awful in the regiments from the Peninsula. Unless something can be done to restore tone to this army, it will melt away before you know it.[51]

Halleck at once ordered Pope to march within the Washington defenses, now commanded by McClellan, he added.[52] Pope marched as far as Ball's Cross Roads, which he saw as a suitable temporary camp for rest and reorganization before returning to the field. He wired Halleck: "We ought not to lose a moment in pushing forward the fresh troops to confront the enemy. In three days we should be able to renew the offensive in the direction of Little River pike beyond Fairfax Court House. We must strike again with fresh men while the enemy is wearied and broken down. I am ready to advance again to the front with fresh troops now here."[53]

Halleck nevertheless ordered Pope to march within the actual fortifications of Washington and then to report to Halleck in person, saying, "A reorganization of an army for the field will be immediately made."[54] At 4 P.M. McDowell and Pope, riding at the head of the column, met McClellan. An officer on the scene remembered:

Their uniforms and that of all the party was covered with dust, their beards were covered with it; they looked worn and serious, but alert and self-possessed . . . both parties bowed, and the cavalcade moved on. . . . Hatch was present near Pope, when McClellan assumed command, and instantly rode a few paces to the head of his column and shouted, "Boys, McClellan is in command again; three cheers!"

The cheers were given in wild delight, and were taken up and passed toward the rear of the column. Warm friend of McClellan as I was, I felt my flesh cringe at the unnecessary affront to the unfortunate commander of that army. But no word was spoken. Pope lifted his hat in a parting salute to McClellan and rode quietly on with his escort.[55]

Hatch took his revenge for Pope's dressings-down a few months earlier.

Pope went the full circle from Washington to Washington with a trail of 12,500 casualties to Lee's 10,500.[56] On September 3 Lincoln personally assured him that he had done well, saying that McClellan had only temporary command of Washington and hinting that Pope would soon command a new field army.[57]

NOTES

1. Pope to Reno, Aug. 27, 1862, OR XII, part 3:704; Pope to Porter, Aug. 27, 1862, OR XII, part 2:71; Pope to Kearny, Aug. 27, 1862, OR XII, part 2:72; Pope to McDowell, Aug. 27, 1862, OR XII, part 2:72.
2. Pope, Final Report, OR XII, part 2:37; Irwin McDowell, "Reports of Maj. Gen. Irwin McDowell, U.S. Army, commanding Third Corps, Army of Virginia, of Operations August 7–September 2," OR XII, part 2:325, 2:335.
3. Pope, Final Report, OR XII, part 2:37.
4. McDowell, OR XII, part 2:336.
5. George D. Bayard, "Reports of Brig. Gen. George D. Bayard, U.S. Army, of Operations July 21–September 2," OR XII, part 2:88, 91.
6. McDowell, OR XII, part 2:335.
7. Pope, Final Report, OR XII, part 2:37.
8. Pope to McDowell, Aug. 28, 1862, OR XII, part 2:74.
9. Pope, Final Report, OR XII, part 2:38.
10. Ibid., 37.
11. See John Gibbon, *Personal Recollections of the Civil War* (New York, 1928; reprint, Dayton, Ohio, 1978), 55. For recent discussions of the Battle of Groveton, see *The American Heritage Picture History of the Civil*

War, narrative by Bruce Catton, (New York, 1960; reprint, 1982), 121–42 (map on 141); *Lee Takes Command: Time-Life History of the Civil War* (Alexandria, Va., 1984), 138–43.

12. Pope, Final Report, OR XII, part 2:38.

13. McDowell, OR XII, part 2:337.

14. Pope, Final Report, OR XII, part 2:37.

15. Porter to Burnside, Aug. 28, 1862, OR XII, part 3:732.

16. Porter to Burnside, Aug. 29, 1862, OR XII, part 3:733.

17. See James Longstreet, "Our March against Pope," in Robert Underwood Johnson and Clarence Clough Buel, eds., *Battles and Leaders of the Civil War,* 4 vols. (New York, 1887), 2:519.

18. Pope to Porter, Aug. 29, 1862, OR XII, part 2:75; Ruggles to Porter, Aug. 29, 1862, OR XII, part 3:733.

19. Pope, Final Report, OR XII, part 2:39.

20. This battle has been fought and refought. For contemporary records see Report of John Pope; Report of Gen. Robert E. Lee on Operations of the Army of Northern Virginia Aug. 13 to Sept. 2, 1862, OR XII, part 2:552; Report of Gen. Thomas J. Jackson, Apr. 27, 1863, OR XII, part 2:642; Report of Gen. Jeb Stuart, Feb. 23, 1863, OR XII, part 2:731. For reminiscences see *Battles and Leaders,* 2:449–541. Also, see T. C. H. Smith, "Memoir and Review of Pope's Campaign in Virginia," in Smith Papers, Ohio Historical Society, Columbus, Ohio. For recent general accounts see Herman Hattaway and Archer Jones, *How the North Won* (Urbana, 1983), 220–36; *The American Heritage Picture History of the Civil War,* 216–23; *Lee Takes Command,* 135–67. For specialized studies see Stephen E. Ambrose, "Henry W. Halleck and the Second Bull Run Campaign," *Civil War History* 6, no. 3 (Sept. 1960), 328; Dennis Kelly, "The Second Battle of Manassas," *Civil War Times Illustrated* 22, no. 3 (May 1983), 9; and L. Van Loan Naisawald, "The Location of Grover's Attack in Relation to the Terrain and Opposing Confederate Brigades," unpub. monograph, Library of the Manassas National Military Park, Manassas, Va.

21. John Codman Ropes, *The Army under Pope,* Campaigns of the Civil War Series (New York, 1881), 86.

22. Pope to McDowell and Porter, Aug. 29, 1862, OR XII, part 2:76.

23. McDowell, OR XII, part 2:338.

24. Ibid.

25. Pope, Final Report, OR XII, part 2:40; David H. Strother, quoted in Henry Steele Commager, ed., *The Blue and the Gray,* 2 vols. (Indianapolis, 1950; rev. and abrd., New York, 1973), 182.

26. Pope to Porter, Aug. 29, 1862, OR XII, part 2:18.

27. Pope, Final Report, OR XII, part 2:40.

28. Pope, *Battles and Leaders,* 2:484.

29. Smith, 166–67.

30. Pope to Porter, Aug. 29, 1862, OR XII, part 2:18.

31. Halleck to McClellan, Aug. 29, 1862, OR XII, part 3:723; McClellan to Halleck, Aug. 29, 1862, OR XII, part 3:723.
32. Ropes, 160–61.
33. Pope, Final Report, OR XII, part 2:41.
34. Pope to Halleck, Aug. 30, 1862, OR XII, part 3:741.
35. Pope, Final Report, OR XII, part 2:42.
36. Ibid.
37. Smith, 193; J. Watts DePeyster, *Personal and Military History of Philip Kearny* (New York, 1869), 421.
38. Pope, Final Report, OR XII, part 2:43–44.
39. Pope to Halleck, Aug. 30, 1862, OR XII, part 2:78–79.
40. Tyler Dennett, ed., *Lincoln and the Civil War in the Diaries and Letters of John Hay* (New York, 1939), 46.
41. "Report of Maj. Gen. George B. McClellan upon the Organization of the Army of the Potomac and of Its Campaigns in Virginia and Maryland from July 26, 1861 to November 7, 1862," H. Ex. Doc. 15, 38th Cong., 1st Sess., 1864, 185.
42. Ibid., 181–82.
43. Pope to Halleck, Aug. 31, 1862, OR XII, part 2:80; Halleck to Pope, Aug. 31, 1862, OR XII, part 3:769.
44. Dennett, 45–46.
45. Pope, Final Report, OR XII, part 2:45; McDowell, OR XII, part 2:344.
46. Pope to Halleck, Sept. 1, 1862, OR XII, part 2:83.
47. Report of John Pope, 26, 252.
48. See T. C. H. Smith, "The Battle of Chantilly," unpub. ms, Smith Papers, Ohio Historical Society, Columbus, Ohio; Charles F. Walcott, "The Battle of Chantilly," paper read before the Military Historical Society of Massachusetts (Boston, 1886), 2:169; and L. Van Loan Naisawald, "The Battle of Chantilly," *Civil War Times Illustrated* 3 (March 1964), 3.
49. Report of George B. McClellan, 182–83.
50. McClellan to Porter, Sept. 1, 1862, OR XII, part 3:787; Porter to McClellan, Sept. 2, 1862, OR XII, part 3:798.
51. Pope to Halleck, Sept. 2, 1862, OR XII, part 3:796–97.
52. Halleck to Pope, Sept. 2, 1862, OR XII, part 3:797; GO 122, AGO, Sept. 2, 1862, OR XII, part 3:807.
53. Pope to Halleck, Sept. 3, 1862, OR XII, part 3:808.
54. Halleck to Pope, Sept. 3, 1862, OR XII, part 3:809.
55. Jacob D. Cox, *Military Reminiscences of the Civil War,* 2 vols. (New York, 1900), 1:244–45.
56. Thomas L. Livermore, *Numbers and Losses in the Civil War in America 1861–65* (New York, 1901; reprint, Bloomington, Ind., 1957), 140. Compare Grant's loss of 17,666 in the futile Battle of the Wilderness in the two days of May 5 and 6, 1864. "The Opposing Forces at the Beginning of Grant's Campaign against Richmond," *Battles and Leaders,* 4:179, 4:182. Grant had supreme command, a free hand, no

political enemies, and all supplies and reinforcements he asked, and was fighting an Army of Northern Virginia weakened by two years of fighting.

57. David Donald, ed., *Inside Lincoln's Cabinet: The Civil War Diaries of Salmon P. Chase* (New York, 1954), 120.

Chapter Twelve

AFTERMATH

JOHN POPE LIVED TO SERVE twenty-four more useful years in the army but whatever he did, however able and far-sighted, could not make him known to the public as anyone but the general who lost the Second Battle of Bull Run. Before he left Washington on July 29 Pope is reported to have commented to Chase that

> he could take command of the Army of Virginia and so operate with it as to attract the attention of the rebel authorities, and induce them to combine all their forces against them, that he could penetrate their country as far as Gordonsville, and cut their line of supplies. That he would then have to fall back to the Rapidan, and fight there; then fall back to the Rappahannock, and fight again there; and that somewhere about the old Bull Run battlefield he would have to fight the third and final battle. That by that time McClellan's Army could be in supporting distance, and that if he were supported he would whip them, and if he were not supported, he would be whipped.[1]

If he really made this comment before going out, he took the field in a questionable spirit for an army commander at the outset of a campaign, as well as in some misunderstanding of his objective. His campaign turned out almost as this prophecy, and now he had to undergo the new experience of taking the consequences of what the authorities and the public saw as failure.

While Pope and Jackson fought at Chantilly, Washingtonians could hear the boom of artillery fifteen miles away. After Pope withdrew to the Washington defenses leaving an unchecked Confederate Army outside, panic followed inevitably in the city. Almost the sole topic in the capital was whether or not Lee would march his army down Pennsylvania Avenue until news came from Maryland that McClellan had fought Lee to a standstill. The fears and worries of the time toppled Pope instantly from the peak on which he stood and disposed of him. Pope complained that he got harsh, hasty treatment as his reward for faithful service, and he had good reason for saying so.

Even before Pope arrived, cabinet members knew about Porter's skulking and Franklin's delays.[2] Chase made an unsuccessful try to get McClellan dismissed,[3] but the president firmly backed Halleck in naming McClellan to command the Washington defenses.[4] Most cabinet members sympathized with Pope, although reluctantly agreeing that he should not stay in command. Secretary of the Navy Welles wrote in his diary, "The general conviction is that he is a failure here, and there is a belief and admission on all hands that he has not been seconded and sustained as he should have been by McClellan, Franklin, Fitz John Porter, and perhaps some others. Personal jealousies and professional rivalries, the bane and curse of all armies, have entered deeply into ours."[5]

By September 4 Pope finished a preliminary report[6] that placed the blame for his defeat at Bull Run squarely on McClellan, Porter, and Franklin as a trio of Democratic conspirators. He read it to Lincoln and Welles that morning. Welles commented:

> It was not exactly a bulletin nor a report, but a manifesto, a narrative, tinged with wounded pride and a keen sense of injustice and wrong. The draft, he said, was rough. It certainly needs modifying before it goes out, or there will be war among the generals, who are more ready to fight each other than the enemy. . . .
>
> Pope and I left together and walked to the Department. He declares all his misfortunes are owing to the persistent determination of McClellan, Franklin, and Porter, aided by Ricketts, Griffin, and some others who were predetermined he should not be successful. They preferred, he said, that the country should be ruined rather than that he should triumph.[7]

On the following day the president and his cabinet met to discuss Pope's report. After some talk the cabinet voted unanimously not to publish it. In the present crisis the administration could not afford to reveal its inside wrangling.[8] This by no means meant an endorsement of McClellan. Welles, himself a Democrat, set down his feelings:

> I cannot relieve my mind from the belief that to him, in great degree, and his example, influence, and conduct are to be attributed some portion of our late reverses, more than to any other person on either side. His reluctance to move or have others move, his inactivity, his detention of Franklin, his omission to send forward supplies unless Pope would send a cavalry escort from the battlefield, and the tone of his conversation and dispatches, all show a moody state of feeling.[9]

Later that day Lincoln penned an order convening a court of inquiry to look into the behavior of Generals Porter, Franklin, and Griffin on August 29-30,[10] which Halleck made into a formal order, naming members of the court and setting a date;[11] McDowell had already asked for a similar court to refute rumors charging him with treasonable conduct.[12] McClellan was too hot to attack at the moment: the country that relied on him to save Washington could not afford to offend him. He was now in chief command of the army as well as Washington.[13]

Halleck suspended Porter, Franklin, and Griffin from their commands until the Court of Inquiry reported its findings. His order also went on to read: "The armies of the Potomac and Virginia being consolidated, Major General Pope will report to the Secretary of War as a witness in a Court of Inquiry."[14] Pope got a copy later that day and was stung. His field consolidation of the Army of the Potomac into the Army of Virginia was reversed without notice. Now he, not McClellan, stood as a commanding general without a command.

Pope wrote Halleck a heated letter asking for public vindication through a complimentary order for his army, which Halleck promised earlier,[15] and also asked to have his report published, saying, "I am sure you will see the propriety of all these requests. Either I have conducted badly or I have not. If I have, I am prepared to shoulder the blame, but if, as both you and the President informed me, my course has met with your entire approval, I am entitled to be shielded from unjust censure."[16] Halleck replied in a soothing letter that he did not yet know what Pope's new command might be and that the president and secretary of war did not think a complimentary order to Pope's army advisable at the time since McClellan's army did not get one after leaving Harrison's Landing: "we think you did the best with the material you had," Halleck concluded.[17]

Appeasement did not work with an angry John Pope, who called on his friend Chase on September 6. Chase noted,

> He expressed strong indignation against Fitz John Porter and McClellan, who had, as he believed, prevented his success. He wanted his Report published, as an act of justice to himself and his army. I stated my objection to present publication, on the ground of injury to service at this critical time, but said that a General Order, thanking the Army for what they had done ought to be promulgated. He said this would be satisfactory (partially so, at least) but that Halleck would not publish one. I said, I would see the President and urge it.[18]

John Pope's sentence for undergoing defeat in battle was command of the newly created Department of the Northwest, which included Iowa, Minnesota, Wisconsin, and the territories of Dakota and Nebraska. Stanton's letter of instructions read:

> The Indian hostilities[19] . . . require the attention of some military officer of high rank in whose ability and vigor the Government has confidence, and you have therefore been selected for this important command. You will proceed immediately to your Department, establish your headquarters in St. Paul, Minnesota, and . . . take such prompt and vigorous measures as shall quell the hostilities and afford peace, security, and protection to the people against Indian hostilities.[20]

In a word, banishment.

With only a short time left in Washington, Pope hurried to start the machinery for bringing Porter before a general court-martial and made a last call at the War Department, where he saw Stanton, Chase, and Welles. Still "angry and vehement,"[21] he left to board his train for St. Paul on Sunday, September 7. That day Chase called on Lincoln asking for a general order commending Pope's army. Lincoln told Chase "he thought it due and said he would speak to Halleck,"[22] but nothing ever followed.

The Pope matter kept bubbling even while Lee's army was marching around Washington and north into Maryland. Lincoln confided to Welles why he had to let Pope go and bring General McClellan back into command in spite of the cabinet's opposition: "I must have McClellan to reorganize the army and bring it out of chaos, but there had been a design, a purpose in breaking down Pope, without regard to the consequences to the country. It is shocking to see and know this; but there is no remedy at present; McClellan has the Army with him."[23]

Lincoln and Welles met again the next day. Lincoln was still preoccupied with the generals' feud, saying,

> We had the enemy in the hollow of our hands on Friday [August 29] if our generals, who are vexed with Pope, had done their duty; all our present difficulties and reverses have been brought upon us by these quarrels of the generals. . . .
>
> Of Pope he spoke in complimentary terms as brave, patriotic, and as having done his duty in every respect in Virginia, to the entire satisfaction of himself and Halleck, who both knew and watched, day and night, every movement. . . . Pope, said the President, did well, but there was here an Army prejudice against him, and it was necessary he should leave. He had gone off very angry, and not without cause, but circumstances controlled us.[24]

Welles noted the comments of General David G. Birney, commanding Second Brigade, First Division, Third Corps, Army of the Potomac, who served with Pope. "The combination against Pope was, Birney says, part of the plan carried out, and the worst feature to him was the great demoralization of his soldiers. They were become rebellious and untamable."[25]

On September 8, the day after Pope left Washington, the *New York Times* let loose the whirlwind by publishing Pope's preliminary report that the president, the cabinet, and the general-in-chief had refused to allow printed. It was done, Pope said, without his "authority or knowledge . . . contrary to his wishes," and he refused to speak of it further.[26] This publication came under discussion at a cabinet meeting on September 12:

> Smith [Interior] complimented Pope's patriotism and bravery, and the President joined in the encomium. Blair [Postmaster General] was unwilling to concede any credit whatever to Pope; said he was a blower and a liar[27] and ought never to have been intrusted with such a command as that in front. The President

admitted Pope's infirmity, but said a liar might be brave and have skill as an officer. He said Pope had great cunning. He had published his report, for instance, which was wrong—an offense for which, if it can be traced to him, Pope must be made amenable—'But,' said he, 'it can never, by any skill, be traced to him.' 'That is the man,' said Blair, 'Old John [he meant Nathaniel] Pope, his father, was a flatterer, a deceiver, a liar, and a trickster; all the Popes are so.'[28]

These top politicians felt nevertheless that the clique of McClellan and friends contributed heavily to Pope's disaster and pointed out that Halleck, whom Pope had not blamed, also had a hand in it. Welles saw Halleck as a "military dictator, not a general, a man of some scholarly attainments, but without soldierly capacity," who turned on Pope when he was out of favor and began supporting McClellan.[29] Even an open enemy of Pope wrote of Halleck, "He remained in Washington, practically inert, while one of the great armies of which he was general-in-chief was suffering sore reverses, almost in sight of the Capitol."[30] Behind Halleck, of course, stood Lincoln, beyond reach, who did not want to "interfere" and so left Pope in Halleck's hands.

Newspaper reporters could not know top-level confidences, but they did their best with human interest stories and articles second-guessing Pope. The supposed dying words of a colonel made good copy: " 'I have fought manfully and now die fearlessly. I am one of the victims of Pope's imbecility and McDowell's treason. Tell the President that to save our country he must not give our flag to such hands.' "[31]

This anecdote led directly to McDowell's request for a court of inquiry. Other soldiers had no good words for Pope: " 'Sir, there was no plan. We knew nothing but what we discovered ourselves. . . . I must ask to be relieved unless General Pope is removed. I cannot see my men murdered. . . . The opinions of the troops are unanimously against him. . . . There is no dissent or disagreement, they will not and cannot fight again under Pope with confidence.' "[32]

As early as September 4, reporters picked up rumors of Pope's charges against McClellan, Porter, and Franklin,[33] which came out in the open when Pope's report was published. A week later one editorial writer could say, "a number of our generals are literally at swords' points with each other, hating and condemning one another quite as cordially as they do the enemy . . . half a dozen at least are intriguing with a view to the next presidential nomination."[34] When Pope blamed everything on a conspiracy of subordinates following McClellan's orders, newspaper readers sensed an attempt to cover up Pope's own incompetence. The verbal artillery fired at Porter raised sympathy for Porter, who had not had a chance to answer. Above all, the matter became a case in the heated tribunal of politics. Pope, symbolizing the Republicans, looked as if he were trying to pin the blame for failure, as well as charges of treason, on the Democrats, symbolized by McClellan and Porter. What followed in the newspapers and elsewhere became a party tug of war in which what actually happened on August 29, and its consequences, became almost irrelevant.

Newspaper editors divided along political lines. When Pope's preliminary report appeared, the *Philadelphia Public Ledger* called it "singularly ill-timed" and no more than "Pope's budget of excuses and accusations."[35] Not so, said the *Chicago Tribune,* contrasting Pope's call for judicial process with S. L. M. Barlow's call to his friend McClellan to take charge of the country and replace unfriendly cabinet members.[36] If some reporters shrugged off the whole campaign as an example of "poor generalship,"[37] most of them took the trouble to go into some analysis, although the choice of targets fell largely along party lines.

A Democratic writer, for instance, wrote that Pope was able but overconfident, should have known that Jackson was getting reinforced, never seemed to know or care where the enemy was, brushed off warnings of enemy approach, and gave almost no orders, which left even corps commanders ignorant of the battle plan, what units were on right or left, and who was in support and reserve.[38] A Republican writer stressed Pope's handicaps: delay on McClellan's part in embarking the Army of the Potomac, resulting withdrawal of Pope from the Rapidan to the Rappahannock, McClellan's further delay in sending out Second and Sixth Corps, Army of the Potomac, which left Manassas Junction unguarded and made Jackson's attack possible.[39] Whatever their politics, however, readers knew that Pope withdrew within the Washington defenses and that Lee's army marched around Washington almost unopposed on its way north. Newspapers largely agreed that Pope had put the capital in jeopardy. It was the win-or-lose judgment of war: Pope's excuses might be convincing, Pope might deserve sympathy, but rebels were nevertheless marching north.

A teasing undercurrent runs through the diary of Gideon Welles, who thought he saw a conspiracy of Chase and Stanton smashed when Pope failed to hold the field. As Welles saw it, Chase and Stanton wanted to persuade Lincoln to replace McClellan with Pope. With Pope in command the two conspirators could control the army for their purposes, whatever those might be. Pope was Chase's protégé, solidly in command under General-in-Chief Halleck, who was in a sense Pope's protégé. In June 1862 Lincoln could have been amenable to such a plan. He was losing his patience with McClellan. He was willing to summon Pope to Washington, probably on Chase's recommendation, willing to summon Halleck to Washington on Pope's recommendation, willing to recall McClellan from the Peninsula on Halleck's recommendation, and willing to allow the transfer of the Army of the Potomac to the Army of Virginia in the guise of reinforcements. When Pope's army collapsed, the conspiracy fell to pieces.[40] Welles asserted, "The defeat of Pope and placing McC in command of the retreating and disorganized forces after the second disaster at Bull Run interrupted the intrigue which had been planned for the dismissal of McClellan, and was not only a triumph for him but a severe mortification and disappointment for both Stanton and Chase."[41]

There is no proof or corroboration of ulterior aims for Chase and Stanton, but Chase's personality and his known part in other intrigues make such an idea a reasonable deduction. Chase thirsted after presidential power and thought Lincoln poorly equipped to be president. Even if Chase did not think of becoming an army-supported dictator, he could hold real power in the Republican party if he controlled an army commanded by a Republican who owed his command to Chase. A bloc of some 100,000 or more armed voters certainly offered temptation to a seasoned political infighter. Other infighters proved the level of intrigue was high. McClellan showed that a general with political shrewdness could make an army into a powerful political bloc and S. L. M. Barlow's invitation to McClellan to march in and take over[42] was not the only such invitation at the time: Jefferson Davis was also invited to take over the Confederacy.

Si qua fata sinant. The fates, however, sent Pope to meet Jackson,

Longstreet to join Jackson, and the Army of Virginia back to Washington in tatters. In the end Lincoln postponed issuing his Emancipation Proclamation, British and French politicians continued to talk about armed intervention, and in the general elections of November 1862 American voters returned more Democrats to office in the North than they did in 1860. The country could trace this in part to what Pope described as "a campaign . . . which has been misunderstood to an extent perhaps unparalleled in the history of warfare."[43]

NOTES

1. D. Taylor to V. B. Horton, Aug. 30, 1871; endorsed as "probably" correct by Salmon P. Chase, Dec. 5, 1871, Salmon P. Chase Papers, Ohio Historical Society, Columbus.
2. David Donald, ed., *Inside Lincoln's Cabinet: The Civil War Diaries of Salmon P. Chase* (New York, 1954), 117.
3. John T. Morse, Jr., ed., *Diary of Gideon Welles, Secretary of the Navy under Lincoln and Johnson,* 3 vols. (Boston, 1911), 1:94.
4. Ibid., 1:104–5.
5. Ibid., 1:114.
6. John Pope, Preliminary Report, Sept. 3, 1862, OR XII, part 2:12–17.
7. Morse, 1:109–10.
8. Donald, 121; Morse, 1:110–11.
9. Morse, 1:107.
10. Draft Order, War Department, Washington, Sept. 5, 1862, signed Abraham Lincoln, RG 153 NA.
11. SO 122, AGO, Sept. 5, 1862, RG 153 NA.
12. Donald, 121.
13. Halleck to McClellan, Sept. 5, 1862, OR XII, part 3:811.
14. SO 223, AGO, Sept. 5, 1862, RG 94 NA.
15. See Halleck to Pope, Sept. 1, 1862, OR XII, part 2:82.
16. Pope to Halleck, Sept. 5, 1862, OR XII, part 3:812.
17. Halleck to Pope, Sept. 5, 1862, OR XII, part 3:812–13.
18. Donald, 123.
19. On August 18, 1862, a bloody uprising broke out among the Sioux in Minnesota.
20. Stanton to Pope, Sept. 6, 1862, OR XII, part 3:617.
21. Morse, 1:112.
22. Donald, 123.
23. Morse, 1:113.
24. Ibid., 1:116.
25. Ibid., 1:117.

26. See *Cincinnati Commercial Advertiser,* Sept. 11, 1862.
27. Research does not show any definite evidence that Pope was basically a liar. A habitual liar could never have held the important military commands that Pope did over so many years. The accuser, Montgomery Blair, did live some years in St. Louis, but he hardly could have known Pope very well because during most of this time Pope was far distant from that city, first in the Mexican War and afterward on the frontier. Blair's reputation for making derogatory remarks about public persons was well known around Washington. He was particularly hostile toward Chase and Stanton, and this feeling apparently extended to their friends. After four years in the cabinet as postmaster general, he resigned at Lincoln's request to keep peace in the cabinet.
28. Morse, 1:126.
29. Ibid., 1:107, 1:122.
30. John M. Schofield, *Forty-Six Years in the Army,* (New York, 1897), 359.
31. See *Philadelphia Public Ledger,* Sept. 11, 1862.
32. See *Cincinnati Enquirer,* Sept. 8, 1862.
33. See *Chicago Tribune,* Sept. 4, 1862.
34. See *Boston Evening Transcript,* Sept. 11, 1862.
35. See *Philadelphia Public Ledger,* Sept. 13, 1862.
36. See *Chicago Tribune,* Sept. 11, 1862.
37. See *New York Herald,* Sept. 8, 1862.
38. See *Cincinnati Enquirer,* Sept. 3, 8, 1862.
39. See *Boston Evening Transcript,* Sept. 3, 1862.
40. See Morse, 1:105, 1:107-9, 1:113, 1:119, 1:120-21.
41. Ibid., 1:108-9.
42. See *Chicago Tribune,* Sept. 11, 1862.
43. Pope, Final Report, OR XII, part 2:46.

Chapter Thirteen

JUDGMENT

ON SEPTEMBER 3 GENERAL JOHN POPE ended his Army of Virginia's campaign by leading his troops out of the field into the shelter of Washington's defense net. Robert E. Lee held the field and continued his northward march as far as Sharpsburg, Maryland. In the ordinary judgment of war Lee "won" and Pope "lost." In this campaign, however, the words *won* and *lost* hardly applied. The real question was whether Pope carried out his mission. His mission was never clear-cut. The only explicit detail was that Lincoln, Stanton, and Halleck did not send Pope out to meet Lee's Army of Northern Virginia and destroy it, although that misunderstanding somehow attached itself to the campaign.

In June 1862 Lincoln wanted Pope to keep Washington safe while McClellan fought at Richmond, wanted Pope to catch Jackson and Ewell, and, if all went well, wanted Pope to help McClellan at Richmond, perhaps using his Army of Virginia as the right wing of a great pincers movement.

McClellan's plan to take Richmond depended on the enemy's sitting still to await attack, but the Confederates attacked first and fought the Army of the Potomac to a standstill. Convinced that he was outnumbered, McClellan changed his base to Harrison's Landing, where he sat refusing to attack again unless reinforced. Lincoln, Stanton, Halleck, and Pope thought the requests for reinforcements wildly overstated and decided that the best thing to do was to bring McClellan's army back to Washington to start over. Pope's original mission became obsolete, so he simply sparred for time by drawing Confederate troops away from Richmond where they could attack McClellan before he got his soldiers safely aboard their transports. This meant the chance of facing the whole Confederate army, which outnumbered Pope two to one. If not heavily reinforced, Pope could not risk attacking anything. Halleck promised to send Pope reinforcements that could only come from the returning Army of the Potomac, a fact which in turn muddled the command problem. Halleck also added the new campaign requirement of keeping communciations open with Fredericksburg at all costs, which severely limited Pope's maneuvering power.

Lincoln never modified or withdrew his June order that called for Pope to catch Jackson and Ewell, or, for that matter, to join McClellan at Richmond. Lincoln also left two very big questions open. Who would command when Pope's army joined McClellan's? What would follow when the two armies came together at Richmond or Washington? Other underlying questions were never answered either. Should Lincoln and Halleck have ordered McClellan to bring his army back to Washington? Should Pope have gone farther south than Culpeper after being held in Washington for more than a month?

Pope recommended McClellan's return from the peninsula and so was in no position to complain when he was saddled with the consequences. Lincoln, Stanton, and Halleck all knew that Pope meant to march to the Rapidan when he left Washington, but they mentioned nothing about going farther south. Pope may have drawn his assignment out a little by relying on Lincoln's June order to catch Jackson and Ewell, who were moving north again when Pope went out at the end of July. Even his harshest critics would have to admit that Pope carried out a mission. While McClellan languidly withdrew from the peninsula, Pope drew Confederate troops away from the Potomac and held them off to the gates of Washington. McClellan then took command of all the troops and marched off after Lee, which may have been what Lincoln had in mind in the first place. Pope's campaign did trim the Confederate Army of Northern Virginia by 10,000 in casualties.[1] Pope's army was able to reinforce the Army of the Potomac by contributing its Second and Third Corps and the Pennsylvania Reserves to the Antietam campaign after only a few days' rest.[2] The Second Battle of Bull Run, which Pope "lost beyond doubt," has tended to overshadow the full-length campaign.

On August 26 Pope had been in the field for four weeks and was doing a good job of holding the Confederates back at the Rappan-hannock in spite of having lost combat use of Second Corps at Cedar Mountain. Then Longstreet and Jackson began Lee's plan of a flanking movement leading to a trap. Jackson raided Manassas Junction and cut Pope's communications with Washington. If, said Pope, McClellan had started his withdrawal on time and had sent Second and Sixth Corps, Army of the Potomac, forward from Alexandria, and if Pope's subordinates had carried out orders, Jackson could never have made his disruptive attack. Despite Pope's assertions he did go out of his way to insult McClellan repeatedly and if he thought about it, could look for nothing but grudging and indifferent help from him. Pope took no steps to see that subordinates carried out orders even though he had at least two days' warning of a coming raid. Pope even watched Jackson's march but drew a wrong conclusion. He heard nothing from his own troops who met the marchers and fought them; he had not set up a proper network for channeling information. When Jackson's raid took place and cut Pope off, Pope had several choices. He could speed north, reopen communications, and turn about, but that would have cost him his chance to trap Jackson, although it was probably the wisest move, or he could go after Jackson. He seems to have tried both at once. Sound military practice said that no commander should pass up a reasonable chance to destroy the enemy. He could attack Longstreet but he did not interpret Jackson's flank march quickly enough.

On August 29, in spite of his own shortcomings, in spite of hindrances and delays, in spite of his ill-assorted makeshift army, in spite of Halleck's uselessness, in spite of McClellan's failure to get Second and Sixth Corps, Army of the Potomac, to the battlefield, Pope nevertheless had his troops fighting at 6:30 A.M. and kept heavy pressure on Jackson the rest of the day. By midafternoon Jackson's left began to give way. A hard blow on Jackson's right would win the battle.

In spite of an indefinite order, Porter was in position near Gainesville where Jackson's right rested and where Porter could see and hear the battle. He deliberately put his troops in the woods and sat the battle out, ignoring a direct order to attack. Longstreet had time to join Jackson and Pope lost his moment of advantage. If Porter had attacked when he should have, Jackson's line would have collapsed and Pope would have won his battle.[3] The real cause of the lost battle was Porter's inaction, and the real cause of his inaction was almost certainly a tacit understanding among the Democrats of the Army of the Potomac not to allow Pope a victory that would make him overshadow the Democrat's idol, McClellan. Pope had fanned the political flames, but even so had a right to expect that no major general would disobey a direct order to attack issued by his commander during the course of a battle.

Porter argued after the event that if he had moved his corps forward he would have sent it to useless destruction because Longstreet had arrived by noon and could have cut Porter's corps with enfilading fire. What time Longstreet did arrive is still unknown and will probably remain unknown. Pope said it made no difference; Porter said it made all the difference; it is still unknown at what time Longstreet arrived.[4] Pope's argument that Porter should have tested the enemy's strength in front of him seems a better military procedure than Porter's inactivity and subsequent rationalization.

It seems fair to Pope to agree that he lost his critical battle through Porter's inaction, and that in spite of this loss he managed his campaign with at least enough success to allow another commander to carry on. The capital was in serious danger, but, at least in part thanks to Pope, not lost. Historians will always debate the military wisdom of calling the Army of the Potomac back from Harrison's Landing instead of replacing McClellan as commander. Pope will always have to bear his share of the blame for enthusiastically recommending the withdrawal that set the whole chain of events in motion.

Pope had admitted shortcomings as a general. He seems to have had only a rudimentary system for collecting field intelligence and no procedures at all for keeping in touch with the enemy. He wrote florid orders that provoked snickers, using phrases like "the first dawn of day," and that were at times dangerously misunderstood. He saw orders as self-executing and rarely bothered to see if anyone obeyed. Pope must have relied heavily on army routine, which was generally reliable, but his risky position called for more than routine precautions.

Even at the summit of his career the personal John Pope is dim. No one ever knew much about how he felt on becoming a general, on getting married, on facing the enemy, on entering Washington's social circle. In public life he spent most of his time smugly explaining how wrong everything was and how easily he could set it right. Pope recedes in history as a kind of two-dimensional figure that poses while roaring and swearing ever more faintly until it disappears.

A reporter caught him at close range just before he began to fade. The general was in full dress uniform, wearing a formal sword, seated in a rocking chair in a second floor parlor over a restaurant near Fourteenth Street and Pennsylvania Avenue in Washington. He was taking great pleasure in testifying for the prosecution before the general court-martial trying Fitz John Porter. For once Pope found himself in a completely agreeable setting. The court was made up of friendly Republicans, including future president James A. Garfield and Judge Advocate Joseph Holt, who later prosecuted the Lincoln conspirators and who, as a onetime Democrat now turned Republican, had all the zeal of a convert.

The reporter caught Pope

leaning backwards, and when not in the act of answering a question, rocking himself assiduously. He is a singularly round and heavy little man. His face is round—round as an apple—and surrounded by a heavy growth of beard and hair; his head is round—his body is round. His voice is a tolerable tenor, with a streak of harshness in it, over which his words, uttered pleasantly enough, have to be rasped as they go. His smile commences pleasantly, but subsides into a sneer, or, rather, perhaps, into quick indifference. His whole appearance would indicate that he is on good terms with self, morally and physically, and that if he should do anything wrong, he would not be unlikely to suspect some one else was chiefly to blame. He talks rapidly, and is rather fond of it, as an exercise or diversion. He uses language with good discrimination of words. His cross-examination has been a very severe ordeal, and he has stood fire well.[5]

The public Pope gave this impression of smug self-satisfaction and condescension.

No one could question his courage. He proved it in the face of the enemy at Monterrey, Buena Vista, and New Madrid, at Cedar Mountain and Bull Run. David Strother, his Virginia topographer, was surprised to find him bright, well-read, curious, with a memory like a blotter. Pope's reports of the 1850s showed how far afield his curiosity could take him.

He was certainly ambitious. Even as a green lieutenant he wanted big assignments and asked for them: to Col. Stephen H. Long's exploring parties, for command of a Chicago depot. Moving easily in the path of his family's political ties, he called on politicians when he needed them and emphasized his political alignment when it suited his ambitions. He cultivated Governor Yates of Illinois and Lincoln, Chase, and Stanton. He took extra care to stay on good terms with his rich father-in-law, who was a representative from Ohio, member of the House Ways and Means Committee, and friend of Salmon P. Chase.

Pope did have a rarely seen private side. Strother noted him as a lively storyteller, cheerful and easy when off duty. On the way to Washington in 1861 Pope and his former commanding officer Sumner kept the weary president-elect and the whole Lincoln train amused with yarns new even to the Rail-Splitter. After being nearly captured at the Battle of Cedar Mountain, Pope was found sitting on a rail fence talking and joking with his three corps commanders, Banks, McDowell, and Sigel. It was in Pope's inheritance to posture, roar, and forget about discretion: he was Judge Nathaniel Pope's son. Always sure of being right, he saw no point in holding back disagreeable truths about others. He touched off Colonel Abert's wrath by criticizing Fremont; he nearly had to face a court-martial for criticizing President Buchanan; he brought ruin on himself by criticizing McClellan.

Some of this conceit carried into Pope's style of command. He gave commands, then stood aside. He assumed that subordinates could see to details because it was their duty to obey. If anything went wrong, someone else was at fault. Such an outlook led Pope to underrate his enemy, get careless, and fall into traps. Since Pope had an unbroken string of victories without casualty lists, he got used to victories and assumed that they would keep coming. In fact, his victories in Missouri, New Madrid, and Corinth were only minor skirmishes. Even granting the excellence of his plans at Island No. 10, he faced an enemy in an exposed position, outnumbered, looking for ways of escape. Pope's aggressiveness and belief in the attack came from this same assumption of superiority. Preparation could take care of itself. Even while extraordinarily successful generals like Napoleon made careful plans to mass forces at the enemy's weak points and made sure of temporary superiority at the point of attack, Pope seemed to think he could win by instinct and that his subordinates would know instinctively what he had in mind. He did make a careful plan for the second day at Bull Run, but without knowing where the enemy was. None of these traits—brains, ambition, pride, curiosity, plain-speaking, wire-pulling, braggadocio, even a little rashness and carelessness—necessarily made a bad general; Patton and MacArthur prove that. Pope, however, had some unequivocally unfavorable traits as well.

His worst trait was his vanity, which compounded most of his other bad characteristics: smugness, self-righteousness, contempt, and carelessness. His enemies must have enjoyed hearing about Stuart's soldiers carrying off Pope's dress uniform. What was a general in the field doing with a dress uniform? His vanity also led to foolish actions. Longstreet remembered how Lee assessed Pope as a general who had such contempt for the enemy that he would gallop into an enemy trap while denying that the enemy had enough wit to set one. When Pope openly and vainly attacked McClellan in speaking to the House of Representatives and the Joint Committee on Conduct of the War, he made his standing a challenge and set himself up as a target for the Democrats. Grant, too, had political backers and political affiliations but managed to keep them out of newspaper range.

Pope's service record reflected his main weaknesses. As Pope well knew, an army can only work through routine and discipline, and discipline called for routing military affairs through military channels so that each level of command knew what was going on. Pope ignored channels, which, as his commanding officers rightly complained, meant that he called on the nonmilitary to exercise military command functions.

He also went out of his way to write up as separate "memoirs" several accounts of what he did individually on assignments commanded by others and in which others took part. After getting rapped on the knuckles for doing this in 1845, he might have realized that it irked his superiors, but he did it again in 1849 and 1851. Since his memoirs strayed into extraneous fields and sometimes gave sharp digs at army officers, a reviewer might well question whether the writer had more in mind than spreading information: the memoirs tended to pounce on mistakes and oversights of others. Pope came out unblemished.

If Pope could have learned that people judge by impressions and not fundamentals, he would have saved himself some disappointments. Popularity called for shallow antics and sleight of hand that Pope thought beneath his dignity. Even so, he did not deserve his deliberate undercutting in the Virginia campaign, but his personality was such that he could never raise sympathy for himself after repeatedly causing resentment through his plain-speaking.

NOTES

1. "The Opposing Forces at the Second Bull Run, August 16th–September 2nd, 1862," in Robert Underwood Johnson and Clarence Clough Buel, eds., *Battles and Leaders of the Civil War,* 4 vols. (New York, 1887), 2:497, 2:500.

2. Third Corps, Army of Virginia, became First Corps, Army of the Potomac, under Maj. Gen. Joseph Hooker. Second Corps, Army of Virginia, became Twelfth Corps, Army of the Potomac, under Maj. Gen. Joseph K. F. Mansfield. The Pennsylvania Reserves became Third Division, First Corps, Army of the Potomac, under Brig. Gen. George G. Meade. See *Battles and Leaders,* 2:598–600.

3. Found as a fact by the Fitz John Porter court, OR XII, part 2, Supp.:1051.

4. See James Longstreet, "Our March against Pope," in *Battles and Leaders,* 2:518–19; see also "The Time of Longstreet's Arrival at Groveton" in *Battles and Leaders,* 2:527–28 and W. Roy Mason, "Marching on Manassas," in *Battles and Leaders,* 2:528–29.

5. *Milwaukee Sentinel,* Dec. 17, 1862.

PART 3

DOWNHILL

Chapter Fourteen

SIDETRACKS

IN POPE'S MIND HIS MILITARY career after 1862 was one long anticlimax caused by the Democrats' conspiracy that cost him a battle, a command, and a top place in the army hierarchy. In reality Pope spent twenty-four more productive years in the service in which he restored civil government to Missouri, took part in Reconstruction, was the army's chief expert in Indian affairs, advised on army reorganization and training, helped Western settlement, and wound up as a respected sage, public speaker, and even adviser to presidents. It was only in history books that Pope dropped out of sight; while he lived he was a very public figure. He may have refought the Second Battle of Bull Run more often than his hearers liked, but Fitz John Porter was always making public noises to remind Pope that Porter had betrayed him.

Packed off to his Minnesota banishment, Pope spent the rest of the Civil War largely as an onlooker who had to read about the great eastern campaigns in the newspapers. After arriving in St. Paul on September 15 Pope commanded his Department of the Northwest with energy and efficiency, but the war that he fought was not the war that he left. A few thousand Indians hardly offered the military challenge of matching wits with West Pointers.

Eight days after Pope reached Minnesota, Colonel Henry H. Sibley with troops of the Third, Sixth, and Seventh Minnesota regiments took care of the Sioux in a pitched battle at Wood Lake, Minnesota,[1] leaving Pope only the duty of setting up federal garrisons at key spots to guard outlying settlements and posting border detachments to keep the Sioux in Dakota Territory from sneaking into Minnesota to reinforce their kin. On December 26 the Sioux

War that brought Pope to Minnesota ended at Mankato, Minnesota, in the army-supervised mass hanging of thirty-eight warriors convicted of atrocities. In a statement that would later seem wildly out of character Pope swore "utterly to exterminate the Sioux"[2] and in 1863 and 1864 planned and directed field campaigns against the Sioux in Dakota in which he seemed dedicated to putting his policy into effect.

In exile Pope obeyed orders like a soldier and gave his best to the distasteful assignment given him, but he nevertheless exercised the soldiers' right to gripe. In his first month in Minnesota he seemed to his adjutant a "bear with a sore head" who was "ambitiously crazy, imagines himself the most talented general in the world and the one most wronged."[3] To Pope, Lincoln was a demon who let him down and then stripped him of honor. The president could have spoken out in Pope's defense but instead hid behind political expediency. Pope wrote of "the feeble, cowardly, and shameful conduct of Lincoln" who had "sold himself or given himself away to the Devil or something worse."[4] When Pope's father-in-law tried to assure Pope that Lincoln was still Pope's friend, Pope snarled,

> He has suffered me to be traduced and maligned for months, he has allowed the falsest and grossest slander to be circulated to the discredit of my personal and professional character, knowing all the while how false it is and yet how much it was injuring me and he has said no word nor permitted me to say a word in my defense. . . . His very professed friendship makes silence conclusive against me. . . . If Lincoln be my friend, I pray to God that I never have such another.[5]

Halleck was another demon, and to Pope a particularly ungrateful one, after Pope had helped him reach general-in-chief. Lincoln was above attack, but Pope plunged into a paper battle with Halleck, charging Halleck with failing to come to Pope's rescue, being soft with McClellan's treachery, and underhandedly planning Pope's banishment to Minnesota. With the distance between them the battle came to a draw, but Halleck had to admit that the newspapers had been roasting him for the very things that Pope charged him with.[6] Like many other sidetracked commanders, Pope wrote copiously in hopes that some reader might help return him to high command. In his own department he outwitted efforts of the

Democrats to have him replaced,[7] and he courted the spotlight as champion of civil liberties when he refused to let the army enforce the Draft Act against Wisconsin rioters, saying, "I have steadily declined to permit the use of any of the troops under my command unless I could be convinced that all other legitimate means had been tried without success. People should not surrender Civil Law to military force. Such, of course, would lead to the complete domination of the military and final overthrow of free institutions."[8]

Reflecting on slow Union progress, Pope also put forward his concept of war as the Union should fight it, with hard blows struck by an iron hand, untempered with the gallantry, chivalry, or promises of forgiveness that Lincoln liked to appear to be recommending. "War means desolation and death, and it is neither humanity nor wisdom to carry it out upon any other theory. The more bitter it is made for the delinquents, the sooner it will end."[9] He wrote two long letters on strategy and military policy to Chase, whom he still thought a sincere and influential friend. In one written on April 22, 1863, he laid out how to apply his theory of war to command and strategy. The Union Army, Pope said, suffered from territorial aims and separate commands. Proper conduct of the war called for a supreme commander "untrammeled by instructions" who should fight against armies, not places, and who should maneuver or force all the Confederate armies to come together at one point where Union forces could fall on them and destroy them. He ended with a proper reminder: "In answer to your request that I should suggest some appropriate command and field of operations for myself, I have only to reply, that I am sure you know that at all times, and in any position, I stand ready to serve the country with zeal and fidelity."[10]

In a letter written on June 15, Pope addressed the use of black soldiers. Chase wanted black soldiers under black officers to garrison the Southern states when conquered. Pope advised that the army could use black soldiers, but for the present only under white officers. He also warned Chase against showing such extraordinary fondness for blacks if he still had political ambitions. Chase was, Pope wrote, "by far the most prominent and powerful member of the Government" and should not jeopardize his future by monomania for the black cause, which would lose him most of the votes in the Northwest. At the end of this letter, too, Pope came back to his real theme: "We need one head to our military operations in the West. We are embarrassed and almost paralyzed by these independent armies and unharmonious operations."[11] Chase had both letters printed and circulated, and Pope was not the only person to recommend unified command. Lincoln understood this need and picked Grant as lieutenant general and supreme commander on March 9, 1864.

In other letters that reflected his experience with Indians in New Mexico in the 1850s and in Minnesota in the recent Sioux War, Pope outlined ideas that he would preach until his retirement and that won him the title of the Army's Indian expert. Pope stressed that Americans must see the Indians as simply other American citizens who had to obey the law too. The tribes were not "nations" entitled to "treaties" approved by a possibly corrupt Senate and carried out by a certainly corrupt Bureau of Indian Affairs. The United States should not pay bounties. Whites only swindled Indians out of their bounty and made them angry enough to attack. The army had to have control of all tribes, otherwise even a peaceful tribe might become hostile if it was more profitable to do so.

The only lasting way to handle them, Pope said, was to round them up, disarm them, support them at government cost, and expose them to "Christianity and education." Instead of putting them on Western reservations in the path of wagon trains and certain trouble, the government should relocate them near settled areas in the East. With proper government support the tribes would not need their hunting grounds and, living close to villages and cities, could learn the ways of whites and merge gradually into nearby communities.[12] Stanton agreed and also had Pope's letter to him printed and circulated. In the late 1860s some of Pope's ideas came close to adoption, but public interest waned as the Indian Wars came to an end, and in the 1880s Pope could only look back on his recommendations, a little ruefully, as prescriptions for a Land of Might-Have-Been.

Pope's essays were fruits of exile written to pass time. The sore head healed gradually. Pope's wife joined him. Their third child, Horton, was born in Milwaukee. Following Pope's plans, efficient and obedient field commanders carried out punitive campaigns against the Sioux. The war in the East gradually turned in favor of the Union. On July 4, 1863, Meade turned the Confederates back at Gettysburg and Grant cleared the Mississippi at Vicksburg. Foreign intervention was no longer a menace. By the end of 1864 Union forces occupied a large part of the Confederacy. Pope's old enemy McClellan was defeated as a candidate for the presidency. Sherman was on his way to the Carolinas after reaching the sea. As early as April Pope's friend Senator Lyman Trumbull of Illinois introduced into the Senate a thirteenth amendment ending slavery.

Toward the end of 1864 Pope received an unexpected telegram from Halleck ordering him to report to the War Department in person. On November 30, sitting across from Grant in City Point, Virginia, Pope learned that he would now command the new Military Division of the Missouri, with headquarters at St. Louis.[13] His banishment had come to an end. Pope liked the assignment. He had strong personal ties with St. Louis, and he might command another field army base there. Confederate General Edmund Kirby Smith, who headed the Trans-Mississippi Department, still had soldiers in the field in Arkansas, Louisiana, and Texas. Despite Grant's success in Virginia, the Union command could not ignore armed forces in the West.

On February 3, 1865, Pope assumed command of his military division, which was the largest Union territorial command, covering Iowa, Kansas, Minnesota, Missouri, and Wisconsin, the territories of Colorado, Nebraska, and Utah, and the Dakota Territory east of the Missouri River.[14] Pope found his most urgent problem in Missouri. The state was free of Confederate troops but still under martial law as proclaimed by Fremont in 1861. No civil courts were open. Military provost marshals took charge of a rough kind of justice in which they acted as prosecutors, judges, and juries. What seemed worse to Pope and Governor Thomas C. Fletcher was that the citizens of Missouri seemed content to let this system go on since the United States paid for it and relieved Missouri of the expense of sheriffs, police, and courts.

At Lincoln's request Pope investigated the system. He wrote a letter to Governor Fletcher restating his belief in superiority of civil government over the military and promising to take the army out of law enforcement as soon as Missourians showed themselves willing to assume this duty again.[15] On March 7, 1865, the governor issued a proclamation calling on the civil courts to open.[16] Pope then issued a special order recalling the army from judicial duties in any county with open civil courts.[17] Lincoln confirmed all proceedings in a letter of March 19.[18] The result was to bring Missouri, a onetime slave state, back into the Union on its old footing without undergoing the agonies of military reconstruction then in the planning stages for former Confederate states. Pope deserves the credit for supervising this painless transition.

With this done, Pope turned to his plans for smashing the trans-Mississippi Confederates as Grant had ordered.[19] By April 8 Pope had completed plans for a campaign based in Little Rock, Arkansas. Thirty thousand troops would cut across country to Marshall, Texas, a Confederate supply depot, and then south to Houston and Galveston.[20] Pope had already requisitioned cavalry horses when news came that Lee had surrendered at Appomattox on April 9.[21] The Civil War was almost over. Pope abandoned plans for his campaign, writing Grant, "It is more than likely that when this news reaches Kirby Smith's army they will disperse to their homes."[22] For the next month Pope concentrated on getting the remaining Confederate forces to surrender, reminding the commanders that a Confederate government no longer existed and that if they remained in the field they risked being classed as freebooters, armed soldiers acting under no recognized command and thus not entitled to terms.[23] Kirby Smith finally surrendered the last Confederate field forces to General E. R. S. Canby at Galveston, Texas, on June 2.[24]

At the war's end Pope found himself a brigadier general in the regular army,[25] but in a topheavy army speedily running out of enlistees. Painful readjustment had to follow the change to peacetime; Pope at least had the satisfaction of being replaced by a leading figure. General William T. Sherman, not a favorite of President Johnson and a Washington-hater, took command of the Military Division of the Missouri. On June 27 Pope stepped down to become Sherman's subordinate.[26] Pope took it well. He would have done the same if he were in Sherman's place; it was the army game. At the welcoming banquet for Sherman, Pope was the principal speaker and to great applause summed up the conduct of the war in terms that greatly appealed to his new chief: "This has been emphatically the people's war. Had its prosecution been left to the politicians and political leaders, either in the civil or military service, it is safe to say that it would long since have been ended in disgrace or ruin."[27]

As the pacified nation threw much of its energy into settling and developing the West, more problems with Indians developed. While Pope still thought of them as objects of punishment for past misdeeds and oversaw further punitive expeditions against them in 1865 and 1866, he also thought that this time of postwar reorganization might be suitable to get official approval of his long-range solution. Grant was satisfied with Pope's acts in Missouri, agreed with Pope that the army should have full charge of all tribes, and was willing to help Pope put his views forward in political circles.[28] In June 1865, while the Lincoln conspiracy trials caught most people's attention, Pope, Grant, and Secretary of War Stanton met quietly in Washington with Secretary of the Interior James Harlan.[29] Pope argued that the United States must end the practices of making "treaties" and awarding bounties, and that since the army had to face the hostile tribes, which were no longer easily identifiable, it should in all justice control all the tribes on and off reservations. Although no minutes of the meeting survive, Stanton and Grant must have agreed with Pope's arguments.

Unfortunately, Secretary Harlan replied, no executive officers but the president could change the treaty system. Representatives of the British Crown had begun it, and President Washington had continued it, so Secretary Harlan could not order it abandoned. Control of all tribes came under existing law, which the secretary of the interior was also powerless to change or disregard.[30] The matter was settled for the moment.

Pope, always busy, turned to another problem that he could handle himself. At the war's end the number of wagon trains heading West grew into a sizeable stream. No matter what trails the wagons took, they ran across Indians. After the Sand Creek Massacre of 1864 travelers could assume that the Plains Indians would be hostile. Pope had had success in enforcing emigrant regulations in his Department of the Northwest. Since wagons got through safely there, he felt that the same system would work in the Department of the Missouri. In 1865 he modified his earlier plan and embodied the newer system in a general order allowing wagon trains to cross his department only if they had at least 20 wagons, 100 able-bodied men, and 20 armed men, and if they reported at the two check points of Fort Riley and Fort Kearney.[31] Pope's regulations stayed in force until the railroads took over westward travel.[32]

In August 1866 Pope knew that he was about to be replaced and transferred. A private plea to Grant saved him from going to the "remote region" of Oregon,[33] but all the wire-pulling that he could do, including personal requests to Stanton, Grant, and Senator Orville H. Browning, and his emphasis that he was well-qualified as an "officer of high rank . . . and had seen service in the war"[34] could not get him the appointment that he really wanted, superintendent of the United States Military Academy at West Point.[35] On August 6 General Winfield Scott Hancock, a hero of Gettysburg and a Democrat, replaced Pope, and on September 1 Pope was mustered out of the service as a major general of volunteers and given extended leave until April 1, 1867.[36] He was still a permanent brigadier general in the regular army, one of ten brigadier generals confirmed and continued in the Army Reorganization Act of 1866.[37]

Although he spent his extended leave at his wife's family's home in Pomeroy, Ohio, Pope kept in touch with current matters. A bill transferring the Bureau of Indian Affairs from the Department of the Interior to the War Department was on its way through Congress at last. Grant favored the bill, as did most senior army officers, and had Pope prepare for him a long state paper written in the form of a report on the "Fetterman Massacre" that took place on the Bozeman Trail in 1866. After repeating his now familiar arguments and pointing out flatly that no one became an Indian agent under the Bureau of Indian Affairs unless he or she wanted to take the money and property issued to Indians in consequence of "treaties," Pope ended his report somberly,

> I have repeatedly warned the government that the Indian war now upon us was inevitable, and that no reliance whatever could be placed upon treaties of peace such as had been negotiated. The peace commissioners promise the Indian, in the first place, that the whites shall not go into the Indian country knowing full well that it is impossible to fulfill such a promise. This is the first and most persistent demand of the Indians, a demand readily conceded but never executed. . . . The Indian has lost confidence in such promises, and only makes a treaty to secure the money and supplies which accompany it. In this unscrupulous manner treaties are made and violated on both sides.[38]

Grant endorsed Pope's report and forwarded it to member of Congress Robert C. Schenck of Ohio, chairman of the House Military Affairs Committee and a former brigadier general of volunteers who served in Pope's Virginia campaign. In spite of its distinguished backing, the bill failed to pass. Too many members of Congress had constituents who needed jobs in the Bureau of Indian Affairs. Pope could only shrug his shoulders and say, "I told you so" when the next Indian outbreak came. He would never come closer to having his system enacted into law.

NOTES

1. Kenneth Carley, "The Sioux Uprising of 1862," Minnesota Historical Society, St. Paul, 1976, 62.
2. Pope to Henry H. Sibley, Sept. 28, 1862, OR XIII: 685–86.
3. Speed Butler to William Butler, Oct. 5, 1862, John Pope Papers, Chicago Historical Society, Chicago, Ill.
4. Pope to William Butler, Sept. 26, 1862, John Pope Papers, Chicago.
5. Pope to Valentine B. Horton, Mar. 9, 1863, Manning F. Force Papers, University of Washington Libraries, Seattle, Wash.
6. Pope to Halleck, Sept. 30, 1862, OR XII, part 2:816–19; Halleck to Pope, Oct. 10, 1862, OR XII, part 3:819–20; Pope to Halleck, Oct. 20, 1862, OR XII, part 3:820–23; Pope to Halleck, Oct. 30, 1862, OR XII, part 3:823–24; Halleck to Pope, Nov. 7, 1862, OR XII, part 3:824; Pope to Halleck, Nov. 20, 1862, OR XII, part 3:825–26; Pope to Halleck, Dec. 3, 1862, OR XII, part 3:826–27.
7. Former Sen. Henry M. Rice and Sen. Morton P. Wilkinson criticized Pope's acts in Minnesota sharply and tried to use their influence to get him removed. Pope to Stanton, Aug. 29, 1863, OR XXII, part 2:493–95; Samuel Miller to Pope, Aug. 24, 1863, OR XXII, part 2:495.
8. Pope to Edward Salomon, June 25, 1864, New York Historical Society, New York.
9. Pope to Richard Yates, Sept. 21, 1862, John Pope Papers, Illinois State Historical Library, Springfield, Ill.
10. Pope to Chase, April 22, 1863, Henry E. Huntington Library, San Marino, Calif.
11. Pope to Chase, June 15, 1863, Henry E. Huntington Library.
12. Pope to Stanton, Aug. 29, 1863, OR XXII, part 2:494; Alfred Sully to AAG, Dept. of the Northwest, Nov. 22, 1864, OR XLI, part 4: 651–52; Pope to J. C. Kelton, AAG, Jan. 12, 1864, OR XXXIV, part 2:69–70. See also St. Paul Daily Press, Dec. 4, 1862. See also Pope to Stanton, Feb. 6, 1864, OR XXXIV, part 3:159, and Halleck to Pope, Apr. 14, 1864, OR XXXIV, part 3:159. For a full study of

Pope's policy, see Richard N. Ellis, *General Pope and U.S. Indian Policy* (Albuquerque, 1970).

13. Grant to Halleck, Nov. 30, 1864, OR XLI, part 4:716.
14. GO 11, Div. of the Missouri, Feb. 3, 1865, OR XLVIII, part 1:734; GO 11, AGO, Jan. 30, 1865, OR XLVIII, 1:716.
15. "The Supremacy of the Law in Missouri," (pamphlet), Jefferson City, Mo., 1865.
16. Ibid., 3.
17. SO 15, Div. of the Missouri, Mar. 17, 1865, OR XLVIII, part 1:1202-3.
18. Lincoln to Pope, Mar. 19, 1865, OR XLVIII, part 1:1215.
19. Grant to Pope, Mar. 21, 1865, OR XLVIII, part 1:1128-29.
20. Pope to Grant, Apr. 8, 1865, OR XLVIII, part 2:53.
21. Pope to Halleck, Apr. 7, 1865, OR XLVIII, part 2:44.
22. Pope to Grant, Apr. 10, 1865, OR XLVIII, part 2:64.
23. Pope to Gen. Grenville Dodge, Apr. 25, 1865, OR XLVIII, part 2:192.
24. Instrument of Surrender, May 26, 1865, OR XLVIII, part 2:600-602.
25. Service Record, John Pope, RG 94 NA.
26. Ibid.
27. *St. Louis Missouri Republican*, July 22, 1865.
28. Pope to Grant, June 14, 1865, OR XLVIII, part 2:879-82; Grant to Pope, June 15, 1865, OR XLVIII, part 2:892
29. Pope to Grant, June 19, 1865, OR XLVIII, part 2:933; Pope to James Harlan, June 19, 1865, OR XLVIII, part 2:933-35.
30. Harlan to Pope, July 6, 1865, OR XLVIII, part 2:1056-58.
31. Ellis, 114-15, 118.
32. Ibid.
33. Pope to Browning, Aug. 28, 1866, John Pope Papers, Illinois State Historical Society, Springfield, Ill.
34. Ibid.
35. See Col. Adam Badeau to Pope, Sept. 21, 1866, "A change cannot be made in the Superintendency of the Military Academy at this time without detriment to the interests of the service," Ulysses S. Grant Papers, Library of Congress, Washington.
36. Service Record, John Pope, RG 94 NA.
37. Act of July 28, 1866, 14 Stat. 332.
38. Reports of the Secretaries of War and Interior, in Relation to the Massacre at Fort Phil Kearney, Washington, S. Ex. Doc. 13, 40th Cong., 1st Sess., 1867, 45-52.

Chapter Fifteen

MAINSTREAM

POPE'S EXTENDED LEAVE CAME to an end on April 15, 1867, when orders came appointing him commanding general of the Third Military District to be one of five district commanders charged with executing the new Reconstruction Acts.[1] After nearly two years of wrangling with President Johnson, who called the former Confederate states already reconstructed, the overwhelming Republican majority in Congress enacted statutes over the president's veto that set up a new reconstruction plan in the hands of Congress and the army.[2]

Pope had no enviable assignment at his headquarters in ruined Atlanta: he had to supervise a lengthy program of Reconstruction. This program included enrolling all adult males, including blacks, as voters; adopting state constitutions that abolished slavery, repudiated Confederate war debts, and guaranteed civil rights to blacks; and electing new state officers and a state legislature that must ratify the Fourteenth Amendment. He might hope for, but could not expect, cooperation of the white residents. It went without saying that congressional leaders wanted their army commanders to guide blacks into voting Republican and to disfranchise enough former Confederates to put state administrations comfortably in Republican hands. Loyalty oaths required of voters could take care of disfranchisement because commanders had power to accept or reject them. After all this, Congress might not even readmit the states to the Union on their old footing.

Pope agreed with the program as necessary to pursue the goals of a war fought not only to preserve the Union, but in the end to abolish slavery and to enfranchise blacks and make them citizens.

He therefore accepted the congressional premise that all state governments in the conquered South were tentative, temporary, subject to control under the laws of war, and only recognized for the time being as a convenience. There would be no elections for state or local office until a state went through the whole procedure: voter registration, election for constitutional convention, election ratifying constitution, election to state office, and ratification of the Fourteenth Amendment. Pope overrode elections held in spite of his orders[3] and went so far as to remove and replace all the city officials of Mobile, Pensacola, and Augusta for defiance of orders.[4] He also would have removed the governor of Georgia for denouncing the Reconstruction Acts if he had not apologized.[5] Moving briskly for civil rights, Pope put black voters on jury panels and removed a judge who refused to follow the order.[6] In words almost echoing Louis XIV, the governor of Georgia was told that Pope had power to make "such orders as I consider necessary" and that such orders had "all the force of law until they are modified or countermanded by higher authority."[7] Between April and December 1867, Pope removed 124 Alabama officials, 13 Florida officials, and 20 Georgia officials.[8]

The general had no visionary thoughts about the permanence of Reconstruction without army enforcement. "These politicians are wily and sagacious," he wrote. "They will make no laws which are not equal on their face to all men. It is in the execution of these laws, which seem to bear equally on all, that wrong will be done. . . . Social exclusion, withdrawal of business relations, open exhibitions of hostility, if not, indeed, actual hostile acts . . . these will be the weapons used against Union men and the colored race."[9]

Unhappily for district commanders their show of absolutism rested on anything but absolute power. They were sworn to carry out acts enacted by a Republican Congress over the president's veto, but the president was their commander-in-chief who could give them lawful orders. Yet the President was a Democrat who had served in the Senate and attended Democratic party caucuses in company with Southern leaders until 1861, and who repeatedly denounced these acts despite his constitutional duty to "take care that the laws be faithfully executed."[10] All this translated into a catastrophic dilemma. Disobeying the president could lead to trial

by court-martial for insubordination. Executing an unlawful statute
could lead to civil suits and ruinous damages, since soldiers as well
as civilians had to answer to the civil courts and could not plead the
unlawful orders of a superior in defense. Congress might make
restitution to the officer but only after trial, judgment, payment,
introduction of a special bill in the House of Representatives,
passage in the House, introduction in the Senate, passage in the
Senate, passage through a conference committee to resolve differ-
ences in House and Senate bills, repassage in House and Senate,
approval by the president, who might be quite another president by
that time, and, at last, issuance of a warrant to the treasurer of the
United States authorizing a check.

Pope and other district commanders found themselves tangled
in legalisms and acting at their own peril. If the Confederates could
secede as a matter of law, they created a separate nation and fought
and lost a "war," in which case military government was proper.
Otherwise, military government might be unconstitutional. The
administration in Washington could not as a matter of policy admit
the legality of secession, even if that policy undercut the military
government. President Johnson's proclamations of April 2, 1866,
and August 20, 1866, declaring hostilities at an end[11] made those
dates conclusive only for the end of fighting and had no effect on
whether what had just gone on was "war" or "rebellion" and when
it ended. On April 3 the Supreme Court, now headed by Pope's
friend Chase, decided that even in wartime a military court had no
jurisdiction to try a civilian if civil courts were open.[12] In 1867
federal and state courts were open in the South, but the Reconstruction plan depended on having provost courts and military commissions available as alternate tribunals if Southern judges proved
obstinate about civil rights.

Pope had hardly settled himself into Atlanta's National Hotel
before he found himself a defendant in an original proceeding in
the United States Supreme Court. Georgia's governor and others
had speedily tried to enjoin the president's agents[13] from enforcing
the Reconstruction Acts, calling them blatantly unconstitutional.
On May 13, 1867, the Court dismissed the petition as involving a
political question, shying away from such yet unanswered questions as whether Georgia was a state in 1867 or had in fact left the
Union and was subject to military government as conquered

territory.[14] It was a close call for Pope, who had been reconstructing with a heavy hand for a month before the Court gave its decision. Further complexities faced the district commanders. Congress and President Johnson were now fighting to the point that members of Congress were getting ready to begin impeachment proceedings. Then district commanders were forced to guess how the impeachment trial would turn out before they could decide whose orders to follow.

Pope knew that Johnson's old political cronies reported to the president every unpopular step taken by Pope and the other district commanders, and that Johnson listened to the complaints sympathetically. Pope also knew that Johnson received Southern deputations at the White House and openly denounced the Reconstruction Acts, both of which seriously undercut the district commanders and encouraged Southern resistance.

Attorney General Henry Stanbery, who drafted Johnson's veto message accompanying the Reconstruction Acts, issued an opinion that district commanders had no power to interfere in state administration unless state authorities asked for help.[15] This opinion would normally bind army officers, but Grant told Pope to ignore the opinion since the army carrying out Reconstruction was a congressional army created under the powers of Congress and not the "Army of the United States" described in the Constitution.[16] That left Pope forced to decide for himself who was right. Congress finally enacted a Third Reconstruction Act that identified the army carrying out Reconstruction as a congressional army, ratified everything the district commanders had done, and practically delivered the South into army hands. This act specified that no officer carrying out Reconstruction was bound by the opinion of any "civil officer of the United States."[17] When President Johnson learned that Stanton took part in drafting the act, he suspended Stanton as secretary of war and put Grant in his place; Grant still held his office of general-in-chief. Was Grant now a "civil officer of the United States" whose opinions district commanders could ignore? Was he commanding general of the Army of the United States or only the congressional army?

Toward the end of 1867 Pope could see the political turmoil getting worse as president, Congress, and now General Grant seemed intent on using Reconstruction for their own ends. Congress wanted

to use the president's failure to enforce the Reconstruction Acts as a
basis for impeachment. The president wanted to defend his action
by resting on the Constitution. Grant, who was now certain of
being the Republican candidate for president in the election of
1868, would take no steps that might harm his popularity. Suddenly the president moved to challenge congress by dismissing
General Dan Sickles and General Phil Sheridan as commanders of
the Second and Fifth Military Districts and replacing them with
reliable Democrats or politically indifferent generals.[18] This caught
the radical Republican leaders Senator Charles Sumner and Representative Thaddeus Stevens unprepared; they did nothing. Grant
also did nothing, but since he had not yet actually declared himself
a Republican, he may have decided to stay out of it. He did have
some inside information: on September 9 he wrote Pope that Pope
might be next.[19]

Pope could almost feel the blade since he had been even stricter
than Sheridan and Sickles, but he went ahead with his Georgia
Constitutional Convention and his plans for the coming convention in Florida. He was pleased with what he had been able to
accomplish so far and was particularly pleased with the speedy
progress made by blacks: "The social and political results of such a
change cannot fail to be important and to a great extent decisive of
the questions which we are seeking to solve."[20] Facing dismissal
after a brave but unrewarded eight months' fight to carry war aims
into practice against Southern sabotage and Northern indifference,
Pope was discouraged. He wrote Grant resignedly on his last day of
duty in Atlanta, "The indications are now that the managers of the
disloyal faction in the South will succeed in breaking down every
general who performs his duty."[21]

On December 27 Pope was relieved from command of the Third
Military District and assigned to command the Department of the
Lakes, with headquarters at Detroit.[22] Pope shrugged his shoulders
and departed. He had nearly completed his full assignments in all
three of his states and resented not being allowed to stay until the
new state governments emerged, but the champion of a Democratic army had to make concessions to politics. Shortly after assuming command Pope wrote Grant asking for reassignment to his old
Third Military District, hoping to see the conclusion of his plans
for state governments.[23] Grant did not reply. Pope assumed com-

mand at Detroit and began to carry out his new, obviously interim, assignment. In 1868 the Canadian border was almost as peaceful as in the twentieth century. The only military activity might come from the Fenians, an Irish group that in 1866 made two unsuccessful attacks on Canada from bases in the United States. As part of their plan to free Ireland from British rule, the Fenians hoped to seize Canada and hold it for ransom. The British could get Canada back only by releasing Irish prisoners held for anti-British acts. Rumors said that the Fenians might try again in 1870. The risk of such a foray was slight, but Pope felt compelled to investigate, hiring the Pinkerton Detective Agency to make an undercover investigation in the border towns of Michigan and Ontario. When a team of Irish Protestant detectives went through the area and reported nothing even after snooping into the basements of Catholic churches to look for concealed weapons, Pope was convinced that he had nothing "serious to be apprehended from Fenians on the frontier."[24]

Pope had little to do but shuffle papers about deserters, back pay, bounties, pensions, and discharges after his investigators proved the Fenians to be no trouble.[25] He was hoping for a change. Since Grant became president in 1869 and Sherman general-in-chief, the resulting promotions all along the line could mean a vacancy for Pope. On April 15, 1870, Pope was happy to be relieved from his command in Detroit and assigned once more to command his old Department of the Missouri from Fort Leavenworth.[26] He would spend thirteen years there, his longest tour of duty in one place, and he would leave there only for a short sunset tour in the West before his retirement.

He took command of his department on May 3, now as subordinate to General Philip Sheridan, who succeeded Sherman as commanding general of the Military Division of the Missouri.[27] Back at Fort Leavenworth Pope again faced problems with Indians. While continuing to disagree with the statutory scheme of divided control, he worked dutifully for resettlement, civilizing, and christianizing, handling the hostile tribes with his troops and leaving the peaceful ones to the Bureau of Indian Affairs. As Pope foresaw, split supervision only led to further trouble, and in the years between 1870 and 1883 four of the fourteen wars that Pope saw as inevitable took place within his Department of the Missouri.[28] Pope planned and supervised the army campaigns that brought them to their ends, although subordinates took the field, led the troops, and got the publicity.

The Red River War broke out in June 1874 when a band of Kiowas, Comanches, and Southern Cheyennes under Chief Quanah Parker attacked a party of trespassing white buffalo hunters in Texas. After a hard campaign on the plains that lasted through the winter, the army forced Parker and his warriors to surrender in April 1875.[29]

The Mexican Border Wars were sporadic outbreaks generally caused by name-calling between Mexicans and their Indian supporters and the Texas Rangers. In 1877 hostilities broke out when a Mexican mob executed three Texas Rangers who had surrendered. Pope called out the Ninth Cavalry, a black unit from New Mexico. The cavalry moved swiftly into Fort Bliss at El Paso and this episode in the war came to an abrupt end.[30]

In 1879 the usually peaceful Utes exploded after patiently enduring white trespassers on their mining lands for ten years. When Nathan Meeker, founder of the teetotaler cooperative settlement of Greeley, Colorado, became an Indian agent and tried to impose his ways on the Utes, they revolted, set forest fires, killed Meeker, and tore down the White River Reservation buildings. The Ninth Cavalry moved in again but this time only acted as wardens and overseers until in 1880 the Utes moved peacefully into their new Uintah Reservation.[31]

After 1880 only the Apaches still fought with America. Victorio had raided southwestern New Mexico in 1879 only to be put down by the Ninth Cavalry. When Victorio died in battle in 1880 Geronimo became chief and led the Chiricahuas in a lightning attack at Cibico Creek near Fort Apache, New Mexico. Pope called the troops from the Ute Reservation and from Fort Wingate near Gallup, New Mexico. The troops drove the Apaches away easily enough since, as Pope had noted thirty years earlier, pitched battles were not the Apache way. The Apache threat hovered over New Mexico and Arizona until Geronimo was cornered and surrendered in 1886.[32]

While trying to stay out of organized politics, John Pope knew that a lifetime in the army meant a lifetime of army politics that he could not afford to disregard. To get on in the service called for the same kind of log-rolling that advancement in Congress did. In 1872 Pope reached fifty. In 1872 Major General George G. Meade died and left a vacancy; the Army Act of 1869 allowed three major generals;[33] all ten of the brigadier generals began to deploy their influential troops. Pope got support from Ohioans. Judge Manning F. Force, his brother-in-law, and Rutherford B. Hayes, already a leading Republican politician, asked President Grant to appoint Pope. Ohio governor Edward F. Noyes and member of Congress Matthew C. Carpenter followed Force and Hayes, saying that Pope should have the place as compensation for the bad treatment given him during the war.[34] Unluckily for Pope, Brigadier General Irwin McDowell was older, was senior on the rank list, and even though a thoroughly inept general who never commanded troops after 1862, managed to rouse more public sympathy and support; he got the appointment. Even though Pope was not happy to be passed over, McDowell was still his friend. It would be the last such vacancy until 1882.

By 1876 the scandals of Grant's administration had given sensational copy to newspapers and had earned Grant the name of heading the most corrupt administration in American history. Like other idealists of the 1870s who did not have to get themselves elected, Pope detested the spoils system used by Grant. To give a political office to some party hack with no visible qualifications seemed morally wrong. Pope saw the cure in a civil service system that filled public offices with persons tested for their abilities, again, like other idealists, not seeing that no one has yet devised a better system to keep incompetents in office. He was delighted when the Republicans nominated his supporter Rutherford B. Hayes for president in 1876 to run on a campaign of civil service reform. Pope wrote Hayes long letters about keeping his administration pure by staffing it only with the noncorrupt and closing the door on machine politicians looking for handouts.

Pope seemed doomed to worship flawed idols. When the 1876 election turned into a deadlock, Hayes surrendered to the machine politicians of his party who tied him into the corrupt bargain that got Hayes the presidency at the price of withdrawing troops and erasing black civil rights in the South as well as disbanding the Southern Republican party. No one heard further about civil service reform. Pope nevertheless kept faith with his ideas and found another idol in James A. Garfield, nominated as Republican candidate for president in 1880. Pope liked Garfield also because he was a member of the court-martial that convicted Porter in 1863. On election night in 1880 one of Garfield's congratulatory telegrams read, "Thanks be to God for the victory. JNO. POPE."[35]

Pope knew that Garfield edged out Grant's stalwarts in the 1880 Republican convention and election and could not help repeating to Garfield the advice he had given Hayes about letting any of Grant's supporters enter the cabinet: "Your position on the question of nominations is sound and true if you stand firmly on it without the shadow of wavering or compromise you will do incalculable benefit to the country and be the greatest and most honored President we have had for fifty years."[36] Pope was always a little naive in trying to advise old friends who now held political office and must have still seen Hayes and Garfield as his young subordinates of '62. Garfield had once openly opposed civil service reform. It could take away the fuel for his tight Ohio machine that payment for favors with appointment to public office kept running. Garfield was also credited with the phrase "Vote early and often." After his assassination his manipulations became public; they matched those of Grant and Hayes.

In 1878 Pope took part in a political issue not colored by his idealism. The Franco-Prussian War had startled the world when in 1870 the Prussians reached the gates of Paris sixty days after France declared war. Believing that flaws in the French military system were the cause of the rout, every country with a military system based on the French system began immediate reorganization. Most of these countries adopted the Prussian system in which a professional officer corps commanded an expanded army raised through compulsory military service. In 1878 Congress decided that the American army might be outdated and set up a Joint Committee on the Army headed by Senator Ambrose E. Burnside of Rhode Island, once the unlucky commander of the Army of the Potomac. Burnside held hearings with testimony by professionals and nonprofessionals. Since Pope had helped to revise the West Point curriculum in 1874,[37] his expertise in reorganization was welcomed.

The proposed army bill reflected the views of General Emory Upton, the leading American theorist on war in the 1870s, who blamed the inexperience of volunteers for Union failures in the

Civil War and saw safety and efficiency in the Prussian army. Under the new bill the army would have 25,000 soldiers headed by a permanent general staff like that of von Moltke. During wars volunteers and conscripts would bring the army up to suitable strength, but regular army officers would command all units.

Pope testified, again in terms of Jeffersonian idealism, but this time his idealistic comments rested on a shrewd understanding of the society from which armies of the future would come. In the democratic United States, Pope said, the Prussian way simply would not do. A professional group exercising all command functions down through those of a platoon lieutenant would create a new class of citizens, privileged, likely indifferent to the country's institutions, and apt to be loyal to commanders alone. An American army had to depend on patriotic officers and soldiers drawn from the citizen body. To Pope's satisfaction the bill failed to pass. If the United States had faced sudden and serious attack between 1878 and 1898, Upton's system would probably have been better, but since there were none the present system was adequate until the army reforms of 1899.

Much of Pope's day by day duty centered around Fort Leavenworth. Pope's lasting memorial is perhaps the Episcopal Chapel that he and his wife paid for with their own funds. Thanks to Pope's efforts, the fort's extensive lands remained intact because railroad executives failed in their efforts to buy them from Congress. During the early years of his command, Pope continued to urge the consolidation of the small, temporary posts in his department into one major post at Fort Leavenworth. In his annual report to Lieutenant General Philip H. Sheridan, commander of the Division of the Missouri, Pope stressed the advantages of the military reservation at Fort Leavenworth because it was large enough to accomodate four regiments and had good communications in all directions by rail and wagon roads.[38]

Pope also stressed the advancement of instruction for the troops by concentrating them. To further this plan, he advised Sheridan that he was concentrating the Twenty-Third United States Infantry at the fort. He further wrote that "if the experiment proves successful . . . it is hoped that the range of instruction be extended, and that the establishment of this regimental school . . . may be perpetual here." "I earnestly recommend that all proper encouragement be given by superior authority to the present experiment here, as in my judgment it cannot fail to be of incalculable benefit to the army by restoring regimental discipline and esprit and by instructing both officers and enlisted men on many subjects extremely necessary that they should know."[39] Pope's suggestions for this school were favorably received by William T. Sherman, General-in-Chief of the Army, and in 1881, at Sherman's request and with Sheridan's help, Pope set up the first two extensions of West Point in infantry and cavalry. In 1883 he was delighted to see the first classes graduate from these extension schools of West Point.[40] In time the Fort Leavenworth schools grew into the Command and General Staff College, still in operation and the army's top service school.

By 1883 the country had pushed memories of the Civil War aside in the race for frontier settlement and industrial growth. Grant, Sherman, Sheridan, Pope, and others of their generation walked in the self-consciousness of historical figures who would soon pass from the scene. In 1882 Congress established sixty-four as the compulsory army retirement age and provided a regular pension system. McDowell had to retire in 1882, and Pope took the necessary political and military steps to see that he filled the resulting vacancy and became a permanent major general, at last having the satisfaction of reaching the permanent rank to which he had been brevetted in 1865. Sherman retired in 1883; Sheridan became general-in-chief. Schofield left the Division of the Pacific to take Sheridan's place as commanding general of the Division of the Missouri and became heir apparent to the general-in-chief.

On October 15 Pope was relieved from duty at Fort Leavenworth and given command of the Division of the Pacific with headquarters at the presidio of San Francisco.[41] He was 61 and so knew that the assignment was largely ceremonial. Military affairs in California and Oregon, and in the territories of Arizona, Utah, and Washington, were scarcely pressing. Life passed agreeably at the presidio in a gentle routine of paperwork now and then interrupted by glances at the white-sailed ships in San Francisco Bay. As the aging general neared retirement, he wrote his only memoir, an article on the Second Battle of Bull Run for *Century* magazine, later incorporated into the *Battles and Leaders* series. He was detached enough until he dealt with Porter, who was still living and also writing articles for the same series on the Peninsular Campaign; to Porter, Pope showed his continued enmity.[42] To posterity, Pope left the final judgment on a "campaign . . . greatly misunderstood"[43] since he had given up trying to correct the misunderstanding in his lifetime.

On March 16, 1886, Pope reached sixty-four and retired[44] to live in St. Louis with his wife, children, Horton, 22, John, 19, Lucretia, 12, and Francis, 9. Two years later his wife died. Pope felt alone. His only close friend left was his brother-in-law, Judge Force.

In the summer of 1892 Pope accepted Force's invitation to visit him at the Ohio Soldiers' and Sailors' Home at Sandusky, Ohio, where Force had been superintendent. Pope was in failing health and died in his sleep at the home on September 23, certified by the home's surgeon as having died from "a complete breakdown of the nervous system, a letting loose of all vital force, which has been very properly called 'nervous prostration.' "[45] His death was announced in a general order[46] and after a full dress military funeral in St. Louis he was buried in the family plot in Bellefontaine Cemetery near his wife, father, and mother. His simple headstone reads, "Sacred to the Memory of John Pope, Major-General U.S. Army."

NOTES

For a summary of presidential Reconstruction see J. G. Randall and David Donald, *The Civil War and Reconstruction,* 2d ed. (Lexington, Mass., 1969), 535–91. For congressional Reconstruction see Walter L. Fleming, *A Documentary History of Reconstruction,* 2 vols. (Cleveland, 1906), and James E. Sefton, *The United States Army and Reconstruction* (Baton Rouge, 1967).

1. GO 18, AGO, Mar. 15, 1867, RG 94 NA.
2. Act of Mar. 2, 1867, 14 Stat. 428; Act of Mar. 23, 1856, 15 Stat. 2.
3. See, for instance, Pope's order cancelling the municipal election in Tuscumbia, Alabama, held before Alabama completed the statutory Reconstruction cycle: SO 2, 3d Mil. Dist., Apr. 16, 1867, RG 98 NA.
4. SO 27, 3d Mil. Dist., May 22, 1867, RG 98 NA; SO 34, 3d Mil. Dist., May 31, 1867, RG 98 NA; GO 25, 3d Mil. Dist., May 29, 1867, RG 98 NA; Report of the Sec. of War, 1867 (Washington, 1868), 364–74.
5. Report of the Sec. of War, 1867, 323–24.
6. Ibid., 333; GO 53, 3d Mil. Dist., Aug. 19, 1867, RG 98 NA.
7. Report of the Sec. of War, 1867, 326–29.
8. Ibid., 364–74.
9. Pope to Grant, July 24, 1867, RG 107 NA.
10. *United States Constitution,* Art. II, sect. 3.

11. Proclamation of Apr. 2, 1866, 14 Stat. 811; Proclamation of Aug. 20, 1866, 14 Stat. 814.
12. *Ex parte Milligan,* 4 Wallace (71 US) 2 (1866).
13. In *Mississippi v. Johnson,* 4 Wallace (71 US) 475 (1867) the Supreme Court refused to enjoin the president from carrying out his constitutional duty of law enforcement.
14. *Georgia v. Stanton,* 6 Wallace (73 US) 50 (1867). The full title of this case was *The State of Georgia v. Edwin M. Stanton, Ulysses S. Grant, and John Pope.*
15. 12 OAG (1870).
16. Grant to Pope, June 28, 1867, Ulysses S. Grant Papers, Library of Congress, Washington. Under Art. I, sect. 8, cl. 12, Congress has power to "raise and support armies." Under Art. II, sect. 2, cl. 1 the president is commander-in-chief of the "Army of the United States." Stanton interpreted the first clause as giving power to Congress to raise armies in addition to the "Army of the United States."
17. Act of July 19, 1867, 15 Stat. 14.
18. Grant to Pope, Sept. 9, 1867, RG 108 NA.
19. Ibid.
20. Pope to Grant, July 24, 1867, RG 107 NA.
21. Pope to Grant, Dec. 27, 1867, RG 108 NA.
22. GO 104, AGO, Dec. 18, 1867, RG 94 NA.
23. Pope to Grant, Feb. 19, 1868, A. B. Comstock Papers, Library of Congress, Washington.
24. Report of the Sec. of War, 1868, 287–88.
25. Report of the Sec. of War, 1869, 101.
26. GO 41, AGO, Apr. 15, 1870, RG 94 NA.
27. Ibid.
28. The Red River War; the Bannock, Sheepeater, Paiute, and Ute Wars; the Mexican Border War; and the wars with Geronimo.
29. Robert M. Utley, *Frontier Regulars: The United States Army and the Indians 1866-1891* (New York, 1973), 213, 219–20, 230, 234.
30. Sec. of War to Sec. of the Interior, Nov. 28, 1877, Nov. 30, 1877, Dec. 14, 1877, Dec. 15, 1877, Dec. 18, 1877, Jan. 11, 1878, Jan. 18, 1878; Sec. of War to R. Q. Mills, Apr. 19, 1878, RG 107 NA.
31. Utley, 333, 335, 338, 340.
32. Ibid., 364, 373.
33. Act of Mar. 3, 1869, 15 Stat. 315.
34. Hayes, Force, et al. to Grant, Nov. 9, 1872; Carpenter to Grant, Nov. 9, 1872; Noyes to Sec. of War, Nov. 9, 1872; Noyes to Sec. of Interior, Nov. 9, 1872, RG 107 NA.
35. Pope to Garfield, Nov. 3, 1880, James A. Garfield Papers, Library of Congress, Washington.
36. Pope to Garfield, May 15, 1881, James A. Garfield Papers.
37. Utley, 235n23, citing *Army and Navy Journal,* Oct. 10, 1874.

38. Report of the Sec. of War, 1877, Report of Brig. Gen. John Pope to Lieut. Gen. Philip H. Sheridan, Sept. 15, 1877, 59.
39. Ibid., 62.
40. GO 42, AGO, May 7, 1881, RG 94 NA; Report of the Sec. of War, 1881, 39, 125; Report of the Sec. of War, 1882, 102; Report of the Sec. of War, 1883, 45, 135.
41. GO 71, AGO, Oct. 15, 1883, RG 94 NA.
42. John Pope, "The Second Battle of Bull Run," in Robert Underwood Johnson and Clarence Clough Buel, *Battles and Leaders of the Civil War,* 4 vols. (New York, 1887), 2:484.
43. Ibid.
44. GO 13, AGO, Mar. 16, 1886, RG 94 NA.
45. J. F. Haynes to M. F. Force, Sept. 27, 1892, Personal File, John Pope, RG 94 NA.
46. GO 67, AGO, Sept. 26, 1892, RG 94 NA.

Appendix A

Keeping the Ashes Hot:
Fitz John Porter

IN AN AFTERMATH of twenty-four years of violent squabbles followed by more than one hundred years of angry argument, the Second Battle of Bull Run was fought and refought in the White House Oval Office, before a general court-martial, before a Board of Review, in hot and nasty letters to and from survivors, in newspapers and magazines, in the smoke-filled chambers of party caucuses, in the committee rooms and on the floors of the House and Senate, in lecture halls, in history books, and, more recently, in Civil War Round Tables.[1]

Through the years Pope and Porter sparred at a distance. Pope saw Porter as the demon who ruined a victory almost in hand. Porter saw Pope as an idiot for whom he was sacrificed. Who was right?

Pope insisted that Porter skulked in the face of the enemy by keeping his Fifth Corps in the woods all afternoon on August 29, 1862, and that Porter was insubordinate in failing to carry out a direct order to attack at 1630. Porter insisted that obeying Pope's order would have meant the useless sacrifice of his corps since Longstreet had taken his position on Jackson's right by 1200 and barred the line of march of Porter's corps to the battlefield. In Porter's story everything rested on Longstreet's arrival time. If Longstreet arrived at or before 1200 Porter could not see himself chargeable for skulking or insubordination.

Moves to punish Porter, Griffin, and Franklin began as early as September 4, 1862, when Lincoln, Stanton, and Halleck had read Pope's battlefield complaints about these generals.[2] A court of inquiry met on September 6 and was adjourned sine die on September 15.[3] Lee's invasion of Maryland and the Battle of Antietam and its aftermath held up proceedings until November.

On November 15 a military commission was called to try the charges against Porter but was dissolved on November 17, probably because Halleck realized that a military commission was not a proper tribunal for trying an officer of his own army for violating the Articles of War.[4] Halleck as general-in-chief then convened a general court-martial to try Porter alone.[5] This time the court would take up charges preferred not by Pope but by Brigadier General Benjamin S. Roberts who served as inspector general of the Army of Virginia.[6] The order for the court named Major General David Hunter president and Major Generals Ethan Allan Hitchcock and Silas Casey, Brigadier Generals Rufus King, James A. Garfield, Napoleon B. Buford, and William W. Morris (later replaced by Brigadier General J. P. Slough) as other members. Colonel Joseph Holt served as judge advocate and recorder.[7] Pope should have been pleased with the court's members. Hunter rode the Lincoln train with him in 1861; Garfield was a Republican member of Congress; King had served Pope faithfully in the Virginia campaign; Holt was also a sound Republican who would later prosecute the Lincoln conspirators.

Roberts's charges against Porter arose under the Ninth Article of War, punishing any officer or soldier who "shall disobey any lawful command of his superior officer,"[8] and under the Fifty-second Article of War punishing any officer or soldier who "shall misbehave himself before the enemy, run away ... etc."[9] Specifications under the Ninth Article of War were (1) disobeying Pope's order of 1830 on August 27 to march to Bristoe Station at 0100 on August 28; (2) disobeying Pope's order of August 29 to attack the enemy's right and rear; and (3) allowing Griffin's and Piatt's brigades to march to Centreville in spite of Pope's order of 2050 on August 29 sending them to the field of battle.[10] Specifications under the Fifty-second Article of War were: (1) retreating from the enemy on August 29 without engaging the enemy and without trying to help Union troops already engaged; (2) failing to bring Fifth Corps to the field on August 29, although knowing that a battle was taking place; and (3) failing to help Union troops engaged with the enemy although knowing that these troops faced defeat and that defeat would endanger Washington.[11] Judge Advocate Holt withdrew a fourth specification under the Fifty-second Article of War charging that Porter willfully made a feeble and half-hearted attack on the enemy on August 30.[12]

The court met on December 3 in a second-floor parlor over a Fourteenth Street restaurant near Pennsylvania Avenue. At Porter's request the court admitted the public and newspaper reporters. Members of the court sat in dress uniform. Newspaper reporters commented on their bright scabbards and plumed hats.[13] Porter's choice of counsel aligned him squarely with the Democratic party and made his trial a political event: Reverdy Johnson, slick Union Democrat, attorney general in 1849, runner of secret missions for Lincoln, and in 1867 counsel for Andrew Johnson in Johnson's impeachment trial; and Charles Eames, noted for constitutional arguments before the Supreme Court and in 1867 also counsel for Johnson.[14]

At the outset Porter's counsel moved to have the record show Pope as the real party who preferred the charges; the motion was denied because the defense must deal only with the charges presented. Porter then pleaded not guilty to all charges and his trial began.[15] Porter was right in moving to have his real accuser named, but in view of widespread newspaper articles saying that Pope wanted only to blame Porter for losing the battle, it was wise to have Roberts prefer the charges.

On December 4 the prosecution called Pope as the first witness. For the next five days Pope testified "with a readiness, accuracy and general consistency and a manliness too"[16] while seated in a rocking chair.[17] He testified that at 1830 on August 27 he ordered Porter to start marching for Bristoe Station the next morning at 0100, but that Porter ordered the march for 0300. Porter's march actually began at 0400 so that the Fifth Corps did not reach Bristoe Station until 1000. To Porter's contention that he could not have made a night march because the night was dark and the road jammed with parked wagons, Pope testified that was not so since others marched and arrived on time.[18]

On August 29, the first day of battle, Pope testified that Porter did absolutely nothing. Could Porter have carried out Pope's order to attack? defense counsel asked. "'Had Porter fallen upon the flank of the enemy,'" Pope replied, "'at any time up to 8:00 p.m. that night, it is my firm conviction that we should have destroyed the army of Jackson.'"[19] Porter disobeyed again on August 30, Pope testified, by letting Griffin's and Piatt's brigades stray off to Centreville after Pope ordered Porter to bring his full command to the battlefield. Was that a clear violation of Pope's order? "'Undoubtedly,'" Pope replied.[20]

Since Porter's whole defense rested on when Longstreet's troops arrived, Porter's counsel wanted to know if Pope thought Longstreet was in position at 1630 on August 29. "'I had feared the junction of those corps at any moment,'" Pope replied, "'as I knew from information that Longstreet was pushing forward to join Jackson. I, therefore, expected that movement of Longstreet certainly during the afternoon of the 29th.'"[21] Could Porter then have carried out Pope's order to attack? "'I did not then believe,'" Pope replied, "'nor do I now believe that at that time any considerable portion of Longstreet's corps had reached the vicinity of the field.' "[22] When did Pope know that Longstreet had arrived? " 'By 7:00 in the evening I knew—that a portion of Longstreet's forces, perhaps one-half of the forces of Porter, certainly not more than two-thirds as Buford estimated it—in all probability, had joined Jackson.' "[23] To add more confusion the Buford dispatch mentioned by Pope that went from General Buford to General Ricketts at 0930 on August 29 read: "Seventeen regiments, one battery, and 500 cavalry passed through Gainesville three-quarters of an hour ago on the Centreville road. I think this division should join our forces now engaged, at once."[24] No one who saw this understood what it meant.

The exact time that Longstreet and troops arrived and took positions where they could support Jackson was lost in a tangle of missing records and failing memories, but most analysts agree that this probably happened by 1200.[25] The exact time was irrelevant. If Porter knew the Army of Virginia was in trouble on August 29, he had a duty to report it to Pope; he reported nothing. The charges against Porter rested on the fact that he did nothing when he knew the Army of Virginia might be in trouble and when he had orders to attack.

Pope's testimony ended with an explanation of why he had almost decided not to take action against Porter. The other officers, Pope said, kept him from arresting Porter on the evening of August 29. By September 2 Pope had in hand the telegram from McClellan asking Porter to cooperate with Pope and knew of the telegrams from Porter to Burnside criticizing Pope. From these documents, Pope testified, he concluded that Porter came to Pope's Army of Virginia with an already formed intent to sabotage Pope's campaign if he could.[26]

After Pope, General Irwin McDowell proved the hardest-hitting prosecution witness. In the late morning of August 29, McDowell testified, Pope sent a joint order to McDowell and Porter. The two generals met at 1200 that day to talk it over. McDowell testified positively that the joint order gave him discretion to give further orders as he was the senior officer and that long before he saw Pope's direct order to Porter to attack at 1630 he himself had ordered Porter to attack the enemy's right flank and rear as soon as the two generals parted.[27]

Defense counsel asked if McDowell knew that some of Longstreet's forces might be at hand. McDowell answered, " 'I did not know anything about Longstreet or Jackson's corps—I had received a note from Buford that seventeen regiments, a battery, and 500 cavalry were marching from Gainesville to Groveton. To whom they belonged or to whom they were going was not a matter of which I was informed.' "[28] If Porter had attacked, would his corps have had any effect on the outcome of battle? " 'I think and thought,' " McDowell replied, " 'that if the corps of General Porter, reputed one of the best—had been added to the efforts made by the others, the result would have been in our favor very decidedly.' "[29] What if Porter attacked and got trounced? " 'To have defeated General Porter in that attack,' " McDowell testified, " 'would have required a large force of the enemy, which would have relieved the attack in front, and I think, would have still resulted in a success to our side—to our army generally.' "[30]

Porter admitted telling McDowell he was unable to "go in anywhere there without getting into a fight;"[31] McDowell answered, " 'Well, that's what we came here for.' "[32] Did McDowell think Porter's remark showed unwillingness to face the enemy? " 'When I left him I thought he was going to engage and would engage the enemy.' "[33] Cross-examination could not shake McDowell, as he kept insisting that on August 29 Porter could have and should have attacked.

The prosecution ended its case by introducing telegrams that Porter sent Burnside on August 27, 28, and 29 while the Army of Virginia was fighting the enemy. Porter was at least foolish in using the military telegraph system. These telegrams sniped at Pope, the Army of Virginia, and Pope's strategy: "I wish myself away from it, with our old Army of the Potomac." "All that talk of bagging Jackson, etc. was bosh. That enormous gap, Manassas, was left open." "Pope went to Centreville . . . at that time not knowing where was the enemy and when Sigel was fighting within eight miles of him and in sight." "It would seem from proper statements of the enemy that he was wandering around loose, but I expect they know what they are doing which is more than anyone here or anywhere knows."[34] The prosecution emphasized these to show Porter's fixed intent to undercut Pope from the outset and to imply that Porter's ideas were almost treasonable. The dispatches inflamed the newspapers and must have influenced members of the court.[35]

On December 24 the defense opened its case. In his examination McDowell testified that he did not remember saying to Porter, "Porter, you are too far out already; this is no place to fight a battle,"[36] though Porter's chief of staff testified he remembered hearing McDowell say it.[37] But McDowell's statement could not change the effect of his unquestioned direct order to Porter to attack.

Brigadier General John F. Reynolds then testified that the fields over which Porter's troops would have had to march to reach the enemy were " 'very broken by ravines and wooded.' "[38] Could a military force nevertheless cross in proper order to face an enemy? Reynolds answered, "'I should think not, in the immediate presence of the enemy.'"[39] But on cross-examination Reynolds backed away. Even though he was "'across broken country,'" Porter was no more than three miles south of the Union left, Reynolds estimated. As late as 1300 Reynolds, who was in action on the Union left, saw only small numbers of Confederate reinforcements filing into the enemy right that faced him.[40] If Porter had then attacked the enemy right flank, what would the effect have been? the judge advocate asked. Reynolds had to reply, "'A vigorous attack made ought to have resulted favorably to our success; ought to have contributed greatly toward it, certainly.'"[41]

Porter's last important witness was the colonel of the Thirteenth New York, a unit in Porter's Fifth Corps. The colonel testified that Porter sent him on reconnaissance at 1300 on August 29. To the north he ran into a very large enemy force already formed in line of battle to the front and right of Fifth Corps. Between 1700 and dusk could Porter have moved to his right in order to reach Jackson's right? "'No, Sir'" he answered, "'it was impossible to have done so.'"[42]

On January 10, 1863, defense counsel read and filed a written defense. The judge advocate filed no written argument and asked for an immediate decision, which the court gave at 1800. First charge: guilty of specifications one, two, and three; not guilty of specifications four and five. Second charge: guilty of specification one except any implication that Porter "retreated"; guilty of specification two except for the words "to the Manassas Junction."[43] The court read its sentence: "Maj. Gen. Fitz John Porter, of the United States Volunteers, *'To be cashiered, and to be forever disqualified from holding any office of trust or profit under the Government of the United States.'*"[44]

The record duly went to the secretary of war and the president. On January 21 Lincoln approved and confirmed the findings and the sentence, which went into effect at once.[45]

Porter heard of Lincoln's action at 1700 on January 22 from a newspaper reporter.[46] Porter's conviction and sentence became a newspaper sensation divided along party lines. The *Cincinnati Daily Enquirer* commented fittingly, "General Porter is a Democrat and a warm, personal friend of McClellan."[47] Those politics worked against McClellan in Lincoln's favor. McClellan would have been his most likely opponent in the presidential race in 1864, but Lincoln held a formal judgment that the Democrats had tried to undermine the war effort.

Porter sat the rest of the war out as a civilian. When the war ended, he wrote both Lee and Longstreet to ask when their troops were ready to fight on August 29, 1862. Longstreet answered on September 23,

1866: before 1200;[48] Lee answered on October 31, 1867: before 1200.[49] Each had had time to learn about Porter's court-martial and Porter's contentions; each was a Democrat.

Porter had already started a tempest by asking Franklin to repeat a statement made in 1862 that Franklin, Reynolds, and General George H. Thomas would testify that they would not believe Pope or Roberts even under oath.[50] Franklin was dull-witted enough to write this in a letter to Grant, then secretary of war, who turned it over to the Senate, who had it printed.[51] Franklin could never placate either Roberts or Pope after this,[52] although Thomas wrote Pope forthrightly that Franklin had no basis for his statement.[53]

Though nothing came of Franklin's letter, Porter wrote Grant asking for a review of his case on the basis of newly discovered evidence. Grant did not reply.[54] Pope found out about Porter's appeal and in turn wrote Grant to protest that no new testimony could possibly change the court's findings and judgment[55] because Lincoln's review in 1863 was the only review allowed by law and was now final. Grant turned Pope's letter over to Porter.[56] Porter used it as another avenue of appeal by answering it in the form of a letter to President Johnson. Johnson did not answer.[57]

Two years later, on June 10, Porter asked Sherman, now general-in-chief, to ask Grant, now president, to appoint a board of officers to review the court-martial.[58] Grant took no action but Pope again heard about Porter's letter and again wrote to protest.[59] Pope also wrote Sherman,[60] who assured Pope that no new hearing was in sight but admitted getting letters from prominent men asking to have Porter's civil disabilities lifted.[61] Porter next had his appeal to Grant printed as a pamphlet. Pope got a copy and read with fury Porter's charge that the only reason for Porter's court-martial was Pope's defeat in Virginia,[62] though it did not specify what part Porter might have had in the defeat. Members of Congress also read the pamphlet, with the result that on February 21, 1870, Senator Zachariah Chandler of Michigan, leader of the Radical Republicans, took the Senate floor to review Pope's Virginia campaign and to castigate McClellan and Porter, ending with the words, "Let Fitz John Porter thank God that he still lives."[63] That stopped any effort to help Porter for several years.

Since he had nothing else to do, Porter nevertheless kept on. By 1874 Porter managed to start a rumor that Grant was keeping his hands off the case only because Pope's Republican friends kept advising Grant not to get involved. This made Pope uncomfortable enough to write Grant denying that he was using political influence. Although the court-martial reached the only possible decision, Pope wrote,

Grant could look into it as he wished, but, "I beg . . . that you yourself, Mr. President, examine as fully into the question as you think justice and mercy demands, or you will order a board of competent officers of high rank, unconnected with the armies or transactions involved, to investigate fully the statements of this new evidence made by General Porter."[64] Grant replied that he had read the new evidence and agreed with Pope. "My conclusion," Grant wrote, "was that no new facts were developed that could be fairly considered and that it was of doubtful legality, whether by the mere authority of the Executive, a rehearing could be given."[65] That ended the Porter affair until Grant left office on March 4, 1877, to be replaced by Rutherford B. Hayes.

Hayes served under Pope in an Ohio regiment, and the two had long been corresponding friends. After Hayes took office, Pope saw shrewdly that Hayes worried about his title and might do almost anything to keep it from being questioned. "His 'title,' you may be surprised to hear," Pope wrote to his brother-in-law, "is his constant fear; and much of his conduct is ruled by the fear of losing his office before his term is out."[66]

Late in 1877 a friend of Porter's, Democrat Senator Theodore Randolph of New Jersey, a member of the Senate Military Affairs Committee, began pestering Hayes to review Porter's case. Since McClellan had been elected governor of New Jersey in 1877 and since Porter lived there, the Porter case was a hot party issue in New Jersey. Hayes called for a formal appeal from Porter, got it, and appointed a board of officers to review Porter's case. The board would take new evidence into account and report "what action, if any in their opinion, justice requires should be taken on said application by the President."[67] The board was headed by Major General John M. Schofield, a sharp critic of Pope's campaigns and administration in Missouri and certainly dedicated to reinterpreting and if possible drawing attention away from the testimony favorable to Pope given in the court-martial proceedings.[68] The other members were Brigadier General Alfred H. Terry and Colonel George W. Getty; Major Asa Bird Gardner served as judge advocate and recorder.[69] The board opened its hearings at West Point on June 25, 1878,[70] since Schofield was superintendent at that time.

Why Hayes, who claimed to be Pope's friend, placed Pope's reputation into the hands of Schofield was a mystery. Although Schofield took no active part in politics, he became general of the army through appointment by Democratic President Grover Cleveland in 1888, clearly for services rendered for putting Porter's case into suitable form for influencing legislators.

By law only superiors acting promptly on a direct appeal could vacate a court-martial judgment. The Schofield Board as a board of review acting twenty-five years later could not. It could, however, give Porter a forum in which he could sound off to the public, and its report and recommendations could influence the president and Congress to take steps within their power. The president could grant a pardon; Congress could set the judgment aside and reinstate Porter in the army. The board obviously served no other purpose. Pope could do nothing. He had no objection to an executive pardon but, "I do contend that what is done shall be an act of clemency pure and simple, and in no manner affecting the righteousness of the verdict against him."[71]

For this second round Porter again enlisted the best lawyers: John C. Bullitt; Joseph H. Choate, known as the "Wizard of the Bar"; and Anson Maltby. The Board's hearings were not adversary proceedings, but, apparently without objection, Porter and his counsel made them adversarial by classifying witnesses as for the "government" or the "petitioner" and by having witnesses testify under oath.[72] The board sat intermittently from June 25, 1878, until March 19, 1879, and in the course of its hearings listened to 142 witnesses. Schofield used the board as an opportunity to bring out anything that would justify setting aside the court-martial judgment of 1863. Porter's job was to present everything backing his claim that on August 29, 1862, sound military judgment called for sitting in the woods in spite of hearing sounds of battle and in spite of holding written orders to attack the enemy.

Longstreet was the key witness since Jackson had died in 1863; Stuart, in 1864; and Lee, in 1870. Longstreet was a shrewd enough lawyer to see that Schofield wanted a whitewash for Porter who, after all, had done just what Longstreet would have wanted him to do. After sixteen years Longstreet's memory for details came back remarkably clearly as his questioners led him through the events. He testified positively that he and his troops were in position to support Jackson by 0900 on August 29, 1862, that all his troops were actually deployed in line of battle by 1100, but that he did not know that Porter's Fifth Corps was in the woods in front of him until 1400.[73]

The board also took in as evidence Stuart's written report of August 29 that he saw in front of him a Union force now known to be Porter's. If that unit marched forward, the report said, its line of march would take it straight into Stuart's observation post, an ideal spot for artillery.[74] But Longstreet's report in 1862 said that only one Confederate division of 6,300 actually faced Porter's Fifth Corps of 12,000.[75] Two other Virginia witnesses said that for most of August 29 they saw only tiny Confederate detachments near Porter's hideaway and that Long-street's troops only got into fighting position around 1500.[76]

McDowell stood a grilling by Porter's counsel who tried without success to get McDowell to blur or weaken his testimony given in the court-martial.[77] At the request of Porter's counsel Schofield tried to subpoena Pope, but Pope refused on the grounds that Schofield had made the proceedings adversary. If Pope answered a subpoena from the Board, his testimony bound no one. If the government or Porter called him, his testimony would bind the party calling him. He appealed to the secretary of war, who passed it on to the president, who left the matter to Pope's discretion. According to Pope, all his onetime friend Hayes "did was simply to decline to order me 'to appear or not to appear' leaving on me the onus of refusing to be bulldozed by a Board he himself had ordered. It is very plain that it is not Porter's case which is being examined but a deliberate attempt to injure me."[78] Pope did not appear.[79] Schofield was obviously regulating the evidence he wanted heard and was unwilling to have his board or Porter bound by what he knew Pope would say.

An unlikely witness did appear. Robert T. Lincoln said that some time in January 1863 he talked to his father about the Porter court-martial. His father showed him a note from Porter to McDowell, which said that Porter "judged by the sound of the firing that our troops were beaten and that he should withdraw his troops from the field."[80] Abraham Lincoln then said, "'the case would have justif-ied . . . a sentence of death.'"[81]

The hearings ended on March 14, 1879. The board deliberated until March 19 and then sent a written report to the secretary of war. In the 1862 court-martial, the board said, Porter's accusers had "radically erroneous opinions" of the facts. Porter did lounge in the woods with a battle-hardened corps of 12,000, yet "Porter's faithful, subordinate and intelligent conduct that afternoon saved the Union Army from the defeat which would otherwise have resulted that day from the enemy's more speedy concentration." Porter's "action had been wise and judicious."[82] Porter had unkind thoughts about Pope and the Army of Virginia but such "evidence of animus in Porter's case ceases to be material in view of the evidence of his soldierly and faithful conduct." The board nevertheless criticized Porter for the "indiscreet and unkind terms in which General Porter expressed his distrust of the capacity of his superior commander."[83] The board recommended rescinding the court-martial judgment and handing back to this "wise and judicious" man his military rank and standing as of January 21, 1863.[84]

Pope felt even more betrayed when Gardner, the board's judge advocate, told him privately that Porter's sponsor, Senator Randolph, in fact "most judiciously selected" the board members while assuring Hayes that they were unbiased.[85] "What I apprehend," Pope wrote his brother-in-law, "is that Hayes, to avoid responsibility, will send them [the Board's findings] without comment to Congress and thus perpetuate or probably perpetuate a horrible injustice."[86] In June Hayes forwarded the Board's report and recommendations to Congress with the flat note: "the proceedings and conclusions of the Board are transmitted for the information of Congress and such action as in your wisdom shall seem expedient and just."[87] In effect Hayes admitted that as president he had gone as far as he could under his executive power. Only Congress had power to take further steps. From then on the Fitz John Porter case was controlled by partisan politics. From 1879 to 1885 Republicans controlled the administration. A Senate bill to set aside the court-martial judgment and give Porter his old rank of colonel nevertheless passed in spite of a bitter speech against it by Senator John A. Logan of Illinois, the founder of the Grand Army of the Republic and Memorial Day.[88] A companion House bill never reached a vote.[89]

In 1881 President Garfield was assassinated. This benefited Porter since Garfield sat on the 1862 court and would have vetoed anything calling its judgment in question. But in 1882 President Chester A. Arthur gave Porter a pardon, removing his civil disabilities.[90] In 1883 another Porter reinstatement bill passed the Senate in spite of another Logan speech against it, but again a companion House bill died.[91] In the next session of Congress bills to reinstate Porter passed both the Senate and the House but this time President Arthur vetoed.[92] Finally in 1885 Grover Cleveland became the first Democrat to reach the White House since 1857, after Porter campaigned for him actively in New Jersey. In 1886 a bill to set aside the court-martial judgment and sentence and reinstate Porter passed Congress and Cleveland signed it on July 1, 1886.[93] On July 6 Cleveland nominated Porter to be a colonel; the Senate consented. On August 7 War Department orders restored Porter's commission as colonel and immediately placed him on the retired list.[94]

The long affair which began in party politics ended in a display of party politics. Porter, now 64, could rejoice weakly with his Democratic well-wishers, such as Schofield and Terry of the "impartial" board, and Ellen McClellan, widow of the general. Pope, also 64 and retired because of age, could brush off the acts of Congress and of Cleveland as political japery. Pope had written Force in 1878, "I have always expected the Democrats, if they got into power, to white-wash Porter as far as could be done, but as it would be done on partisan grounds, I cared nothing about it as such action would scarcely alter public opinion on the subjection."[95]

NOTES

1. The testimony in the Fitz John Porter trial of 1862–63 appears in full in OR XII, part 2, supp.:821–1134. The findings, judgment, and sentence, and presidential affirmation in 1863 appear in OR XII, part 2:506–12.

  The proceedings of the Schofield Board of Review in 1878 appear in "Proceedings and Report of the Board of Army Officers Convened by Special Orders No. 78, Headquarters of the Army, Adjutant General's Office, Washington, D.C., April 12, 1878, in the Case of Fitz John Porter," 3 vols, S. Ex. Doc. 37, 56th Cong., 1st Sess., 1879.

  The order convening the board, the board's report, President Hayes's letter referring the report to Congress, and President Arthur's pardon remitting Fitz John Porter's civil disabilities also appear in OR XII, part 2:512–36

  The best study of the Fitz John Porter case is Henry Gabler, "The Fitz John Porter Case: Politics and Military Justice" (Ph.D. diss., City University of New York, 1979). Another book on the subject is Otto Eisenschiml, *The Celebrated Case of Fitz John Porter* (Indianapolis, 1950).

2. John Pope, Preliminary Report, Sept. 3, 1862, OR XII, part 2:12–17; Pope to Halleck, Sept. 3, 1862, OR XII, part 2:19.

3. Order Creating a Board of Inquiry, War Department, Sept. 5, 1862 (in Lincoln's handwriting and signed by him), RG 153 NA; SO 122, AGO, Sept. 5, 1862, RG 153 NA; SO 223, AGO, Sept. 5, 1862, RG 94 NA.

4. SO 350, AGO, Nov. 17, 1862, OR XII, part 2:506; SO 362, AGO, Nov. 25, 1862, OR XII, part 2:507.

5. SO 362, AGO, Nov. 25, 1862, OR XII, part 2:507.

6. See OR XII, part II, supp. (hereafter 1862 Proceedings), 824.

7. SO 362, AGO, Nov. 25, 1862, RG 94 NA.

8. Act of Apr. 10, 1806, 2 Stat. 359, sec. 9.

9. Ibid., sec. 52.

10. See 1862 Proceedings, 824–26.

11. Ibid., 827.

12. Ibid.

13. *Milwaukee Sentinel,* Dec. 17, 1862.

14. Ibid.

15. 1862 Proceedings, 828–29.

16. See note 13.
17. Ibid.
18. 1862 Proceedings, 830–31.
19. Ibid., 834.
20. Ibid., 835.
21. Ibid., 851.
22. Ibid., 852.
23. Ibid., 853.
24. Buford to Ricketts, Aug. 29, 1862, OR XII, part 3:730.
25. See Report of Brig. Gen. Cadmus Wilcox, Oct. 11, 1862, OR XII, part 2:898; Report of Brig. Gen. David R. Jones, Dec. 8, 1862, OR XII, part 2:279; John Codman Ropes, *The Army under Pope,* Campaigns of the Civil War Series (New York, 1881), 112; and Douglas Southall Freeman, *Lee's Lieutenants: A Study in Command,* 3 vols. (New York, 1942), 2:112.
26. OR XII, part 2, Supp.: 840–41.
27. Ibid., 907.
28. Ibid., 908.
29. Ibid., 912–13.
30. Ibid., 917.
31. Ibid., 912–13.
32. Ibid.
33. Ibid.
34. Ibid., 919, 925, 933. See also *Milwaukee Sentinel,* Dec. 18, 1862.
35. Ibid.
36. OR XII, part 2, supp.: 906.
37. Ibid., 956.
38. Ibid., 991.
39. Ibid.
40. Ibid., 993.
41. Ibid.
42. Ibid., 1012.
43. Ibid., 1051, 1075–112.
44. Ibid., 1051.
45. Ibid., 1052; Presidential Order, Jan. 21, 1863.
46. *New York Daily Tribune,* Jan. 22, 1863.
47. *Cincinnati Enquirer,* Jan. 23, 1863; see also *Chicago Tribune,* Jan. 23, 1863.
48. Longstreet to Porter, Sept. 23, 1866, "Proceedings and Report of the Board of Army Officers . . . in the Case of Fitz John Porter," 3 vols., S. Ex. Doc. 37, 46th Cong., 1st Sess., 1879, 1:552 (hereafter 1878 Report).
49. 1878 Report, 1:551.
50. Franklin to Grant, Sept. 30, 1867, 1878 Report, 1:489–90.
51. See Franklin to Roberts, Apr. 6, 1868, and Pope to Thomas, Dec. 21, 1869, Manning F. Force Papers, University of Washington Libraries, Seattle.
52. Ibid.

53. Thomas to Pope, Jan. 5, 1870, Force Papers.
54. Porter to Grant, Sept. 16, 1867, 1878 Report, 1:474–76.
55. Ibid., 1:476–79.
56. See Porter to Andrew Johnson, Oct. 16, 1867, 1878 Report, 1:479–86.
57. Ibid.
58. Porter to Sherman, June 10, 1869, 1878 Report, 1:457–59.
59. Pope to Grant, Dec. 8, 1869, Force Papers.
60. Pope to Sherman, Dec. 10, 1869, William T. Sherman Papers, Library of Congress, Washington.
61. Sherman to Pope, Dec. 13, 1869, Force Papers.
62. Fitz John Porter, "Appeal to the President of the United States for a Re-Examination of the Proceedings of the General Court-Martial in His Case" (Morristown, N.J., 1869).
63. Speech of Zachariah Chandler, Feb. 20, 1871, *Congressional Globe,* 41st Cong., 2d Sess., 1444–47.
64. Pope to Grant, Apr. 18, 1874, Force Papers.
65. Grant to Pope, May 9, 1874, Force Papers.
66. Pope to Force, Apr. 11, 1879, Force Papers.
67. SO 78, AGO, Apr. 12, 1878, OR XII, part 2:512–13.
68. See John M. Schofield, *Forty-Six Years in the Army,* (New York, 1897), 359, 459–66.
69. See Note 67.
70. 1878 Report, 1:1–2.
71. Pope to Force, Jan. 15, 1878, Force Papers.
72. See Pope to Schofield, Oct. 21, 1878, and Schofield to Pope, Oct. 21, 1878, 1878 Report, 3:1027; see also Pope to G. W. McCrary, Oct. 22, 1878, and McCrary to Pope, Oct. 23, 1878, Force Papers.
73. 1878 Report, 2:124.
74. Report of Maj. Gen. Jeb Stuart, Feb. 28, 1863, OR XII, part 2:735–36.
75. Report of Lieut. Gen. James Longstreet, Oct. 10, 1862, OR XII, part 2:565.
76. Lewis B. Carraco and Rev. John Landstreet, 1878 Report, 2:921–22, 2:996.
77. 1878 Report, 1:764–67, 1:805–11.
78. Pope to Force, Nov. 12, 1878, Force Papers.
79. See Note 72.
80. 1878 Report, 2:854–55.
81. Ibid.
82. 1878 Report, 3:1719.
83. Ibid., 3:1720.
84. Ibid.
85. Gardner to McDowell, Mar. 15, 1879, Force Papers.
86. Pope to Force, Mar. 31, 1879, Force Papers.
87. Letter of Transmittal, Rutherford B. Hayes, June 5, 1879, OR XII, part 2:535.

88. S.R. 1139, 46th Cong, 2d Sess.; Speech of John A. Logan, March 2–5, 1880, *Congressional Record,* 46th Cong., 2nd Sess., app.
89. H.R. 3764, 46th Cong., 2d Sess.
90. Pardon, signed by Chester A. Arthur, May 4, 1882, OR XII, part 2:535–36.
91. S.R. 1844, H.R. 6136, 47th Cong., 2d Sess.
92. S.R. 158, H.R. 1015, 48th Cong., 1st Sess.; *Congressional Record,* 48th Cong., 1st Sess., 5932–33, 5935. The House passed the act over Arthur's veto. A try in the Senate failed.
93. H.R. 67, 49th Cong., 1st Sess.; *Congressional Record,* 49th Cong., 1st Sess., 6085, 6108, 6115, 6128; Act of July 1, 1886, Stat.
94. SO 182, AGO, August 7, 1886, RG 94 NA.
95. Pope to Force, Jan. 15, 1878, Force Papers.

Appendix B

Pope's Generalship

CRITICS OF POPE HAD as many views of his generalship as there were critics, though most blamed Pope for his own downfall. After more than 100 years since the tense days of 1862 one small summary can hardly cover all of Pope's critics—and this review will deal with only a selected group.

Critics zeroed in on the Second Battle of Bull Run. Since Pope lost that one, his critics went into their analyses knowing that they were dealing with a defeated general. Such knowledge had to affect their thinking and sharpen their talents for finding fault. Nearly everyone looked at Pope's Virginia campaign as if it were the only campaign he ever took part in, and as if it took place under ideal circumstances in which all Pope had to do was growl a command and watch his subordinates carry it out. They forgot, or glossed over, his makeshift army that had never before fought as a unit, his third-rate subordinates, his mission, orders from Washington that restricted his movement, and the political situation.

Popularizers[1] generally came down hard on Pope. The nature of their writing called for heroes and villains, geniuses and simpletons, drama, suspense, glitter, and sparkling prose. Pope lost, therefore he was an ignoramus who must be drubbed in print. Bruce Catton found Pope a man "simply over his depth"[2] who "lost track of what was happening"[3] and "would send [troops] into action according to a map traced by fantasy."[4] If this were true, why go into so much detail over happenings in fantasyland? Catton, or his team of researchers, probably read a good deal about the background of Pope's campaign, but never bothered to detail what hurdles Pope had to clear before he could get action started. Some generals won or lost through the fortunes of war, Catton admitted, but Pope lost through his own fault in Catton's eyes.

Shelby Foote never disclosed his sources, and in footnote-free prose wrote that while Pope "kept his mind, if not his eye, on the prize within his reach,"[5] he "mishandled" his army,[6] "acted as a dunderhead,"[7] and, in the reporter's favorite word, got himself "outgeneraled."[8] Foote provided no explanation for how or why Pope was "outgeneraled." For all that Foote's text indicated, it was because Pope was so disposed.

Fletcher Pratt specialized in the military. He had nothing better to say about Second Bull Run, although he did give Pope credit for good planning and rapid execution at Island No. 10. Of Second Bull Run, Pratt might as well have quoted the others. Pope had "clean forgotten Thoroughfare Gap."[9] "His orders might as well have been written in Chinese."[10] In the end he was "hopelessly outgeneraled."[11] Although Pratt spent a good many pages on details of the battle and accompanied his commentary with a map, in the end he too failed to take into account the obstacles facing Pope other than those put in his way by the enemy.

Professional historians[12] were kinder to Pope even though they disliked him as a man. They could see his campaign set within the total geographic-political-cultural matrix of the Civil War, and as historians they knew that sometimes there was nothing to do but echo Virgil and say *sunt lacrimae rerum.* They generally were unable to analyze the qualities of generalship probably because most did not have enough professional military knowledge or advice to pick out critical detail.

Herman Hattaway and Archer Jones described Pope as bombastic and incompetent without going into much detail and criticized him more for his General Orders five, seven, and eleven—for living off the land and handling Virginians roughly—than they did for any specific mistakes in handling his army.[13]

James M. McPherson largely echoed his forerunners in putting heavy emphasis on Pope's address to his troops and in resolving the question of Porter's conduct by adopting Porter's claim that Longstreet was in position at noon on August 30, 1862. He did give weight to the Pope-McClellan feud, but in the end was content to call Pope a bragging bungler without going into the background of the whole campaign.[14]

J. G. Randall and David Donald gave a satisfactory number of details about Bull Run, but criticized Pope. When Pope reached Washington, they said, "his aptness for command had been by no means demonstrated"[15] in spite of his successes in the West. They claimed that when Pope commanded in Virginia "a furious offensive action by Pope on the 30th failed chiefly because of Pope's errors, not for any lack of Union morale,"[16] except they did not outline those errors.

Military historians other than professional soldiers[17] showed better understanding. Russell F. Weigley joined the chorus against Pope, perhaps because he admired Lee. Lee "outgeneraled Pope—his Second Manassas campaign was a show piece of Napoleonic warfare. A campaign of maneuver which drew the enemy into a disadvantageous position and then stunned him in a climactic battle."[18] But Weigley noted that while Pope did not use the tactics of maneuver, he had a defensive mission, was tied to Fredericksburg so that he could not maneuver, and did not necessarily have to follow his chase of Jackson with a formal battle.

Kenneth P. Williams, alone among historians, championed Pope. In careful analysis Williams found Pope superior to McClellan in all ways: strong, willing to dig in and hold, ready to attack but obedient to orders even when, as in holding the Rappahannock line, he disagreed with Halleck.[19] Williams even found no fault with Pope's orders and his decision to attack again on August 30, saying that Pope would have profited from his mistakes since other generals did; Pope simply had no chance.[20]

Professional soldiers who were also writers[21] knew the perplexities of command and the tangle of orders, politics, supplies, delays, personality clashes, stupidity, coincidence, and good or bad luck that ran with campaigns. They also knew the military doctrine supplying the mental framework within which a commander planned strategy, which most historians had never heard of. English Major General J. F. C. Fuller, who wrote widely on military history, found that Lee had "handsomely but not decisively defeated Pope,"[22] but said that Lee's "campaign though successful was tactically unremunerative" because of heavy Confederate losses. The inference was that Pope was a respectable opponent even for Lee and that Pope's campaign greatly weakened Confederate strength.

Major Matthew F. Steele in *American Campaigns* wrote,

> Pope's first movements on finding the Confederate Army in his rear, were . . . certainly judicious. McDowell with about 40,000 men [actually 30,000] was sent to Gainesville and Heintzelman to Greenwich to support him. These forces could cut off Jackson's retreat, and with the Bull Run Mountains to hold, could keep back the rest of Lee's Army which was two days march behind Jackson. In fact here [Gainesville] was the key to the situation. Here Pope had the opportunity to place his whole army between Lee's separate wings, and the choice of holding either wing with a containing force, and falling on the other with the bulk of his troops.[23]

The idea sounds plausible, apparently Pope did not think it safe or realistic with the force he had.

Regarding the Second Battle of Bull Run, Steele felt that Pope ought not to have resumed the battle on the thirtieth. Instead, "he ought to have taken up a strong defensive position that day and resisted Lee's attack until he was reinforced by the corps of Franklin and Sumner which were on their way from Alexandria."[24] When Pope launched his attack he did not know when these two corps would arrive. In addition, standing on the defensive did not fit Pope's fighting temperament, especially when he thought he had the enemy at a disadvantage.

John Codman Ropes, although a civilian, was a student of Civil War military affairs, and his book, *The Army under Pope,* is a semi-official report of Pope's Virginia campaign. While no uncritical admirer of the general, Ropes supported Pope. In the campaign "The battles had all been fought creditably, so far as the actual fighting went. . . . The last battle was a defeat, but it was nothing more. Lee, moreover, had suffered greatly as was soon shown at South Mountain and Antietam."[25] Ropes also spoke kindly of the general:

> Pope was a vigorous, active, resolute man. He had many of the peculiarly military virtues, courage, persistence, confidence in himself. He was outgeneraled, it is true, but it must be remembered that he was much hampered in his movements by General Halleck's obstinate adherence to the line of the Rappahannock, and that he was opposed by the best generals of the enemy. When he met his antagonists, he fought them with a courage and persistency which exhorted their admiration.[26]

Emory Upton became the Civil War's Clausewitz and wrote a full review of the ups and downs of Pope and McClellan on their seesaw. His bias toward professionalism to the exclusion of politics and politicians led him to be gentle with both McCellan and Pope who were, after all, professionals. Upton nevertheless blamed Pope by implication for Pope's defeat at Bull Run. Pope, Upton said, sided with the politicians who cut McClellan's campaign short and then agreed to have the Army of Virginia join the Army of the Potomac at the Rappahannock. Upton felt the proper place was either Harrison's Landing or Washington since at the Rappahannock the enemy was at Pope's rear.[27] But "had General Pope been left to himself, it is probable that he would have conducted his army back to Bull Run or to the defenses where the concentration could have been effected in safety; but on the 21st General Halleck telegraphed that in forty-eight hours he could be made strong enough, adding, 'Don't yield an inch if you can help it.'"[28]

In addition to Halleck's wrong-headedness, Upton blamed Pope's subordinates McDowell and Sigel who should, as a matter of routine, have sent out patrols for five miles ahead of their lines. If they had, they would have found the enemy maneuvering near them.[29] Upton approved Pope's deployments and movements, but emphatically denied that McClellan or McClellanism had anything to do with the Army of Virginia's woes. To Upton, the board hearings of 1878 cleared that up.[30]

The official army view in the twentieth-century found Pope incompetent and Porter innocent. In a textbook for use in ROTC training the writers said,

> Pope marched and counter-marched his forces for two days trying to find the elusive Confederates. At the same time the Union commander failed to take Lee's forces into account. As a result he walked into Lee's trap. . . . Pope attacked Jackson, posted behind an abandoned railroad embankment, but again the attack consisted of a series of piecemeal frontal assaults which were repulsed with heavy casualties. By then Porter's V Corps from the Army of the Potomac had reached the field and was ordered to attack Jackson's right (south) flank. By this time, also, Longstreet's column had burst through Thoroughfare Gap, and deploying on Jackson's right, it blocked Porter's move.[31]

Lee had the advantage of a unified command, the writers said, that Halleck should have furnished for the Union armies. Pope could not help this, but even so, he ignored information about the enemy and made piecemeal frontal assaults on a strongly defended position.[32]

The consensus among nearly all critics was that Pope bungled the Second Battle of Bull Run, although few could say exactly when, where, how, and why. None took into account the overall effect of the Virginia campaign or any of Pope's successes elsewhere. But what really makes a good general? So far as politics and popular opinion are concerned a good general wins victories, no matter how; a bad general loses, no matter how. But what of generals who won and lost? Did the Battle of Waterloo wipe out Napoleon's record? When Rommel was forced out of North Africa did the desert sands cover forever his brilliant tactics?

In 1861 and 1862 Pope took the offensive in Missouri and along the Mississippi with power and dash, chafing at the restraints upon him in the Corinth campaign. Grant, Sherman, and Thomas, who were with Pope in the Corinth campaign, had nothing better to show in 1862 than Pope's victories; Grant even had to explain a near-disaster at Shiloh. Grant's capture of Vicksburg in 1863 was really just a replay of Pope's river crossing at Island No. 10.

Pope's mission in his Virginia campaign was at bottom a delaying action, like that of Fabius against Hannibal, to draw the enemy on until Union forces could concentrate and attack. The tactics did work despite Bull Run; McClellan's army did get back to Washington safely; Pope's army did reinforce McClellan's; the combined forces turned Lee's offensive. As Russell F. Weigley pointed out, Pope's campaign spotlighted the weakness of Lee's strategy. The Confederates tried to fight a defensive war because Union forces outnumbered them, but Lee's tactics in trying to entrap Union armies led him to take the offensive after he succeeded; that took him into offensive campaigns the Confederacy could not afford. Pope's casualties in the Virginia campaign ran to 13 percent of his strength (16,054); Lee's, to 19 percent (9,197).[33]

In 1863 and 1864 Pope planned the Indian campaigns that succeeded in spite of the small numbers of troops available. The one criticism that he seemed to draw was that he was not an alarmist; he analyzed the Indian capabilities in Minnesota and Dakota accurately and set out methodically to hand out punishment.

In late 1864 Pope took over Missouri and its enormous department at Grant's personal request. Grant, an acknowledged successful general, cheerfully entrusted to Pope administration of a still unruly area as well as command of an army to be raised within it to take on all of what was left of Confederate strength west of the Mississippi. The commanding general must have thought Pope well able to handle the job since there were other Union commanders who would have liked it, but Pope's generalship appealed to Grant.

Between 1870 and 1883 Pope laid out the campaign strategy for four Indian wars in his department, all chiefly successful, all carried on without any feedback from Pope's superiors. The implication must be that Sheridan and Sherman found Pope's plans and methods acceptable. Though an Indian war was not the same as a war with an enemy of equal number powered with weapons of equal strength, it was a special field calling for special skills that Pope had.

Since no professional had ever made an overall study of Pope's generalship, any new critic would have to approach such a study with inference and common sense. In a fair appraisal Pope came out as equal to most of his contemporaries and better than some. He was no Napoleon, but if he had been given the same chances others had—to learn from mistakes, to command a harmonious unified army, time to make plans, time for training, freedom to maneuver, freedom from Washington second-guessing—he would very likely, as Kenneth P. Williams said, have turned out an outstanding commander. Pope never had the free hand that Grant had in 1864 and never had a supporter, as Sherman had in Grant, who would toss him a theater of war and tell him to go experiment in it. In history Pope still had to wait for a professional soldier-historian who would look over the whole record.

NOTES

1. The popularizers cited here are Catton, Foote, and Pratt, for an audience that wanted bright colors and nothing hard to read.
2. Bruce Catton, *A Centennial History of the Civil War,* 3 vols. (Garden City, N.Y., 1961-65), 2:422.
3. Ibid., 2:428.
4. Ibid. See also Bruce Catton, *The Army of the Potomac: Mr. Lincoln's Army* (New York, 1962), 26-52.
5. Shelby Foote, *The Civil War: A Narrative,* 3 vols. (New York, 1958), 1:622.
6. Ibid., 1:622.
7. Ibid., 1:642.
8. Ibid.
9. Fletcher Pratt, *Ordeal by Fire* (New York, 1935; reprint, New York, 1948), 141.
10. Ibid., 141-42.
11. Ibid., 147.
12. The professional historians (other than military historians) cited here are Hattaway and Jones, McPherson, and Randall and Donald, for an audience willing to follow details and ponder causes and effects.
13. Herman Hattaway and Archer Jones, *How the North Won: A Military History of the Civil War,* (Urbana, 1983), 211, 212, 226, 229.
14. James M. McPherson, *The Battle Cry of Freedom: The Civil War Era,* vol. 6 of *The Oxford History of the United States* (New York, 1988), 524-34.
15. J. G. Randall and David Donald, *The Civil War and Reconstruction,* 2d ed. (Lexington, Mass., 1969), 217.
16. Randall and Donald, 218.
17. The military historians cited here are Ropes, Weigley, and Williams, who specialized in military history and wrote for an audience that knew the basic technicalities.
18. Russell L. Weigley, *The American Way of War: A History of United States Military Strategy and Policy* (New York, 1973), 109.
19. Kenneth P. Williams, *Lincoln Finds a General,* 5 vols. (New York, 1949-59), 1:357.
20. Ibid.
21. The professional soldiers cited here are Fuller, Steele, and Upton.
22. Maj. Gen. J. F. C. Fuller, *Decisive Battles of the U.S.A.* (New York, 1953), 213.

23. Maj. Matthew F. Steele, *American Campaigns,* 2 vols., War Dept. Doc. 324 (Washington, 1909), 255.
24. Ibid., 257.
25. John Codman Ropes, *The Army under Pope,* Campaigns of the Civil War Series (New York, 1881), 170.
26. Ibid., 171.
27. Emory Upton, *The Military Policy of the United States,* War Dept. Doc. 290 (Washington, 1912), 316–76.
28. Ibid., 333.
29. Ibid., 339.
30. Ibid., 342–45.
31. Maurice Matloff, ed., *American Military History* (reprinted and partially revised, 1973), Washington, 226.
32. Ibid., 227.
33. Weigley, 109.

Bibliography

OFFICIAL REPORTS, FEDERAL AND STATE DOCUMENTS
AND PUBLICATIONS

"Cadets Arranged in Order of Merit in Their Respective Classes as Determined at the General Examination in June 1840." West Point, 1840.

McDowell, Irwin. "Reports of Maj. Gen. Irwin McDowell, U.S. Army, Commanding Third Corps, Army of Virginia, of Operations August 7–September 2." OR XII, part 2:325–35.

McClellan, George B. "The Report of Major General George B. McClellan upon the Organization of the Army of the Potomac and of Its Campaign in Virginia and Maryland from July 26, 1861 to November 7, 1862." H. Ex. Doc. 15, 38th Cong., 1st Sess., 1864.

Minnesota in the Civil and Indian Wars 1861–1863. 2 vols. St. Paul Board of Commissioners, 1890, 1899.

Pope, John, Brvt. Capt. "The Report of an Exploration of the Territory of Minnesota." S. Ex. Doc. 42, 31st Cong., 1st Sess. Mar. 22, 1850.

Pope, John. Final Report. Jan. 27, 1863. OR XII, part 2:20–50.

———. "Official Communications from General Pope concerning Indian Affairs." General Order 11. Aug. 5, 1865.

———. Preliminary Report. Sept. 3, 1862. OR XII, part 2:12–17.

"Report of the Exploration of a Land Route from the Red River to the Rio Grande." Pacific Railroad Surveys, 12 vols. H. Ex. Doc. 129, 1855–60.

Pope, Nathaniel, ed. *The Laws of Illinois Territory.* 2 vols. Kaskaskia, 1815.

"Proceedings of a General Court-Martial which Convened at the City of Washington, in the District of Columbia, by Virtue of the following Special Order: SO 362, AGO, Nov. 25, 1862." OR XII, part 2 Supp.:821ff.

"Proceedings and Report of the Board of Army Officers Convened by Special Order no. 78, Headquarters of the Army, Adjutant General's Office, Washington, D.C., April 12, 1878, in the Case of Fitz John Porter." 3 vols. S. Ex. Doc. 37, 46th Cong., 1st Sess., 1879.

"Reports of the Joint Committee on the Conduct of the War." 8 vols. 37th Cong. 3d Sess., 1863; 38th Cong., 2d Sess., 1865–66.

The War of the Rebellion: A Compilation of the Official Records of the Union and Confederate Armies. 70 vols. Washington, 1880–1901.

Woods, Samuel, Brevt. Maj. "Report of Brevet Major Samuel Woods in Relation to His Expedition to the Pembina Settlement." H. Ex. Doc. 51, 31st Cong., 1st Sess.

Woods, Samuel. Records of the Adjutant General's Office 1780s to 1917. RG 94, Letters Received 603 W. 1849.

MANUSCRIPTS AND MISCELLANEOUS PAPERS

Salmon P. Chase Papers, Ohio Historical Society, Columbus.

A. B. Comstock Papers, Library of Congress, Washington.

Cox, Merlin G. "John Pope, Fighting General from Illinois." Ph.D. diss. University of Florida, 1956.

Manning F. Force Papers, University of Washington Libraries, Seattle.

John C. Fremont Papers, Bancroft Library, University of California, Berkeley.

Gabler, Henry. "The Fitz John Porter Case: Politics and Military Justice." Ph.D. diss. City University of New York, 1979.

James A. Garfield Papers, Library of Congress, Washington.

Ulysses S. Grant Papers, Library of Congress, Washington.

Henry E. Huntington Library Collections, San Marino, Calif.

Edmund M. Kern Manuscript Field Book. Henry E. Huntington Library Collections, San Marino, Calif.

Robert T. Lincoln Papers, Library of Congress, Washington.

Literary Society of Cincinnati. Minutes. Public Library of Cincinnati and Hamilton County.

National Archives:

    Office of Exploration and Surveys, RG 48, Misc. Records 1845–56 (Pope's artesian well experiments).

    Office of the Chief of Engineers, Letters Received, Topographical Bureau, RG 77, vol. 4

    Office of the Chief of Engineers, Letters Sent RG 77, vol. 14 (Pope's railroad explorations).

Records of the Adjutant General's Office, War Records Division, RG 94 (includes John Pope's personal file).

Records of the Office of the Secretary of War, RG 107.

New York Historical Society Collections, New York.

John Pope Papers, Chicago Historical Society, Chicago.

John Pope Papers, Illinois State Historical Library, Springfield.

John Pope Papers, Rutherford B. Hayes Library, Fremont, Ohio.

Nathaniel Pope Papers, Illinois State Historical Library, Springfield.

Porter, Fitz John. "Appeal to the President of the United States for a Re-examination of the Proceedings of the Court-Martial in His Case." Morristown, N.J., 1869.

Philip H. Sheridan Papers, Library of Congress, Washington.

William T. Sherman Papers, Library of Congress, Washington.

Franz Sigel Papers, New York Historical Society, New York.

Smith, T. C. H. "The Battle of Chantilly." MS. T. C. H. Smith Papers, Ohio Historical Society, Columbus.

"The Supremacy of the Law in Missouri." Pamphlet. Jefferson City, 1865.

Thiele, Thomas F., "The Evolution of Cavalry in the American Civil War 1861–1865." Ph.D. diss. University of Michigan, 1951.

T. C. H. Smith Papers, Ohio Historical Society, Columbus.

Lyman Trumbull Papers, Illinois State Historical Library, Springfield.

Walcott, Charles F. "The Battle of Chantilly." Paper read before the Military Historical Society of Massachusetts. Boston, 1886.

ADDRESSES, ARTICLES, AND DIARIES

Ambrose, Stephen E. "Henry W. Halleck and the Second Bull Run Campaign," *Civil War History* 6, no. 3 (Sept. 1960).

Angle, Paul. "Nathaniel Pope, 1784–1850, A Memoir." Illinois State Historical Society, Pub. no. 43. Springfield, 1936.

Beale, Rev. G. W. "Colonel Nathaniel Pope and His Descendants." *William and Mary Quarterly,* 12:192 (July 1903).

Chandler, Zachariah. Senate speech, Feb. 20, 1871. *Congressional Globe,* 41st Cong., 2d Sess., 1444–47.

Force, Manning F. "Major General John Pope." *History,* vol. 4, 1905.

Force, Manning F. "John Pope #1127 Class of 1842." An address at the annual reunion of the Association of Graduates of West Point, June 9, 1893.

Heintzelman, Samuel P. "Diary and Field Notes." Manuscript Division, Library of Congress, Washington.

Hennessy, John. *The Federal High Command and Fitz John Porter's Attack,* monograph, 1982. Manassas National Battlefield Park Library, Manassas, Va.

Kelly, Dennis. "Second Manassas: The Battle and Campaign." *Civil War Times Illustrated* 22, no. 3 (May 1983).

Leasure, Colonel Daniel. "Personal Observations and Experiences in the Pope Campaign in Virginia." Papers read before the Minnesota Commandery of the Military Order of the Loyal Legion of the United States. St. Paul, 1887.

Logan, John A. Senate speech, Mar. 2–5, 1880. *Congressional Record,* 46th Cong., 2d Sess., app.

Myers, Lee. "Pope's Wells." *New Mexico Historical Review* (Oct. 1963): 282.

Naisawald, H. Van Loan. "The Location of Grover's Attack in Relation to the Terrain and Opposing Confederate Brigades," unpub. monograph. Library of the Manassas National Battlefield Park, Manassas, Va.

——. "The Battle of Chantilly." *Civil War Times Illustrated* 3 (Mar. 1964): 3

Pope, John. "The Indian Question." Address before the Social Science Society, Cincinnati, May 20, 1878. Newberry Library, Chicago.

Pope, John. "The Second Battle of Bull Run." In Robert Underwood Johnson and Clarence Clough Buel, eds. *Battles and Leaders of the Civil War.* 4 vols. New York, 1887, 2:449–94.

NEWSPAPERS AND MAGAZINES

Boston Evening Transcript
Chicago Tribune
Cincinnati Commercial Advertiser
Cincinnati Daily Gazette
Cincinnati Enquirer
Columbus Daily Enquirer, Columbus, Ga.
Frank Leslie's Illustrated Magazine
Harper's Weekly
Illinois State Journal, Springfield
Meigs County Telegraph, Pomeroy, Ohio
Milwaukee Sentinel
New York Daily Tribune
New York Herald
Philadelphia Public Ledger
St. Louis Missouri Republican
St. Paul Daily Press
St. Paul Pioneer and Democrat
Washington Star
Weekly Missouri Democrat, St. Louis

BOOKS

The American Heritage Picture History of the Civil War. Narrative, Bruce Catton. New York, 1960; reprint, 1982.

Baringer, William E. *A House Dividing: Lincoln as President Elect.* Springfield, Ill., 1945.

Bauer, K. Jackson. *The Mexican War 1846-1848.* New York, 1974.

Boatner, Mark Mayo. *The Civil War Dictionary.* New York, 1959.

Browning, Orville Hickman. *The Diary of Orville Hickman Browning.* Eds. Theodore Calvin Pease and James G. Randall. Springfield, Ill., 1925-33.

Carley, Kenneth A. *The Sioux Uprising of 1862.* St. Paul, Minn., 1976.

Catton, Bruce. *The Army of the Potomac: Mr. Lincoln's Army.* New York, 1962.

———. *A Centennial History of the Civil War.* 3 vols. Garden City, N.Y., 1961-65.

Clausewitz, Carl von. *Vom Kriege.* 3 vols. Berlin, 1832; *On Wars.* Trans. Col. J. J. Graham. London. 1873.

Commager, Henry Steele, ed. *The Blue and the Gray.* 2 vols. Indianapolis, 1950; revised and abridged, New York, 1973.

Cox, Jacob D. *Military Reminiscences of the Civil War.* 2 vols. New York, 1900.

———. *The Second Battle of Bull Run.* Cincinnati, Ohio, 1882.

Cullum, George W. *Biographical Register of the Officers and Graduates of the United States Military Academy.* 2 vols. New York, 1868.

Dennett, Tyler, ed. *Lincoln and the Civil War in the Diaries and Letters of John Hay.* New York, 1939.

DePeyster, John Watts. *Personal and Military History of Philip Kearny.* New York, 1869.

Donald, David, ed. *Inside Lincoln's Cabinet—The Civil War Diaries of Salmon P. Chase.* New York, 1954.

Eby, Cecil B., Jr. *A Virginia Yankee in the Civil War—The Diaries of David Hunter Strother.* Chapel Hill, N.C., 1981.

Eisenschiml, Otto. *The Celebrated Case of Fitz John Porter.* Indianapolis, 1950.

Ellis, Richard N. *General Pope and U.S. Indian Policy.* Albuquerque, 1970.

Ervin, Edgar. *Pioneer History of Meigs County, Ohio to 1949.* Pomeroy, Ohio, 1949.

Fiske, John. *The Mississippi Valley in the Civil War.* Boston, 1900.

Fleming, Thomas. *West Point: The Men and the Times of the United States Military Academy.* New York, 1969.

Fleming, Walter L. *A Documentary History of Reconstruction.* 2 vols. Cleveland, 1906.

Folwell, William Watts. *History of Minnesota.* 4 vols. St. Paul, 1921–30.

Foote, Shelby. *The Civil War, A Narrative.* 3 vols. New York, 1958.

Force, Manning F. *From Fort Henry to Corinth.* Campaigns of the Civil War Series. New York, 1882.

Freeman, Douglas Southall. *Lee's Lieutenants: A Study in Command.* 3 vols. New York, 1942–44.

——. *R. E. Lee.* 4 vols. New York, 1934.

French, Samuel G. *Two Wars: An Autobiography.* Nashville, 1901.

French, Samuel Livingston. *The Army of the Potomac from 1861 to 1863.* New York, 1906.

Frost, J. *The Mexican War and Its Warriors.* New Haven, 1849.

Fuller, Maj. Gen. J. F. C. *Decisive Battles of the U.S.A.*

General Taylor and His Staff. Philadelphia, 1848.

Gibbon, John. *Personal Recollections of the Civil War.* New York, 1928; reprint, Dayton, Ohio, 1978.

Goetzmann, William H. *Army Exploration in the American West 1803–1863.* New Haven, Conn., 1959.

Gordon, George H. *Brook Farm to Cedar Mountain.* Boston, 1883.

——. *History of the Campaign of the Army of Virginia from Cedar Mt. to Alexandria.* Boston, 1880.

Grant, Ulysses S. *Personal Memoirs of U.S. Grant.* 2 vols. Ed. E. B. Long. New York, 1885; reprint, Cleveland, 1952

Halleck, Henry W. *Elements of Military Art and Science.* Boston, 1846.

Hassler, Warren W., Jr. *The Commanders of the Army of the Potomac.* Baton Rouge, La., 1962.

Hattaway, Herman, and Archer Jones. *How the North Won: A Military History of the Civil War.* Urbana, Ill., 1983.

Haupt, Herman. *Reminiscences of General Herman Haupt.* Milwaukee, 1901.

Hunt, Elvid, and Walter E. Lorence. *History of Fort Leavenworth 1827–1937.* 2d ed. Ft. Leavenworth, Kans., 1937.

Johnson, Robert Underwood, and Clarence Clough Buell, eds. *Battles and Leaders of the Civil War.* 4 vols. New York, 1887.

Jomini, Baron Antoine Henri de. *Precis de l'Art de la Guerre.* Brussels, 1836.

——. *Vie Politique et Militaire de Napoleon.* Trans. Henry W. Halleck. New York, 1864.

Jones, Robert Huhn. *The Civil War in the Northwest: Nebraska, Wisconsin, Iowa, Minnesota and the Dakotas.* Norman, Okla., 1956.

Lamon, Ward H. *The Life of Abraham Lincoln: From His Birth to His Inauguration as President.* Boston, 1872.

——. *Recollections of Abraham Lincoln.* Chicago, 1893.

Lavender, David. *Climax at Buena Vista.* Philadelphia, 1966.
Lee Takes Command: Time-Life History of the Civil War. Alexandria, Va., 1984.
Leech, Margaret. *Reveille in Washington.* New York, 1941.
Lewis, Lloyd, *Captain Sam Grant.* New York, 1950.
Lincoln, Abraham. *The Collected Works of Abraham Lincoln.* 8 vols. Ed. Roy P. Basler. New Brunswick, N.J., 1953.
Livermore, Thomas L. *Numbers and Losses in the Civil War in America 1861–65.* Boston, 1901; reprint, Bloomington, Ind., 1957.
Longstreet, James. *Manassas to Appomattox.* Philadelphia, 1896.
Lossing, Benjamin F. *The Pictorial Field Book of the Civil War.* 2 vols. Hartford, Conn., 1874.
McClellan, George B. *McClellan's Own Story.* New York, 1887.
McCullough, William Wallace, Jr. *Dr. William Dennis Kelley, 1825–1888, Texas Physician and Surgeon.* Galveston, 1961.
McPherson, James M. *The Battle Cry of Freedom: The Civil War Era.* Vol. 6 of *The Oxford History of the United States.* New York, 1988.
Matloff, Maurice, ed. *American Military History.* Reprinted and partially revised. Washington, 1973
Military Historical Society of Massachusetts. *The Virginia Campaign of General Pope in 1862.* Boston, 1886.
Morse, John T., Jr., ed. *The Diary of Gideon Welles, Secretary of the Navy under Lincoln and Johnson.* 3 vols. Boston, 1911.
Nevins, Allan. *Fremont, The West's Greatest Adventurer.* 2 vols. New York, 1928; rev. ed., *Fremont, Pathmarker of the West.* 2 vols. New York, 1955.
——, and Henry Steele Commager. *A Pocket History of the United States.* 7th ed. New York, 1981.
——. *The War for the Union.* 2 vols. New York, 1959–60.
Parrish, William E. *Turbulent Partnership: Missouri and the Union 1861–1865.* Columbia, Mo., 1963.
Pratt, Fletcher. *Ordeal by Fire.* New York, 1935; reprint, New York, 1948.
——. *Stanton, Lincoln's Secretary of War.* New York, 1953.
Randall, James G., and David Donald. *The Civil War and Reconstruction.* 2d ed. Lexington, Mass., 1969.
Roddis, Louis H. *The Indian Wars of Minnesota.* Cedar Rapids, Iowa, 1956.
Ropes, John Codman. *The Army under Pope.* Campaigns of the Civil War Series. New York, 1881.
——, and William R. Livermore. *The Story of the Civil War.* 4 vols. New York, 1894–1913.
Schofield, John M. *Forty-Six Years in the Army.* New York, 1897.

Schurz, Carl. *The Reminiscences of Carl Schurz.* 3 vols. New York, 1907.
Scott, Winfield. *Infantry Tactics.* Washington, 1834.
Scribner, B. F. *Campaign in Mexico.* Philadelphia, 1850.
Searcher, Victor. *Lincoln's Journey to Greatness.* New York, 1960.
Sefton, James E. *The United States Army and Reconstruction.* Baton Rouge, 1967.
Sherman, William T. *Memoirs of William T. Sherman.* New York, 1875; reprint, Bloomington, Ind., 1957.
Starr, Stephen Z. *The Union Cavalry in the American Civil War.* 3 vols. Baton Rouge, La., 1979–85.
Steele, Maj. Matthew F. *American Campaigns.* 2 vols. War Dept. Doc. 324, Washington, 1909.
Stevens, Hazard. *The Life of Isaac Ingalls Stevens.* 2 vols. New York, 1900.
Thomas, Benjamin. *Abraham Lincoln.* New York, 1952.
Upham, Warren. *Minnesota Geographical Names.* Minnesota Historical Society Collections, vol. 17. St. Paul, 1920
Upton, Emory. *The Military Policy of the United States.* War Dept. Doc. 290, Washington, 1912.
Utley, Robert M. *Frontier Regulars: The United States Army and the Indians 1866–1891.* New York, 1973.
Villard, Henry. *Memoirs of Henry Villard.* 2 vols. Boston, 1904.
Walworth, Reuben H. *The Hyde Genealogy.* 2 vols. Albany, N.Y., 1864.
Warden, Robert B. *The Private Life and Public Services of Salmon Portland Chase.* Cincinnati, Ohio, 1874.
Weigley, Russell L. *The American Way of War: A History of United States Military Strategy and Policy.* New York, 1973.
Williams, Kenneth P. *Lincoln Finds a General.* 5 vols. New York, 1949–59.
Williams, T. Harry. *Lincoln and His Generals.* New York, 1952.

Index

Note on the Authors

Wallace J. Schutz and Walter N. Trenerry are Civil War enthusiasts and members of the Twin Cities Civil War Round Table of Minneapolis and St. Paul.

WALLACE J. SCHUTZ is a graduate of the University of Minnesota, a co-founder and the first president of the Twin Cities Civil War Round Table, and a successful wholesaler of automotive products. Pope has been his passion. He has covered nearly every inch of ground where Pope and his armies marched and he has interviewed nearly everyone connected in some way with Pope.

WALTER N. TRENERRY is a graduate of Harvard University and Harvard Law School, has served in the army, been an active practicing attorney, and served as president of the Minnesota Historical Society and of the Twin Cities Civil War Round Table. He has published many legal and historical articles and is the author of *Murder in Minnesota*.